Guided Reading
and Study Workbook

Prentice Hall
Physical
Science
Concepts in Action
With Earth and Space Science

PEARSON

Prentice
Hall

Boston, Massachusetts
Upper Saddle River, New Jersey

Guided Reading and Study Workbook

Prentice Hall
Physical Science
Concepts in Action
With Earth and Space Science

ISBN 0-13-069978-0

15 16 17 18 V004 11 10

Contents

Chapter 1   Science Skills

Section 1.1 What Is Science?
(pages 2–6)

This section describes the characteristics of science and technology. It also discusses the big ideas of physical science.

Reading Strategy (page 2)

Previewing Skim the section to find out what the main branches of natural science are. Complete the concept map based on what you have learned. For more information on this Reading Strategy, see the **Reading and Study Skills** in the **Skills and Reference Handbook** at the end of your textbook.

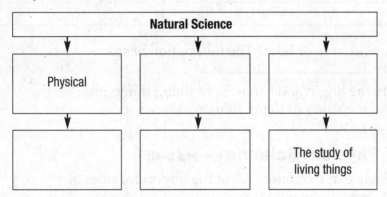

Science From Curiosity (pages 2–3)

1. Define science. _____

_____

2. The questions that lead to scientific discovery are provided by _____.

3. Is the following sentence true or false? The results of every scientific experiment are quantitative. _____

Science and Technology (page 3)

4. Is the following sentence true or false? The use of knowledge to solve practical problems is known as curiosity. _____

5. How are science and technology related? _____

_____

Branches of Science (page 4)

6. Name the two general categories that the study of science can be divided into.

a. _____   b. _____

7. Circle the letters of each branch of natural science.

a. physical science   b. Earth and space science

c. social science   d. life science

Chapter 1   Science Skills

8. Circle the letter of each sentence that is true about the field of chemistry.

    a. Chemists study reactions involving matter.

    b. Chemists study the composition of matter.

    c. Chemists study the structure of matter.

    d. Chemists study the properties of matter.

9. The study of matter, energy, and the interactions between the two through forces and motion is known as _____.

10. Identify the topics that are included in the science of geology.

    _____

    _____

11. Is the following sentence true or false? The foundation of space science is astronomy. _____

12. Scientists who study the origin and behavior of living things are called biologists, and the study of living things is known as

    _____.

The Big Ideas of Physical Science (pages 5–6)

13. Is the following sentence true or false? All of the important rules of nature have already been discovered. _____

14. Circle the letter of each sentence that is true about the diameter of the observable universe.

    a. It is one hundred million meters.

    b. It is seven hundred billion meters.

    c. It is seven hundred million billion meters.

    d. It is seven hundred million billion billion meters.

15. Name the two characteristics of matter.

    a. _____

    b. _____

16. The basic building blocks of matter are called _____.

17. Is the following sentence true or false? A force causes a change in time. _____

18. Describe kinetic energy. _____

    _____

19. Two general types of energy are kinetic energy and _____ energy.

Science and Your Perspective (page 6)

20. Is the following sentence true or false? The scientific facts of today will not change in the future. _____

Chapter 1   Science Skills

Section 1.2 Using a Scientific Approach
(pages 7–11)

This section describes scientific methods and how they are used to understand the world around you.

Reading Strategy (page 7)

Using Prior Knowledge Before you read, add to the web diagram what you already know about scientific methods. After you read the section, revise the diagram based on what you have learned. For more information on this Reading Strategy, see the **Reading and Study Skills** in the **Skills and Reference Handbook** at the end of your textbook.

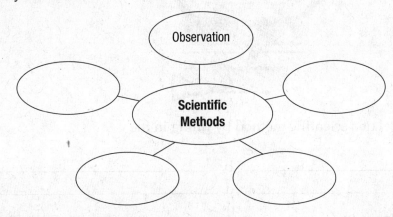

Scientific Methods (pages 7–9)

1. Identify the goal of any scientific method. _____

   _____

2. Name three types of variables in an experiment.

   a. _____ b. _____ c. _____

3. Is the following sentence true or false? If the data from an experiment do not support your hypothesis, you can revise the hypothesis or propose a new one. _____

4. How does a scientific theory differ from a hypothesis? _____

   _____

Match the following vocabulary terms to the correct definition.

Definition	Vocabulary Terms
_____ 5. Information that you obtain through your senses	a. theory
_____ 6. A well-tested explanation for a set of observations	b. hypothesis
_____ 7. A proposed answer to a question	c. observation

Chapter 1   Science Skills

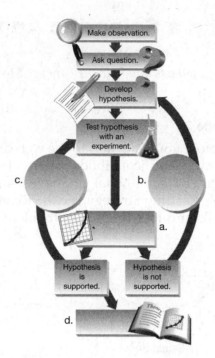

8. Complete the model of a scientific method by filling in the missing steps.

   a. _____   b. _____

   c. _____   d. _____

Scientific Laws (page 9)

9. Is the following sentence true or false? A scientific law attempts to explain an observed pattern in nature. _____

10. All scientists may accept a given scientific law, but different scientists may have different _____ to explain it.

Scientific Models (page 10)

11. Why do scientists use scientific models? _____
    _____

12. Circle the letters that correctly state what scientists do if data show that a model is wrong.

    a. Change the model.   b. Replace the model.

    c. Ignore the data.   d. Revise the data.

Working Safely in Science (page 11)

13. Circle the letters of safety precautions to follow whenever you work in a science laboratory.

    a. Study safety rules.   b. Never ask questions.

    c. Read all procedural steps.   d. Understand the procedure.

14. Why should you wash your hands after every experiment? _____
    _____

Chapter 1   Science Skills

Section 1.3 Measurement
(pages 14–20)

This section discusses units of measurement, making and evaluating measurements, and calculations with measurements.

Reading Strategy (page 14)

Previewing Before you read the section, rewrite the green and blue topic headings in this section as questions in the table below. As you read, write answers to the questions. For more information on this Reading Strategy, see the **Reading and Study Skills** in the **Skills and Reference Handbook** at the end of your textbook.

Measurement
Why is scientific notation useful?

Using Scientific Notation (pages 14–15)

1. Scientific notation expresses a value as the product of a number between 1 and 10 and _____.

2. Circle the letter of the value that is expressed as 3×10^8.

   a. 300   b. 300,000

   c. 30,000,000   d. 300,000,000

3. Why is scientific notation useful? _____

_____

SI Units of Measurement (pages 16–18)

4. Circle the letters of elements that are required for a measurement to make sense.

   a. scientific notation   b. numbers

   c. exponents   d. units

5. Is the following sentence true or false? Units in the SI system include feet, pounds, and degrees Fahrenheit. _____

Match the SI base unit with the quantity that is used to measure.

SI Base Unit	Quantity
_____ 6. meter	a. Mass
_____ 7. kilogram	b. Time
_____ 8. kelvin	c. Length
_____ 9. second	d. Temperature

SI Prefixes			
Prefix	Symbol	Meaning	Multiply Unit By
giga-	G		1,000,000,000
mega-	M	million (10^6)	
kilo-	k	thousand (10^3)	1000
deci-	d		0.1
centi-		hundredth (10^{-2})	0.01
	m	thousandth (10^{-3})	0.001
	μ	millionth (10^{-6})	0.000001
nano-		billionth (10^{-9})	0.000000001

10. Complete the table of SI prefixes by filling in the missing information.

11. A ratio of equivalent measurements that is used to convert a quantity expressed in one unit to another unit is called a(n) _____ .

Limits of Measurement (page 19)

12. Circle the letter of each expression that has four significant figures.

    a. 1.25×10^4 b. 12.51

    c. 0.0125   d. 0.1255

13. Is the following sentence true or false? The precision of a calculated answer is limited by the least precise measurement used in the calculation. _____

14. Calculate the density if the mass of a solid material is measured as 15.00 grams and its volume is measured as 5.0 cm^3? Round off your answer to the proper number of significant figures.

    _____

15. Describe the difference between precision and accuracy. _____

    _____

    _____

Measuring Temperature (page 20)

16. Circle the letter of the base unit of temperature in SI.

    a. degree Fahrenheit (°F)   b. degree Celsius (°C)

    c. candela (cd)   d. kelvin (K)

17. Write the formula used to convert degrees Celsius to kelvins.

    _____

Chapter 1   Science Skills

Section 1.4 Presenting Scientific Data
(pages 22–25)

This section describes how scientists organize and communicate data.

Reading Strategy (page 22)

Comparing and Contrasting After you read this section, compare the types of graphs by completing the table. For more information on this Reading Strategy, see the **Reading and Study Skills** in the **Skills and Reference Handbook** at the end of your textbook.

Type of Graph	Description	Used For
Line graph		
Bar graph		
Circle graph		

Organizing Data (pages 22–24)

1. Circle the letters of tools that scientists use to organize their data.
   - a. the Internet
   - b. newspapers
   - c. tables
   - d. graphs

2. The simplest way to organize data is to present them in a(n) _____.

3. Circle the letter of the place on a line graph where the manipulated variable is generally plotted.
   - a. the y-axis
   - b. the rise
   - c. the x-axis
   - d. the run

4. On a line graph, the ratio of the change in the y-variable to the corresponding change in the x-variable is called the line's _____.

5. Circle the letters of the relationships that are direct proportions.
   - a. distance traveled versus time at a constant speed
   - b. the mass of a substance versus its volume
   - c. the time to travel a given distance versus average speed
   - d. the number of fingers in your classroom versus the number of people

Chapter 1   Science Skills

6. Is the following sentence true or false? An inverse proportion is one in which the product of the two variables is constant. _____

7. Identify each data organizing tool shown below.

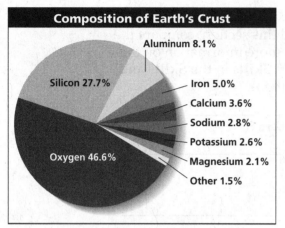

a.

Average Annual Precipitation for Selected U.S. Cities	
City	**Average Annual Precipitation (cm)**
Buffalo, N.Y.	98.0
Chicago, Ill.	91.0
Colorado Springs, Colo.	41.2
Houston, Tex.	117.0
San Diego, Calif.	25.1
Tallahassee, Fla.	166.9
Tucson, Ariz.	30.5

b.

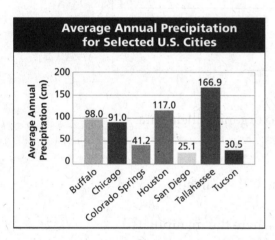

c.

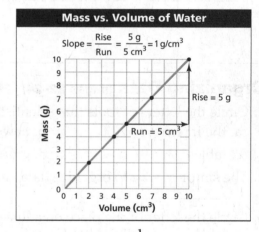

d.

a. _____   b. _____

c. _____   d. _____

Communicating Data (page 25)

8. Name two ways that scientists can report results of their experiments.

   a. _____   b. _____

9. Is the following statement true or false? Scientists always interpret a given set of data the same way. _____

10. Why is peer review an important part of scientific research? _____

_____

Chapter 1   Science Skills

WordWise

Answer the questions by writing the correct vocabulary term in the blanks. Use the circled letter in each term to find the hidden vocabulary word. Then write a definition for the hidden word.

Clues	Vocabulary Terms
The study of matter, energy, and their interactions	_ Ⓞ _ _ _ _ _
The closeness of a measurement to the actual value of what is being measured	_ _ _ _ _ _ _ Ⓞ
A gauge of how exact a measurement is	Ⓞ _ _ _ _ _ _ _ _
The ratio of a vertical change to the corresponding horizontal change in a line	_ _ Ⓞ _ _
An instrument used to measure temperature	_ _ _ _ _ _ _ _ Ⓞ _ _
The use of knowledge to solve practical problems	_ _ _ Ⓞ _ _ _ _ _
A representation of an object or event	_ _ _ Ⓞ _
A system of knowledge and the methods used to find that knowledge	Ⓞ _ _ _ _ _ _
A statement that summarizes a pattern found in nature	_ _ _ _ _ _ Ⓞ _ _ _ _ _
Information that you obtain through your senses	_ _ Ⓞ _ _ _ _ _ _ _

Hidden word: _ _ _ _ _ _ _ _ _

Definition: _____

Chapter 1   Science Skills

Using Scientific Notation

Light travels through space at a speed of 3.00×10^8 meters per second. How long does it take for light to travel from the sun to Earth, which is a distance of 1.50×10^{11} meters?

Math Skill:
Scientific Notation

You may want to read more about this **Math Skill** in the **Skills and Reference Handbook** at the end of your textbook.

1. Read and Understand

What information are you given?

Speed = 3.00×10^8 m/s

Total distance = 1.50×10^{11} m

2. Plan and Solve

What unknown are you trying to calculate?

Time = ?

What formula contains the given quantities and the unknown?

$$\text{Time} = \frac{\text{Total distance}}{\text{Average speed}}$$

Replace each variable with its known variable and known value.

$$\text{Time} = \frac{1.50 \times 10^{11} \text{ m}}{3.00 \times 10^8 \text{ m/s}}$$

$$= \frac{1.50}{3.00} \times (10^{11-8})(\text{m}/(\text{m}/\text{s}))$$

$$= 0.50 \times 10^3 \text{ s} = 5.00 \times 10^2 \text{ s}$$

3. Look back and check

Is your answer reasonable?

Yes, the number calculated is the quotient of distance and speed, and the units (s) indicate time.

Math Practice

On a separate sheet of paper, solve the following problems.

1. The flow of water in a stream is 210,000 liters per hour. Use scientific notation to calculate the amount of water that flows in a week (168 hours).

2. The density of a liquid is 8.03×10^{-1} kilogram per liter. What is the mass (in kg) of liquid in a full 100,000 liter tank?

3. How many balloons, each containing 6.02×10^{23} particles of helium gas, can be filled from a tank that contains 1.204×10^{25} helium particles?

Chapter 2   Properties of Matter

Section 2.1 Classifying Matter
(pages 38–44)

This section explains how materials are classified as pure substances or mixtures. It discusses types of pure substances and mixtures.

Reading Strategy (page 38)

Summarizing As you read, complete the classification of matter in the diagram below. For more information on this Reading Strategy, see the **Reading and Study Skills** in the **Skills and Reference Handbook** at the end of your textbook.

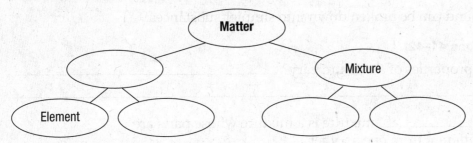

Pure Substances (page 39)

1. Is the following sentence true or false? Every sample of a pure substance has exactly the same composition and the same properties. _____

2. What are the two categories of pure substances?

   a. _____   b. _____

Elements (pages 39–40)

3. What is an element? _____

   _____

4. Is the following sentence true or false? The smallest particle of an element is an atom. _____

5. Why does an element have a fixed, uniform composition? _____

   _____

6. Circle the letter before each element that is a gas at room temperature.

   a. carbon   b. oxygen

   c. mercury   d. nitrogen

Match each element to its correct symbol.

Element	Symbol
_____ 7. aluminum	a. C
_____ 8. gold	b. Al
_____ 9. carbon	c. Au

Chapter 2   Properties of Matter

Compounds (page 40)

10. What is a compound? _____

_____

11. Circle the letter of each sentence that is true about compounds.

   a. A compound always contains at least two elements.

   b. The substances that make up a compound are always joined in a fixed proportion.

   c. A compound has the same properties as the elements from which it is formed.

   d. A compound can be broken down into simpler substances.

Mixtures (pages 41–42)

12. Why do the properties of a mixture vary? _____

_____

13. A(n) _____ mixture is a mixture whose parts are noticeably different from one another.

14. Is the following sentence true or false? A homogeneous mixture is a mixture in which it is difficult to distinguish the substances from one another. _____

Solutions, Suspensions, and Colloids (pages 42–44)

15. A mixture can be classified as a solution, a suspension, or a colloid based on the size of its _____ particles.

16. Circle the letter of the term that identifies the homogeneous mixture that forms when sugar is dissolved in a glass of hot water.

   a. solution   b. suspension

   c. colloid   d. substance

17. Complete the table about solutions, suspensions, and colloids.

Solutions, Suspensions, and Colloids			
Type of Mixture	Relative Size of Largest Particles	Homogeneous or Heterogeneous?	Do Particles Scatter Light?
Solution			No
	Intermediate	Homogeneous	
	Large		Yes

18. Circle the letter before each example of a colloid.

   a. windshield wiper fluid   b. fog

   c. homogenized milk   d. muddy water

19. Is the following sentence true or false? If salt water is poured through a filter, the salt will be trapped on the filter.

_____

Chapter 2   Properties of Matter

Section 2.2 Physical Properties
(pages 45–51)

This section discusses physical properties and physical changes. It also explains how physical properties can be used to identify materials, select materials, and separate mixtures.

Reading Strategy (page 45)

Building Vocabulary As you read, write a definition for each term in the table below. For more information on this Reading Strategy, see the **Reading and Study Skills** in the **Skills and Reference Handbook** at the end of your textbook.

Defining Physical Properties	
Physical Property	**Definition**
Viscosity	
Malleability	
Melting Point	

Examples of Physical Properties (pages 45–47)

1. A physical property is any characteristic of a material that can be observed or measured without changing the _____ of the substances in the material.

2. Explain why a wooden spoon is a better choice than a metal spoon for stirring a boiling pot of soup. _____

_____

3. Is the following sentence true or false? A liquid with a high viscosity flows more slowly than a liquid with a low viscosity at the same temperature. _____

4. Is the following sentence true or false? Discovering which of two materials can scratch the other is a way to compare the hardness of the materials. _____

Match each term to its definition.

Term	Definition
_____ 5. viscosity	a. The ability of a solid to be hammered without shattering
_____ 6. conductivity	b. The temperature at which a substance changes from a liquid to a gas
_____ 7. malleability	c. The resistance of a liquid to flowing
_____ 8. melting point	d. The ability to allow heat to flow
_____ 9. boiling point	e. The ratio of the mass of a substance to its volume
_____ 10. density	f. The temperature at which a substance changes from a solid to a liquid

Chapter 2   Properties of Matter

11. Which of the substances in the table below are gases at room temperature?

a. _____   b. _____   c. _____

Melting and Boiling Points of Some Substances		
Substance	**Melting Point**	**Boiling Point**
Hydrogen	−259.3°C	−252.9°C
Nitrogen	−210.0°C	−195.8°C
Ammonia	−77.7°C	−33.3°C
Octane (found in gasoline)	−56.8°C	125.6°C
Water	0.0°C	100.0°C
Acetic acid (found in vinegar)	16.6°C	117.9°C

Using Physical Properties (page 48)

12. Describe three steps that can be used to identify a material. _____

_____

_____

13. Is the following sentence true or false? Usually, people consider only one property when choosing a material. _____

Using Properties to Separate Mixtures (page 50)

14. Two processes that are commonly used to separate mixtures are _____ and _____.

15. Explain how filtration separates materials based on the size of their particles. _____

_____

_____

16. Explain why distillation works for converting seawater into fresh water.

_____

_____

_____

Recognizing Physical Changes (page 51)

17. Is the following sentence true or false? In a physical change, some of the substances in a material change, but the properties of the material stay the same. _____

18. Explain why the boiling of water is a physical change. _____

_____

19. Circle the letter for each process that is a reversible physical change.

a. wrinkling a shirt   b. freezing water

c. cutting hair   d. peeling an orange

Chapter 2   Properties of Matter

Section 2.3 Chemical Properties
(pages 54–58)

This section discusses chemical properties and describes clues that may show that a chemical change has taken place.

Reading Strategy (page 54)

Relating Text and Visuals As you read, complete the table by finding examples of the clues for recognizing chemical changes in Figures 19 and 20. For more information on this Reading Strategy, see the **Reading and Study Skills** in the **Skills and Reference Handbook** at the end of your textbook.

Recognizing Chemical Changes	
Clue	**Example**
Change in color	
Production of gas	
Formation of precipitate	

Observing Chemical Properties (pages 54–55)

1. Is the following sentence true or false? The substances in paraffin do not change when a candle burns. _____

2. Circle the letters of the compounds formed when a candle burns.

   a. paraffin

   b. hydrogen

   c. water

   d. carbon

3. What is a chemical property? _____

_____

4. Is the following sentence true or false? Flammability is a material's ability to burn in the presence of carbon dioxide. _____

5. The property that describes how readily a substance combines chemically with other substances is _____.

6. Circle the letter of each property that is a chemical property.

   a. hardness   b. density

   c. flammability   d. reactivity

7. Is the following sentence true or false? Nitrogen is a more reactive element than oxygen. _____

Chapter 2   Properties of Matter

8. Why isn't iron used to make coins? _____

_____

9. What is the benefit of pumping nitrogen gas into seawater that is stored in steel tanks? _____

_____

_____

Recognizing Chemical Changes (pages 56–57)

10. A(n) _____ change occurs when a substance reacts and forms one or more new substances.

11. What are three examples of chemical changes?

a. _____   b. _____

c. _____

12. Circle the letters of examples of evidence for a chemical change.

a. a change in color

b. a filter trapping particles

c. the production of a gas

d. the formation of a solid precipitate

Match each example to evidence of a chemical change.

Example	Chemical Change
_____ 13. Lemon juice is added to milk.	a. the production of a gas
_____ 14. A silver bracelet darkens when exposed to air.	b. the formation of a precipitate
_____ 15. Vinegar is mixed with baking soda.	c. a change in color

Is a Change Chemical or Physical? (page 58)

16. Is the following sentence true or false? When iron is heated until it turns red, the color change shows that a chemical change has taken place. _____

17. When matter undergoes a chemical change, the composition of the matter _____.

18. When matter undergoes a physical change, the composition of the matter _____.

19. Complete the following table about chemical changes.

Chemical Changes		
Type of Change	Are New Substances Formed?	Example
Chemical		
Physical		

Chapter 2   Properties of Matter

WordWise

Answer the questions by writing the correct vocabulary term in the blanks.
Use the circled letter in each term to find the hidden vocabulary word. Then,
write a definition for the hidden word.

Clues	Vocabulary Terms
A mixture that results when substances dissolve to form a homogeneous mixture	Ⓞ _ _ _ _ _ _
A substance that can be broken down into two or more simpler substances	_ _ _ _ _ Ⓞ _ _
A change in which the composition of matter stays the same	_ _ _ Ⓞ _ _ _ _
A solid that forms and separates from a liquid mixture	_ _ _ _ _ Ⓞ _ _ _ _
A substance that cannot be broken down into simpler substances	Ⓞ _ _ _ _ _ _
The ability of a material to allow heat to flow	_ _ Ⓞ _ _ _ _ _ _ _ _
A classification for matter that always has the same composition	_ _ _ _ Ⓞ _ _ _ _ _ _ _ _
The ability of a material to burn	_ _ _ _ _ _ _ _ Ⓞ _ _
A homogeneous mixture containing particles that scatter light	_ Ⓞ _ _ _ _ _
The temperature at which a substance changes from a liquid to gas	_ _ _ _ _ _ _ _ _ Ⓞ _

Hidden Term: _ _ _ _ _ _ _ _ _ _

Definition: _____

_____

Chapter 2   Properties of Matter

Melting and Boiling Points

Math Skill:
Data Tables

Melting and Boiling Points of Some Substances		
Substance	Melting Point	Boiling Point
Hydrogen	−259.3°C	−252.9°C
Nitrogen	−210.0°C	−195.8°C
Water	0.0°C	100.0°C
Acetic acid (found in vinegar)	16.6°C	117.9°C
Table salt	800.7°C	1465°C

You may want to read more about this **Math Skill** in the **Skills and Reference Handbook** at the end of your textbook.

Which of the substances in the table above are solids at a temperature of −40°C?

1. Read and Understand

What information are you given?

Temperature = −40°C

The melting and boiling points of five substances are listed in the table.

2. Plan and Solve

What unknown are you trying to find?

Which of the five substances are solids at −40°C?

What guideline can you use?

Any substance that is a solid at −40°C must have a melting point greater than −40°C.

Check the melting point of each substance in the table to find out whether it satisfies the guideline.

Water, acetic acid, and table salt are solids at −40°C.

3. Look Back and Check

Is your answer reasonable?

Because water, acetic acid, and table salt have melting points equal to or greater than 0°C, they will all be solids at a temperature well below 0°C.

Math Practice

On a separate sheet of paper, solve the following problems.

1. Which substance in the table is a liquid at 105°C? _____

2. Which substance in the table has a melting point closest to room temperature (20°C)? _____

3. Which substance in the table boils at the lowest temperature? _____

4. Which substance has the smallest temperature range as a liquid, hydrogen or nitrogen? _____

Chapter 3   States of Matter

Section 3.1 Solids, Liquids, and Gases
(pages 68–73)

This section explains how materials are classified as solids, liquids, or gases. It also describes the behavior of these three states of matter.

Reading Strategy (page 68)

Comparing and Contrasting As you read about the states of matter, replace each letter in the diagram below with one of these phrases: *definite volume, definite shape, variable volume,* or *variable shape*. For more information on this Reading Strategy, see the **Reading and Study Skills** in the **Skills and Reference Handbook** at the end of your textbook.

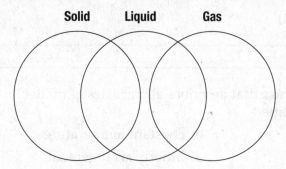

Solid   Liquid   Gas

Describing the States of Matter (pages 68–70)

1. What are three common states of matter?
   a. _____ b. _____ c. _____

2. Is the following sentence true or false? The fact that a copper wire can be bent shows that some solids do not have a definite shape.
   _____

3. Circle the letter of each phrase that describes how particles at the atomic level are arranged within most solids.
   a. randomly arranged   b. packed close together
   c. arranged in a regular pattern   d. spaced far apart

4. Is the following sentence true or false? A liquid takes the shape of its container. _____

5. What is the state of matter in which a material has neither a definite shape nor a definite volume? _____

6. Compare and contrast the arrangement of particles at the atomic level for a liquid and a solid. _____
   _____

7. What determines the shape and volume of a gas? _____
   _____

8. On the sun, where temperatures are extremely high, matter exists in a state known as _____.

Chapter 3   States of Matter

9. The state of matter that can exist at extremely _____
temperatures is called a Bose-Einstein condensate.

10. Complete the table about states of matter.

States of Matter		
State	**Shape**	**Volume**
	Definite	
Liquid		
		Not definite

Kinetic Theory (page 71)

11. Describe kinetic energy. _____
_____

12. Circle the letter of the phrase that describes all particles of matter
in the kinetic theory of matter.

   a. randomly arranged   b. constant temperature

   c. in constant motion   d. orderly arrangement

Explaining the Behavior of Gases (pages 72–73)

13. Is the following sentence true or false? There are forces of
attraction among the particles in all matter. _____

14. Why can scientists ignore the forces of attraction among
particles in a gas under ordinary conditions? _____
_____
_____

15. Is the following sentence true or false? Because of the constant
motion of the particles in a gas, the gas has a definite shape
and volume. _____

Explaining the Behavior of Liquids (page 73)

16. Do forces of attraction have a stronger effect on the behavior of the
particles in a gas or in a liquid? _____

17. Circle the letter of each factor that affects the behavior of liquids.

   a. fixed location of particles

   b. constant motion of particles

   c. orderly arrangement of particles

   d. forces of attraction among particles

Explaining the Behavior of Solids (page 74)

18. Solids have a(n) _____ volume and shape because
particles in a solid vibrate in _____ locations.

Chapter 3   States of Matter

Section 3.2 The Gas Laws
(pages 75–81)

This section discusses gas pressure and the factors that affect it. It also explains the relationships between the temperature, volume, and pressure of a gas.

Reading Strategy (page 75)

Identifying Cause and Effect As you read, identify the variables that affect gas pressure, and write them in the diagram below. For more information on this Reading Strategy, see the **Reading and Study Skills** in the **Skills and Reference Handbook** at the end of your textbook.

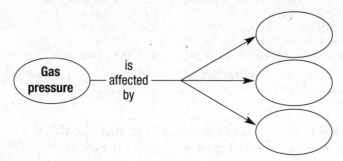

Pressure (pages 75–76)

1. What is pressure? _____

2. Circle the letter of each unit used to express amounts of pressure.

   a. newton   b. joule

   c. pascal   d. kilopascal

3. What causes the pressure in a closed container of gas? _____

_____

Factors that Affect Gas Pressure (pages 76–77)

4. Name the factors that affect the pressure of an enclosed gas.

   a. _____ b. _____ c. _____

5. Is the following sentence true or false? In a closed container, increasing the temperature of a gas will decrease the force with which particles hit the walls of the container. _____

6. What effect does raising the temperature of a gas have on its pressure, if the volume of the gas and the number of its particles are kept constant? _____

7. How does reducing the volume of a gas affect its pressure if the temperature of the gas and the number of particles are constant?

_____

_____

8. Increasing the number of particles of a gas will _____ its pressure if the temperature and the volume are constant.

Chapter 3   States of Matter

Charles's Law (page 78)

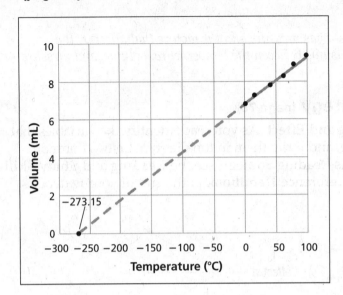

9. Jacques Charles recorded the behavior of gases on a graph like the one above. The data shows that the volume of a gas increases at the same rate as the _____ of the gas.

10. A temperature equal to 0 K on the Kelvin temperature scale is known as _____.

11. What does Charles's law state? _____

_____

Boyle's Law (page 79)

12. If the temperature and number of particles of gas in a cylinder do not change, and the volume of the cylinder is reduced by half, the pressure of the gas will be _____ as the original pressure.

13. Boyle's law states that there is an inverse relationship between the pressure and volume of a gas. Circle the letter of the correct expression of this relationship.

    a. $P_1V_1 = P_2V_2$

    b. $P_1V_2 = P_2V_1$

    c. $\dfrac{P_1}{V_1} = \dfrac{P_2}{V_2}$

    d. $P_1P_2 = V_1V_2$

The Combined Gas Law (pages 80–81)

14. Circle the letters of the factors that are included in the expression of the combined gas law.

    a. temperature   b. number of particles

    c. volume   d. pressure

Chapter 3   States of Matter

Section 3.3 Phase Changes
(pages 84–91)

This section explains what happens when a substance changes from one state of matter to another and describes six phase changes.

Reading Strategy (page 84)

Summarizing As you read, complete the description of energy flow during phase changes in the diagram below. For more information on this Reading Strategy, see the **Reading and Study Skills** in the **Skills and Reference Handbook** at the end of your textbook.

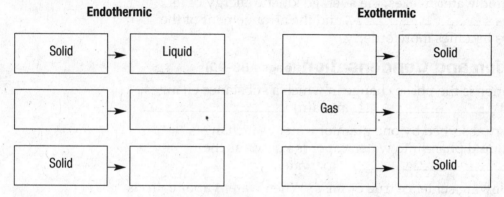

Characteristics of Phase Changes (pages 84–86)

1. What is a phase change? _____
_____

Match each term with the letter of the phase-change description that best describes it.

	Term	**Phase-Change**
_____	2. freezing	a. Solid to gas
_____	3. sublimation	b. Liquid to gas
_____	4. condensation	c. Gas to solid
_____	5. melting	d. Liquid to solid
_____	6. deposition	e. Gas to liquid
_____	7. vaporization	f. Solid to liquid

8. What happens to the temperature of a substance during a phase change? _____

9. Is the following sentence true or false? The temperature at which a substance freezes is lower than the temperature at which it melts. _____

10. Circle the letter that describes the behavior of a substance during a phase change.

   a. neither absorbs nor releases energy   b. always absorbs energy

   c. always releases energy   d. either absorbs or releases energy

Chapter 3   States of Matter

11. A substance absorbs energy from its surroundings during a(n) _____ change.

12. The energy absorbed by one gram of ice as it melts is known as the _____ for water.

13. As water freezes, it releases heat to its surroundings. Freezing is an example of a(n) _____ change.

Melting and Freezing (page 88)

14. Is the following sentence true or false? Water molecules have a more orderly arrangement in ice than in liquid water. _____

15. When liquid water freezes, the average kinetic energy of its molecules _____, and the arrangement of the molecules becomes more orderly.

Vaporization and Condensation (pages 88–90)

16. Vaporization is the phase change in which a substance changes from a(n) _____ into a(n) _____.

17. The energy absorbed by one gram of water as it changes from its liquid phase into water vapor is known as the _____ for water.

18. Is the following sentence true or false? When water vapor collects above the liquid in a closed container, the pressure caused by the collisions of this vapor and the walls of the container is called vapor pressure. _____

19. The phase change in which a substance changes from a gas into a liquid is called _____.

20. Compare and contrast the processes of evaporation and boiling by completing the table below.

Evaporation and Boiling			
Process	**Phase Change**	**Where It Occurs**	**Temperature**
Evaporation			
Boiling			

21. Is the following sentence true or false? A gas absorbs energy as it changes into a liquid. _____

Sublimation and Deposition (page 91)

22. Dry ice can change directly from a solid to a gas without forming a liquid first. This process is an example of _____.

23. What is deposition? _____

_____

Chapter 3   States of Matter

WordWise

Answer the questions by writing the correct vocabulary term in the blanks.
Use the circled letter in each term to find the hidden vocabulary word. Then,
write a definition for the hidden word.

Clues   **Vocabulary Terms**

What is the process that changes a   _ _ _ O _ _ _ _ _ _ _
substance from a liquid to a gas below
the substance's boiling point?

Which gas law states that the   _ _ _ O _ _ _ ' _ _ _ _ _
volume of a gas is directly
proportional to its temperature?

What is the phase change in which a   _ O _ _ _ _ _ _ _ _
substance changes directly from a gas
to a solid?

In what state does matter have   O _ _ _ _
both a definite shape and a definite
volume?

What is the phase change in which   _ _ _ _ _ O _ _ _ _
a substance changes from a gas to
a liquid?

What is the phase change in which   _ O _ _ _ _ _ _ _ _ _
a substance changes directly from a
solid to a gas?

During what type of phase change   _ _ _ _ _ _ O _ _ _
does a substance release energy to
its surroundings?

During what type of phase change   O _ _ _ _ _ _ _ _ _ _
does a substance absorb energy from
its surroundings?

Hidden Term: _ _ _ _ _ _ _ _ _

Definition: _____

_____

Chapter 3   States of Matter

The Combined Gas Law

A gas in a cylinder has a pressure of 235 kPa at a volume of 5.00 L. The volume is reduced to 1.25 L. The temperature does not change. Find the new pressure of the gas.

Math Skill:
Calculating with
Significant Figures

You may want to read more about this **Math Skill** in the **Skills and Reference Handbook** at the end of your textbook.

1. Read and Understand

What information are you given?

$V_1 = 5.00$ L $V_2 = 1.25$ L $P_1 = 235$ kPa

2. Plan and Solve

What unknown are you trying to calculate? P_2

What expression can you use?

$$\frac{P_1 V_1}{T_1} = \frac{P_2 V_2}{T_2}$$

Cancel out the variable that does not change and rearrange the expression to solve for P_2.

$$P_1 V_1 = P_2 V_2 \qquad P_2 = \frac{P_1 V_1}{V_2}$$

Replace each variable with its known value.

$$P_2 = 235 \text{ kPa} \times \frac{5.00 \text{ L}}{1.25 \text{ L}} = 940 \text{ kPa}$$

3. Look Back and Check

Is your answer reasonable?

The volume of a gas is inversely proportional to its pressure if the temperature and number of particles are constant. The volume decreased by a factor of four, from 5.00 L to 1.25 L. The answer, 940 kPa, is four times the original pressure, 235 kPa.

Math Practice

On a separate sheet of paper, solve the following problems. The number of particles remains constant for all problems.

1. A gas has a pressure of 340 kPa at a volume of 3.20 L. What happens to the pressure when the volume is increased to 5.44 L? The temperature does not change.

2. A gas has a pressure of 180 kPa at a temperature of 300 K. At what temperature will the gas have a pressure of 276 kPa? The volume does not change.

3. At 47°C, a gas has a pressure of 140 kPa. The gas is cooled until the pressure decreases to 105 kPa. If the volume remains constant, what will the final temperature be in Kelvins? In degrees Celsius?

Chapter 4   Atomic Structure

Section 4.1 Studying Atoms
(pages 100-105)

This section discusses the development of atomic models.

Reading Strategy (page 100)

Summarizing As you read, complete the table about atomic models. For more information on this Reading Strategy, see the **Reading and Study Skills** in the **Skills and Reference Handbook** at the end of your textbook.

Atomic Models		
Scientist	Evidence	Model
	Ratio of masses in compounds	
	Deflected beam	
Rutherford		Positive, dense nucleus

Ancient Greek Models of Atoms (page 100)

1. Democritus named the smallest particles of matter _____ because they could not be divided.

2. List the four elements that Aristotle included in his model of matter.

    a. _____   b. _____

    c. _____   d. _____

Dalton's Atomic Theory (page 101)

3. Is the following sentence true or false? John Dalton gathered evidence for the existence of atoms by measuring the masses of elements that reacted to form compounds. _____

4. What theory did Dalton propose to explain why the elements in a compound always join in the same way? _____

_____

5. Circle the letters of the sentences that represent the main points of Dalton's theory of atoms.

    a. All elements are composed of atoms.

    b. In a particular compound, atoms of different elements always combine the same way.

    c. All atoms have the same mass.

    d. Compounds contain atoms of more than one element.

Chapter 4   Atomic Structure

Thomson's Model of the Atom (pages 102–103)

6. Objects with like electric charges _____, and objects with opposite electric charges _____.

7. What happened to the beam when Thomson placed a pair of charged metal plates on either side of the glass tube? _____

_____

8. Thomson concluded that the particles in the glowing beam had a(n) _____ charge because they were attracted to a positive plate.

9. Is the following sentence true or false? Thomson's experiments provided the first evidence for the existence of subatomic particles.

_____

10. Describe Thomson's model. _____

_____

Rutherford's Atomic Theory (pages 104–105)

11. What is an alpha particle? _____

_____

12. Fill in the table to show what Rutherford hypothesized would happen to the paths of alpha particles as they passed through a thin sheet of gold.

Rutherford's Hypothesis	
Most particles would travel _____ from their source to a screen that lit up when struck.	Particles that did not pass straight through would be _____ _____

13. Circle the letters of the sentences that describe what happened when Marsden directed a beam of particles at a piece of gold foil.

a. Fewer alpha particles were deflected than expected.

b. More alpha particles were deflected than expected.

c. None of the alpha particles were deflected.

d. Some alpha particles bounced back toward the source.

14. Circle the letter of the sentence that states what Rutherford concluded from the gold foil experiment.

a. An atom's negative charge is concentrated in its nucleus.

b. Thomson's model of the atom was correct.

c. An atom's positive charge is concentrated in its nucleus.

d. An atom's positive charge is spread evenly throughout the atom.

Chapter 4   Atomic Structure

Section 4.2 The Structure of an Atom
(pages 108–112)

This section compares the properties of three subatomic particles. It also discusses atomic numbers, mass numbers, and isotopes.

Reading Strategy (page 108)

Monitoring Your Understanding Before you read, list in the table shown what you know about atoms and what you would like to learn. After you read, list what you have learned. For more information on this Reading Strategy, see the **Reading and Study Skills** in the **Skills and Reference Handbook** at the end of your textbook.

What I Know About Atoms	What I Would Like to Learn	What I Have Learned

Properties of Subatomic Particles (pages 108–109)

1. What are three subatomic particles?

   a. _____   b. _____   c. _____

2. Circle the letter that identifies a subatomic particle with a positive charge.

   a. nucleus   b. proton

   c. neutron   d. electron

3. Why did Chadwick conclude that the particles produced by his experiment were neutral in charge? _____

   _____

   _____

Comparing Subatomic Particles (pages 109–110)

4. Circle the letters of properties that vary among subatomic particles.

   a. color   b. mass

   c. charge   d. location in the atom

5. Circle the letter of the expression that accurately compares the masses of neutrons and protons.

   a. mass of 1 neutron = mass of 1 proton

   b. mass of 2000 neutrons = mass of 1 proton

   c. mass of 1 electron = mass of 1 proton

   d. mass of 1 neutron = mass of 1 electron

Chapter 4   Atomic Structure

Atomic Number and Mass Number (page 110)

6. Is the following sentence true or false? Two atoms of the same element can have different numbers of protons. _____

7. What is an atomic number? _____

_____

_____

8. Circle the letters that identify quantities that are always equal to an element's atomic number.

   a. number of nuclei

   b. number of protons

   c. number of neutrons

   d. number of electrons

9. Is the following sentence true or false? Two different elements can have the same atomic number. _____

10. What is the mass number of an atom? _____

_____

_____

11. Complete the equation in the table below.

Number of neutrons = _____ − _____

Isotopes (page 112)

12. Every atom of a given element has the same number of _____ and _____.

13. Every atom of a given element does not have the same number of _____.

14. What are isotopes? _____

_____

_____

15. All oxygen atoms have 8 protons. Circle the letter of the number of neutrons in an atom of oxygen-18.

   a. 8   b. 9

   c. 10   d. 18

16. Is the following sentence true or false? Isotopes of oxygen have different chemical properties. _____

17. Water that contains hydrogen-2 atoms instead of hydrogen-1 atoms is called _____.

Chapter 4   Atomic Structure

Section 4.3 Modern Atomic Theory
(pages 113–118)

This section focuses on the arrangement and behavior of electrons in atoms.

Reading Strategy (page 113)

Sequencing After you read, complete the description in the flow chart below of how the gain or loss of energy affects electrons in atoms. For more information on this Reading Strategy, see the **Reading and Study Skills** in the **Skills and Reference Handbook** at the end of your textbook.

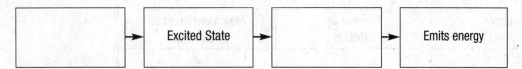

Bohr's Model of the Atom (pages 113–116)

1. Circle the letter of the sentence that tells how Bohr's model of the atom differed from Rutherford's model.

   a. Bohr's model focused on the nucleus.

   b. Bohr's model focused on the protons.

   c. Bohr's model focused on the neutrons.

   d. Bohr's model focused on the electrons.

2. Is the following sentence true or false? In Bohr's model of the atom, electrons have a constant speed and move in fixed orbits around the nucleus. _____

3. What can happen to an electron in an atom when the atom gains or loses energy? _____

   _____

4. What evidence do scientists have that electrons can move from one energy level to another? _____

   _____

5. Is the following sentence true or false? When electrons release energy, some of the energy may be released as visible light.

   _____

Electron Cloud Model (page 116)

6. Is the following sentence true or false? Bohr's model was correct in assigning energy levels to electrons. _____

7. When trying to predict the locations and motions of electrons in atoms, scientists must work with _____.

8. What is an electron cloud? _____

   _____

Chapter 4   Atomic Structure

9. Is the following sentence true or false? Scientists use the electron cloud model to describe the exact location of electrons around the nucleus. _____

Atomic Orbitals (page 117)

10. Is the following sentence true or false? An orbital is a region of space around the nucleus where an electron is likely to be found. _____

11. An electron model is a good approximation of _____.

Use this table to answer questions 12 and 13.

Energy Level	Number of Orbitals	Maximum Number of Electrons
1	1	2
2	4	8
3	9	18
4	16	32

12. Higher energy levels have _____ orbitals than lower energy levels do.

13. What is the relationship between the number of orbitals and the maximum number of electrons in an energy level? _____
_____

Electron Configurations (page 118)

14. What is an electron configuration? _____
_____

15. Circle the letter of the number of energy levels needed for a lithium atom's three electrons when the atom is in its ground state.

    a. zero   b. one

    c. two   d. three

16. Is the following sentence true or false? An excited state is less stable than a ground state. _____

17. Circle the letters of each sentence that is true when all of the electrons in an atom are in orbitals with the lowest possible energies.

    a. The electrons are in the most stable configuration.

    b. The electrons are in an unstable configuration.

    c. The atom is in an excited state.

    d. The atom is in its ground state.

Chapter 4   Atomic Structure

WordWise

*Solve the clues to determine which vocabulary terms from Chapter 4
are hidden in the puzzle. Then find and circle the terms in the puzzle.
The terms may occur vertically, horizontally, or diagonally.*

```
e  m  a  s  s  n  u  m  b  e  r  u  n
n  l  o  r  b  i  t  a  l  x  a  p  i
r  e  e  n  l  t  p  t  s  p  b  k  s
g  n  a  c  a  s  r  d  c  r  h  l  o
b  e  l  d  t  g  o  f  l  s  g  a  t
l  r  t  s  o  r  t  g  r  n  b  t  o
n  g  z  b  m  o  o  p  l  q  d  c  p
p  y  q  p  i  u  n  n  m  a  s  s  e
s  l  n  m  c  n  n  u  c  l  e  u  s
t  e  u  e  n  d  r  i  o  l  k  m  r
r  v  c  l  u  s  v  a  b  t  o  p  k
z  e  l  x  m  t  w  e  s  r  n  u  e
p  l  e  m  b  a  r  l  e  t  a  b  d
b  s  a  q  e  t  z  o  c  m  r  n  k
r  t  s  i  r  e  h  j  n  s  f  l  t
```

Clues	Hidden Words
Dense, positively charged mass in the center of an atom	_____
Positively charged subatomic particle found in the nucleus	_____
Neutral subatomic particle found in the nucleus	_____
Number of protons in an atom of an element	_____
Sum of the protons and neutrons in the nucleus of an atom	_____
Atoms of the same element having different numbers of neutrons	_____
Possible energies that electrons in an atom can have	_____
Visual model of the most likely locations for electrons in an atom	_____
Region of space where an electron is likely to be found	_____
Term for an atom whose electrons have the lowest possible energies	_____

Chapter 4   Atomic Structure

Electrons and Orbitals

Use the table on page 117 of your textbook to find the
ratio of the maximum number of electrons to the number
of orbitals for each of four energy levels.

Math Skill:
Ratios and Proportions

You may want to read
more about this **Math
Skill** in the **Skills and
Reference Handbook**
at the end of your
textbook.

1. Read and Understand

What information are you given?

The number of orbitals and the maximum number
of electrons per energy level

2. Plan and Solve

What unknown are you trying to calculate?

The ratio of the maximum number of electrons to
the number of orbitals in energy levels 1 through 4

*What mathematical expression can you use to calculate
the unknown?*

$$\frac{\text{maximum number of electrons}}{\text{number of orbitals}}$$

Level 1: $\dfrac{2}{1} = \dfrac{2}{1}$ Level 3: $\dfrac{18}{9} = \dfrac{2}{1}$

Level 2: $\dfrac{4}{2} = \dfrac{2}{1}$ Level 4: $\dfrac{32}{16} = \dfrac{2}{1}$

3. Look Back and Check

Is your answer reasonable?

The ratio is the same for all four energy levels. Also, each
orbital can contain only two electrons.

Math Practice

On a separate sheet of paper, solve the following problems.

1. Calculate the maximum number of electrons for energy levels
   5 and 6. Energy level 5 contains 25 orbitals; energy level 6
   contains 36 orbitals.

2. Energy level 7 can contain a maximum of 98 electrons. How many
   orbitals are there in energy level 7?

3. A sodium atom has 11 electrons. How many orbitals in a sodium
   atom contain electrons?

Chapter 5   The Periodic Table

Section 5.1 Organizing the Elements
(pages 126–129)

This section explains how Mendeleev organized elements into a periodic table. It also discusses the predictions he made about undiscovered elements and how the discovery of those elements supported his version of the table of the table.

Reading Strategy (page 126)

Identifying Main Ideas As you read, complete the table by identifying the main idea for each topic. For more information on this reading strategy, see the **Reading and Study Skills** in the **Skills and Reference Handbook** at the end of your textbook.

Topic	Main Idea
Mendeleev's proposal	
Mendeleev's prediction	
Evidence supporting Mendeleev's table	

The Search for Order (page 126)

1. Is the following sentence true or false? The first elements to be identified were mainly gases. _____

2. As the number of known elements grew, so did the need to organize them into groups based on their _____.

3. Circle the letter of each category that the French chemist Antoine Lavoisier used to classify elements.

   a. gases   b. metals

   c. liquids   d. nonmetals

Mendeleev's Periodic Table (pages 127–129)

4. Is the following sentence true or false? Mendeleev needed to organize information about 63 elements. _____

5. Mendeleev's strategy for classifying elements was modeled on a(n) _____.

6. Circle the letter of each type of information Mendeleev knew about each element.

   a. name

   b. number of protons

   c. relative mass

   d. properties

Chapter 5   The Periodic Table

7. Mendeleev arranged the elements into rows in order of _____ so that elements with similar properties were in the same column.

8. Is the following sentence true or false? A periodic table is an arrangement of elements in columns, based on a set of properties that repeat from row to row. _____

Group I	Group II	Group III	Group IV	Group V	Group VI	Group VII	Group VIII
H = 1							
Li = 7	Be = 9.4	B = 11	C = 12	N = 14	O = 16	F = 19	
Na = 23 K = 39	Mg = 24 Ca = 40	Al = 27.3 — = 44	Si = 28 Ti = 48	P = 31 V = 51	S = 32 Cr = 52	Cl = 35.5 Mn = 55	Fe = 56, Co = 59, Ni = 59, Cu = 63.
(Cu = 63) Rb = 85	Zn = 65 Sr = 87	— = 68 Yt = 88	— = 72 Zr = 90	As = 75 Nb = 94	Se = 78 Mo = 96	Br = 80 — = 100	Ru = 104, Rh = 104, Pd = 106, Ag = 108.
(Ag = 108) Cs = 133	Cd = 112 Ba = 137	In = 113 Di = 138	Sn = 118 Ce = 140	Sb = 122 —	Te = 125 —	I = 127 —	— — — —
(—) —	— —	— Er = 178	— La = 180	— Ta = 182	— W = 184	— —	Os = 195, Ir = 197, Pt = 198, Au = 199.
(Au = 199) —	Hg = 200 —	Tl = 204 —	Pb = 207 Th = 231	Bi = 208 —	U = 240		

9. Mendeleev published the table above in 1872. Why did Mendeleev leave some locations in his periodic table blank? _____

_____

10. Circle the letters of two elements that have similar properties.
    a. zinc (Zn)   b. chlorine (Cl)
    c. nitrogen (N)   d. bromine (Br)

11. How did Mendeleev decide where to place arsenic (As) and selenium (Se)?

_____

_____

12. Is the following sentence true or false? Mendeleev was the first scientist to arrange elements in a periodic table. _____

13. Describe a test for the correctness of a scientific model. _____

_____

14. Mendeleev used the _____ located near the spaces in his table to predict properties for undiscovered elements.

15. The close match between Mendeleev's predictions and the actual properties of new elements showed _____.

16. Circle the letter of each element that was discovered after Mendeleev published his periodic table that supported Mendeleev's predictions and provided evidence validating the table.
    a. gallium   b. scandium
    c. germanium   d. aluminum

Chapter 5   The Periodic Table

Section 5.2 The Modern Periodic Table
(pages 130–138)

This section explains the organization of the modern periodic table and discusses the general properties of metals, nonmetals, and metalloids.

Reading Strategy (page 130)

Previewing Before you read, complete the table by writing two questions about the periodic table on pages 132–133. As you read, write answers to your questions. For more information on this reading strategy, see the **Reading and Study Skills** in the **Skills and Reference Handbook** at the end of your textbook.

Questions About the Periodic Table	
Question	**Answer**

The Periodic Law (pages 131–133)

1. Is the following sentence true or false? In the modern periodic table, elements are arranged by increasing number of protons. _____

2. Explain why the number of elements per period varies. _____
_____

3. Properties of elements repeat in a predictable way when atomic numbers are used to arrange elements into groups. This pattern of repeating properties is called the _____.

Atomic Mass (page 134)

4. Label the four types of information supplied for chlorine in the diagram.

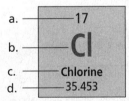

a. _____   b. _____

c. _____   d. _____

5. Define atomic mass. _____

_____

6. Circle the letter of each sentence that is true about a carbon-12 atom.

   a. It has 6 protons and 6 neutrons.

   b. Scientists assigned a mass of 6 atomic mass units to the carbon-12 atom.

   c. It is used as a standard for comparing the masses of atoms.

   d. An atomic mass unit is defined as one twelfth the mass of a carbon-12 atom.

7. Is the following sentence true or false? Most elements exist as a mixture of two or more isotopes. _____

8. The mass of an atom of chlorine-37 is _____ than the mass of an atom of chlorine-35.

9. Is the following sentence true or false? All values are equally important in a weighted average. _____

Classes of Elements (pages 135–136)

10. Name the three categories into which elements are classified based on their general properties.

   a. _____

   b. _____

   c. _____

11. Is the following sentence true or false? All metals react with oxygen in the same way. _____

12. An important property of transition elements is their ability to form compounds _____.

13. Circle the letter of each sentence that is true about nonmetals.

   a. Nonmetals are poor conductors of heat and electric current.

   b. Many nonmetals are gases at room temperature.

   c. Some nonmetals are extremely reactive and others hardly react at all.

   d. Nonmetals that are solids tend to be malleable.

Variation Across a Period (page 138)

14. Across a period from left to right, the elements become _____ metallic and _____ nonmetallic in their properties.

15. Circle the letter of each Period 3 element that is highly reactive.

   a. sodium   b. silicon

   c. chlorine   d. argon

Chapter 5   The Periodic Table

Section 5.3 Representative Groups
(pages 139–145)

This section discusses how the number of valence electrons affects the properties of elements. It also describes properties of elements in Groups 1A through 8A.

Reading Strategy (page 139)

Monitoring Your Understanding As you read, record an important fact about each element listed in the table. For more information on this reading strategy, see the **Reading and Study Skills** in the **Skills and Reference Handbook** at the end of your textbook.

Element	Important Fact
Magnesium	
Aluminum	
Chlorine	

Valence Electrons (page 139)

1. An electron that is in the highest occupied energy level of an atom is a(n) _____ electron.

2. Elements within a group have the _____ number of valence electrons.

The Alkali Metals (page 140)

3. The reactivity of alkali metals _____ from the top of Group 1A to the bottom.

4. Sodium is stored under oil because it _____.

The Alkaline Earth Metals (page 141)

5. Differences in reactivity among alkaline earth metals are shown by the way they react with _____.

Find and match two properties to each element listed.

	Alkaline Earth Metal	Property
_____	6. magnesium	a. Helps build strong teeth and bones
_____	7. calcium	b. Helps plants produce sugar
		c. Is used to make lightweight bicycle frames
		d. Is the main ingredient in limestone

Chapter 5   The Periodic Table

The Boron Family (page 142)

8. List the four metals in Group 3A.

    a. _____   b. _____

    c. _____   d. _____

9. Circle the letter of each sentence that is true about aluminum.

    a. It is the most abundant metal in Earth's crust.

    b. It is often found combined with oxygen in bauxite.

    c. It is more reactive than sodium and magnesium.

    d. It is a good conductor of electric current.

The Carbon Family (page 142)

10. List the two metalloids in Group 4A.

    a. _____   b. _____

11. Except for water, most of the compounds in your body contain

    _____.

The Nitrogen Family (page 143)

12. List the nonmetals in Group 5A.

    a. _____   b. _____

13. Name two elements in the nitrogen family that are contained in fertilizer.

    a. _____   b. _____

The Oxygen Family (page 143)

14. List the nonmetals in Group 6A.

    a. _____   b. _____   c. _____

15. Name the most abundant element in Earth's crust.

    _____

The Halogens (page 144)

16. List the four nonmetals in Group 7A.

    a. _____   b. _____

    c. _____   d. _____

17. Halogens have similar _____ properties but different _____ properties.

The Noble Gases (page 145)

18. Name three characteristics of noble gases.

    a. _____   b. _____   c. _____

19. How can an element that does not react easily with other elements be useful? _____

_____

Chapter 5   The Periodic Table

WordWise

Match each definition with the correct term by writing the definition's number in the grid. When you have filled in all the boxes, add up the numbers in each column, row, and the two diagonals. Hint: The sum should be 15 in each case.

Definitions

1. An arrangement of elements in columns based on a set of properties that repeat from row to row

2. A pattern of repeating properties that occurs when atomic numbers are used to arrange elements into groups

3. One twelfth the mass of a carbon-12 atom

4. Elements that are good conductors of heat and electric current

5. Elements that form a bridge between the elements on the left and right sides of the periodic table

6. Elements that are poor conductors of heat and electric current

7. Elements with properties that fall between those of metals and nonmetals

8. An electron that is in the highest occupied energy level of an atom

9. Colorless, odorless, and extremely unreactive gases

diagonal
= _____

nonmetals _____	periodic table _____	valence electron _____	= _____
metalloids _____	transition metals _____	atomic mass unit _____	= _____
periodic law _____	noble gas _____	metals _____	= _____

= _____   = _____   = _____   diagonal
= _____

Chapter 5   The Periodic Table

Calculating Average Atomic Mass

Carbon has two stable isotopes. Carbon-12 has an assigned atomic mass of 12.0000 and a percentage in nature of 98.93%. The atomic mass of carbon-13 is 13.0034 and its percentage in nature is 1.070%. What is the average atomic mass for carbon?

**Math Skill:
Percents and
Decimals**

You may want to read more about this **Math Skill** in the **Skills and Reference Handbook** at the end of your textbook.

1. Read and Understand

What information are you given?

carbon-12: atomic mass = 12.0000, % in nature = 98.93
carbon-13: atomic mass = 13.0034, % in nature = 1.070

2. Plan and Solve

What unknown are you trying to calculate?

Average atomic mass for carbon = ?

What equation can you use?

(atomic mass C-12) (% C-12) + (atomic mass C-13) (% C-13)
= average atomic mass of C

Convert the percentages to decimals and multiply the atomic mass of each isotope by the decimal representing its percentage in nature.

(12.0000) (0.9893) = 11.8716 rounded to 11.87
(13.0034) (0.01070) = 0.1391364 rounded to 0.1391

Add the products of the two multiplications to find the average atomic mass for carbon.

11.87 + 0.1391 = 12.0091 rounded to 12.01

3. Look Back and Check

Is your answer reasonable?

Because almost all the carbon atoms in nature are carbon-12 atoms, the average atomic mass of carbon (12.01) is close to the atomic mass of carbon-12 (12.0000).

Math Practice

On a separate sheet of paper, solve the following problems.

1. The element boron has two stable isotopes. Boron-10 has an atomic mass of 10.0129 and a percentage in nature of 19.78% The atomic mass of boron-11 is 11.0093 and its percentage in nature is 80.22% What is the average atomic mass for boron?

2. Nitrogen has two stable isotopes, nitrogen-14 and nitrogen-15. Nitrogen-14 has an atomic mass of 14.0031. Its percentage in nature is 99.63%. What is the percentage in nature of nitrogen-15?

Chapter 6   Chemical Bonds

Section 6.1 Ionic Bonding
(pages 158–164)

This section describes the formation of ionic bonds and the properties of ionic compounds.

Reading Strategy (page 158)

Sequencing As you read, complete the concept map to show what happens to atoms during ionic bonding. For more information on this Reading Strategy, see the **Reading and Study Skills** in the **Skills and Reference Handbook** at the end of your textbook.

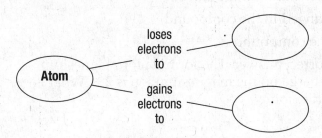

Stable Electron Configurations (page 158)

1. Describe the type of electron configuration that makes an atom stable and not likely to react. _____

_____

_____

2. Describe an electron dot diagram. _____

_____

Ionic Bonds (pages 159–161)

3. Some elements achieve stable electron configurations through the transfer of _____ between atoms.

4. By losing one valence electron, a sodium atom achieves the same electron arrangement as an atom of _____.

5. Circle the letter that states the result of a sodium atom transferring an electron to a chlorine atom.

   a. Each atom ends up with a more stable electron arrangement.

   b. The sodium atom becomes more stable, but the chlorine atom becomes less stable.

   c. The chlorine atom becomes more stable, but the sodium atom becomes less stable.

   d. Each atom ends up with a less stable electron arrangement.

6. Is the following sentence true or false? An ion is an atom that has a net positive or negative electric charge. _____

7. An ion with a negative charge is called a(n) _____.

Chapter 6   Chemical Bonds

8. An ionic bond forms when _____ are transferred from one atom to another.

9. Is the following sentence true or false? The lower the ionization energy, the easier it is to remove an electron from an atom. _____

Ionic Compounds (pages 161–164)

10. Circle the letter of each piece of information provided by the chemical formula of an ionic compound.

    a. which elements the compound contains

    b. the charge on each ion in the compound

    c. how the ions are arranged in the compound

    d. the ratio of ions in the compound

11. Circle the letter of the correct answer. The formula for magnesium chloride is $MgCl_2$. The charge on the magnesium ion is 2+. What is the charge on each chloride ion?

    a. 2−   b. 1−

    c. 0   d. 1+

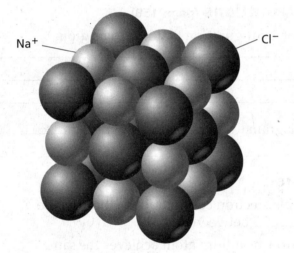

12. Look at the arrangement of ions in a sodium chloride crystal. How many sodium ions surround each chloride ion in this three-dimensional structure?

    a. 3   b. 4

    c. 6   d. 8

13. The shape of an ionic crystal depends on _____.

14. Identify two factors that determine the arrangement of ions in an ionic crystal.

    a. _____   b. _____

15. Is the following sentence true or false? The attractions among ions within a crystal lattice are weak. _____

Section 6.2 Covalent Bonding
(pages 165–169)

This section discusses the formation of covalent bonds and the factors that determine whether a molecule is polar or nonpolar. It also discusses attractions between molecules.

Reading Strategy (page 165)

Relating Text and Visuals As you read the section, look closely at Figure 9. Complete the table by describing each type of model shown. For more information on this Reading Strategy, see the **Reading and Study Skills** in the **Skills and Reference Handbook** at the end of your textbook.

Molecular Models	
Model	**Description**
Electron dot	
Structural formula	
Space-filling	
Electron cloud	

Covalent Bonds (pages 165–167)

1. Describe a covalent bond. _____

_____

2. Circle the letters of molecular models that show orbitals of atoms overlapping when a covalent bond forms.

    a. electron dot   b. structural formula

    c. space-filling   d. electron cloud

3. Describe a molecule. _____

_____

4. Is the following sentence true or false? In a covalent bond, the atoms are held together by the attractions between the shared electrons and the protons in each nucleus. _____

5. Circle the correct answer. Nitrogen has five valence electrons. How many pairs of electrons must two nitrogen atoms share in order for each atom to have eight valence electrons?

    a. zero   b. one

    c. two   d. three

Chapter 6   Chemical Bonds

Unequal Sharing of Electrons (pages 167–168)

6. In general, elements at the _____ of a group have a greater attraction for electrons than elements at the _____ of a group have.

7. In a hydrogen chloride molecule, the shared electrons spend more time near the _____ atom than near the _____ atom.

8. Describe a polar covalent bond. _____

_____

_____

9. When atoms form a polar covalent bond, the atom with the greater attraction for electrons has a partial _____ charge.

10. Is the following sentence true or false? In a molecule of a compound, electrons are always shared equally by both atoms. _____

11. Circle the letter of each factor that determines whether a molecule is polar or nonpolar.

    a. the number of atoms in the molecule

    b. the type of atoms in the molecule

    c. the number of bonds in the molecule

    d. the shape of the molecule

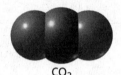
CO_2

H_2O

12. Compare the shapes of carbon dioxide and water molecules. Circle the letter of the polar molecule.

    a. carbon dioxide   b. water

13. Is the following sentence true or false? In a water molecule, the hydrogen side of the molecule has a partial positive charge, and the oxygen side has a partial negative charge. _____

Attraction Between Molecules (page 169)

14. Water has a higher boiling point than carbon dioxide because attractions between polar molecules are _____ than attractions between nonpolar molecules.

15. Is the following sentence true or false? Attractions among nonpolar molecules explain why nitrogen can be stored as a liquid at low temperatures and high pressures. _____

Section 6.3 Naming Compounds and Writing Formulas
(pages 170–175)

This section explains how to name and write formulas for ionic and molecular compounds.

Reading Strategy (page 170)

Predicting Before you read, predict the meaning of the term *polyatomic ion,* and write your prediction in the table. After you read, if your prediction was incorrect, revise your definition. For more information on this Reading Strategy, see the **Reading and Study Skills** in the **Skills and Reference Handbook** at the end of your textbook.

Vocabulary Term	Before You Read	After You Read
Polyatomic ion		

Describing Ionic Compounds (pages 171–173)

1. Is the following sentence true or false? The name of an ionic compound must distinguish the compound from other ionic compounds containing the same elements. _____

2. What information is provided by the formula for an ionic compound? _____
_____

3. Circle the letter of the word that describes a compound made from only two elements.

   a. ionic   b. binary

   c. diatomic   d. polar

4. Is the following sentence true or false? Names of anions are formed by placing the suffix *-ide* after part of the name of the nonmetal.
_____

5. When a metal forms more than one ion, the name of the ion contains a Roman numeral to indicate the _____ on the ion.

6. What is a polyatomic ion? _____
_____

7. Is the following sentence true or false? Because all compounds are neutral, the total charges on the cations and anions in the formula of an ionic compound must add up to zero. _____

Chapter 6   Chemical Bonds

8. Circle the letter of the correct answer. The formula for sodium sulfide is Na_2S. The sodium ion has a charge of 1+. What must the charge on the sulfide ion be?

a. 1+   b. 0

c. 1−   d. 2−

Some Polyatomic Ions			
Name	**Formula**	**Name**	**Formula**
Ammonium	NH_4^+	Acetate	$C_2H_3O_2^-$
Hydroxide	OH^-	Peroxide	O_2^{2-}
Nitrate	NO_3^-	Permanganate	MnO_4^-
Sulfate	SO_4^{2-}	Hydrogen sulfate	HSO_4^-
Carbonate	CO_3^{2-}	Hydrogen carbonate	HCO_3^-
Phosphate	PO_4^{3-}	Hydrogen phosphate	HPO_4^{2-}

9. Circle the letter that identifies the number of ammonium ions needed to form a compound with one phosphate ion.

a. one   b. two

c. three   d. four

Describing Molecular Compounds (pages 174–175)

10. What information is provided by the name and formula of a molecular compound? _____

_____

_____

11. Describe the general rule for naming molecular compounds. _____

_____

_____

12. Is the following sentence true or false? The formula for a molecular compound is written with the symbols for the elements in the same order as the elements appear in the name of the compound. _____

13. Circle the letter that identifies the method of naming the number of atoms in molecular compounds.

a. prefix   b. suffix

c. number   d. symbol

14. In the formula of a molecular compound, the number of atoms of an element in the molecule is represented by a(n) _____.

Chapter 6   Chemical Bonds

Section 6.4 The Structure of Metals
(pages 176–181)

This section discusses metallic bonds and the properties of metals. It also explains how the properties of an alloy are controlled.

Reading Strategy (page 176)

Relating Cause and Effect As you read, complete the concept map to relate the structure of metals to their properties. For more information on this Reading Strategy, see the **Reading and Study Skills** in the **Skills and Reference Handbook** at the end of your textbook.

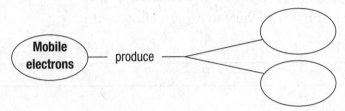

1. Circle the letter of the metal with the highest melting point.
   a. gold   b. vanadium
   c. titanium   d. tungsten

2. Is the following sentence true or false? The properties of a metal are related to bonds within the metal. _____

Metallic Bonds (pages 176–177)

3. Describe a metallic bond. _____
   _____

4. The cations in a metal form a lattice. What holds the lattice in place? _____
   _____

5. Is the following sentence true or false? The more valence electrons a metal has, the stronger its metallic bonds will be. _____

Explaining Properties of Metals (page 177)

6. Some of the properties of metals can be explained by the
   _____ of the electrons within a metal lattice.

7. Name two important properties of metals that can be explained by metallic bonding.
   a. _____   b. _____

Alloys (pages 178–181)

8. Circle the letter of the percentage of gold in jewelry that is labeled 18-karat gold.
   a. 18 percent   b. 50 percent
   c. 75 percent   d. 100 percent

Chapter 6   Chemical Bonds

9. Is the following sentence true or false? When a metal such as copper is mixed with gold, the gold becomes softer. _____

10. Describe an alloy. _____
_____

11. How do the hardness and strength of bronze compare to the hardness and strength of copper alone and tin alone? _____
_____
_____

12. Name two factors that scientists can vary to design alloys with specific properties.

a. _____

b. _____

13. Complete the following table.

Comparing Bronze and Brass			
Alloy	**Component Metals**	**Comparative Hardness of Bronze and Brass**	**Comparative Speed of Weathering**
Bronze	Copper, tin		Weathers more slowly
Brass		Softer	

14. When carbon is added to iron, the lattice becomes _____ than a lattice that contains only iron.

15. Circle the letters of the elements that all types of steel contain.

a. carbon   b. chromium

c. iron   d. manganese

16. Circle the letters of each correct description of stainless steel.

a. Stainless steel contains more carbon than chromium.

b. Chromium forms an oxide that protects stainless steel from rusting.

c. Stainless steel is more brittle than steels that contain more carbon.

d. Stainless steel contains more than 3 percent carbon by mass.

17. Explain why pure aluminum is not the best material for the body of a plane.
_____
_____

18. What type of alloy is used to make airplane parts that need to be extremely lightweight? _____

Chapter 6   Chemical Bonds

WordWise

Unscramble the terms from the following list to fit each of the clues given below.

claimlet	ecumelol	levoctan
lorpa	loyal	marfulo
mooctyliap	nocii	nonia
odbn	starscly	tonica

Clues   **Vocabulary Terms**

A type of bond that holds cations and anions together   _____

A type of bond in which two atoms share a pair of   _____
valence electrons

A neutral group of atoms that are joined together by   _____
one or more covalent bonds

A term describing a covalent bond in which electrons   _____
are not shared equally

An ion that contains a covalently bonded group of atoms   _____

An ion with a negative charge   _____

An ion with a positive charge   _____

A notation that shows what elements a compound   _____
contains and the ratio of the atoms or ions of these
elements in the compound

Solids whose particles are arranged in a lattice structure   _____

A mixture of two or more elements, at least one of which   _____
is a metal

A type of bond that exists between a metal cation and the   _____
shared electrons that surround it

The force that holds atoms or ions together   _____

Chapter 6   Chemical Bonds

Writing Formulas for Ionic Compounds

What is the ratio of the ions in magnesium iodide?
What is the formula for magnesium iodide?

1. Read and Understand

What information are you given?

The name of the compound is magnesium iodide.

2. Plan and Solve

List the symbols and charges for the cation and anion.

Mg ion has a charge of 2+ and I ion has a charge of 1−.

Determine the ratio of ions in the compound.

Mg with a 2+ charge needs two I ions, each with a charge of 1−.
The ratio of the ions in the compound is 1 to 2.

Write the formula for magnesium iodide.

MgI_2

3. Look Back and Check

Is your answer reasonable?

Each magnesium atom loses two electrons and each iodine atom gains one electron. So there should be a 1-to-2 ratio of magnesium ions to iodide ions.

Math Practice

On a separate sheet of paper, solve the following problems.
Refer to Figures 16, 17, and 19 to help you solve the problems.

1. What is the formula for magnesium fluoride?

2. What is the formula for iron(III) chloride?

3. What is the formula for mercury(II) sulfide?

4. What is the formula for potassium dichromate?

5. What is the formula for barium nitrate?

© Pearson Education, Inc., publishing as Pearson Prentice Hall. All rights reserved.

Math Skill: Ratios and Proportions

You may want to read more about this **Math Skill** in the **Skills and Reference Handbook** at the end of your textbook.

Chapter 7   Chemical Reactions

Section 7.1 Describing Reactions
(pages 192–198)

This section discusses the use of chemical equations and how to balance them. It also demonstrates the use of calculations in chemistry.

Reading Strategy (page 192)

Monitoring Your Understanding Preview the Key Concepts, topic headings, vocabulary, and figures in this section. List two things you expect to learn. After reading, state what you learned about each item you listed. For more information on this Reading Strategy, see the **Reading and Study Skills** in the **Skills and Reference Handbook** at the end of your textbook.

What I Expect to Learn	What I Learned

Chemical Equations (pages 192–193)

1. Is the following sentence true or false? The new substances formed as a result of a chemical reaction are called products. _____

2. Circle the letter of each sentence that is a correct interpretation of the chemical equation $C + O_2 \longrightarrow CO_2$.

   a. Carbon and oxygen react and form carbon monoxide.

   b. Carbon and oxygen react and form carbon dioxide.

   c. Carbon dioxide yields carbon and oxygen.

   d. The reaction of carbon and oxygen yields carbon dioxide.

3. Is the following sentence true or false? The law of conservation of mass states that mass is neither created nor destroyed in a chemical reaction. _____

4. Circle the letter of the correct answer. According to the equation $C + O_2 \longrightarrow CO_2$, how many carbon atoms react with 14 molecules of oxygen to form 14 molecules of carbon dioxide?

   a. 1   b. 7

   c. 14   d. 28

5. In the reaction represented by the equation $C + O_2 \longrightarrow CO_2$, the mass of carbon dioxide produced equals _____

   _____.

Chapter 7   Chemical Reactions

Balancing Equations (pages 194–195)

6. Is the following sentence true or false? A chemical equation must be balanced in order to show that mass is conserved during a reaction. _____

7. Circle the letter of the name given to the numbers that appear before the formulas in a chemical equation.

   a. subscripts   b. mass numbers

   c. atomic numbers   d. coefficients

8. Is the following sentence true or false? Because the equation $N_2H_4 + O_2 \longrightarrow N_2 + H_2O$ has two nitrogen atoms on each side, the equation is balanced. _____

Counting With Moles (pages 195–196)

9. Chemists use a counting unit called a(n) _____ to measure amounts of a substance because chemical reactions often involve large numbers of small particles.

10. Circle the letter of the correct answer. If one carbon atom has an atomic mass of 12.0 amu and one oxygen atom has an atomic mass of 16.0 amu, what is the molar mass of carbon dioxide?

    a. 28.0 amu   b. 44.0 amu

    c. 28.0 g   d. 44.0 g

11. Circle the letter of the correct answer. To convert grams of carbon dioxide to moles of carbon dioxide, you must multiply by which conversion factor?

    a. $\dfrac{44.0 \text{ g } CO_2}{1 \text{ mol } CO_2}$ b. $\dfrac{1 \text{ mol } CO_2}{44.0 \text{ g } CO_2}$

    c. $\dfrac{28.0 \text{ g } CO_2}{1 \text{ mol } CO_2}$ d. $\dfrac{1 \text{ mol } CO_2}{28.0 \text{ g } CO_2}$

Chemical Calculations (pages 197–198)

12. Complete the table.

Formation of Water			
Equation	$2H_2$ +	O_2 $\longrightarrow$	$2H_2O$
Amount	2 mol	1 mol	
Molar Mass	2.0 g/mol		18.0 g/mol
Mass (Moles × Molar Mass)		32.0 g	36.0 g

13. Circle the letter of the correct answer. One mole of oxygen has a mass of 32 grams. What is the mass of four moles of oxygen?

    a. 128 g   b. 144 g

    c. 128 amu   d. 144 amu

Chapter 7   Chemical Reactions

Section 7.2 Types of Reactions
(pages 199–205)

This section discusses how chemical reactions are classified into different types.

Reading Strategy (page 199)

Previewing Skim the section and begin a concept map like the
one below that identifies types of reactions with a general form.
As you read, add the general form of each type of reaction. For more
information on this Reading Strategy, see the **Reading and Study Skills**
in the **Skills and Reference Handbook** at the end of your textbook.

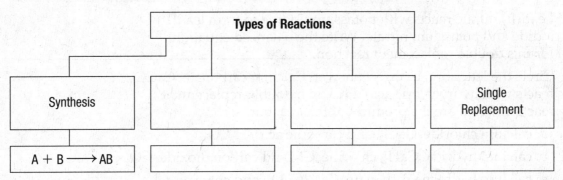

Classifying Reactions (pages 199–204)

1. Name five general types of chemical reactions. _____
_____

2. Circle the letter of each equation that represents a synthesis reaction.

   a. $2Na + Cl_2 \longrightarrow 2NaCl$

   b. $2NaCl \longrightarrow 2Na + Cl_2$

   c. $2H_2O \longrightarrow 2H_2 + O_2$

   d. $2H_2 + O_2 \longrightarrow 2H_2O$

3. Is the following sentence true or false? A decomposition reaction is
   the opposite of a synthesis reaction. _____

4. Write the equation for the decomposition of calcium carbonate into calcium oxide
   and carbon dioxide. _____

5. Circle the letter of the correct answer. Copper reacts with silver
   nitrate in a single-replacement reaction. What are the products of
   this reaction?

   a. copper(II) nitride and silver oxide

   b. copper(II) nitrate and silver

   c. copper(II) oxide and silver nitrate

   d. copper, nitrogen, and silver oxide

Chapter 7   Chemical Reactions

6. What is a double-replacement reaction? _____

_____

7. Complete the chart by filling in the general forms of the reactions shown.

General Forms	
Single-Replacement Reaction	**Double-Replacement Reaction**

8. Lead(II) nitrate reacts with potassium iodide to form lead(II) iodide and potassium nitrate. Write the balanced equation for this double-replacement reaction. _____

9. Circle the letter of the correct answer. Calcium carbonate, $CaCO_3$, reacts with hydrochloric acid, HCl, in a double-replacement reaction. What are the products of this reaction?

a. calcium chloride, $CaCl_2$, and carbonic acid, H_2CO_3

b. calcium hydride, CaH_2, chlorine, Cl_2, and carbon dioxide, CO_2

c. calcium hydrogen carbonate, $Ca(HCO_3)_2$, and chlorine, Cl_2

d. calcium perchlorate, $Ca(ClO_4)_2$, and methane, CH_4

10. Is the following sentence true or false? A combustion reaction is a reaction in which a substance reacts with carbon dioxide, often producing heat and light. _____

11. Methane, CH_4, burns in oxygen to form carbon dioxide and water. Write the balanced equation for this reaction. _____

12. Is the following sentence true or false? The reaction that forms water can be classified as either a synthesis reaction or a combustion reaction. _____

Reactions as Electron Transfers (pages 204–205)

13. What is an oxidation-reduction reaction? _____

_____

14. Calcium reacts with oxygen to form calcium oxide. Which reactant is oxidized in this reaction? _____

15. Is the following sentence true or false? When calcium reacts with oxygen, each calcium atom gains two electrons and becomes a calcium ion with a charge of 2–. _____

16. Is the following sentence true or false? Oxygen must be present in order for an oxidation-reduction reaction to take place. _____

17. The process in which an element gains electrons during a chemical reaction is called _____.

Chapter 7   Chemical Reactions

Section 7.3 Energy Changes in Reactions
(pages 206–209)

This section discusses how chemical bonds and energy relate to chemical reactions.

Reading Strategy (page 206)

Comparing and Contrasting As you read, complete the Venn diagram below to show the differences between exothermic and endothermic reactions. For more information on this Reading Strategy, see the **Reading and Study Skills** in the **Skills and Reference Handbook** at the end of your textbook.

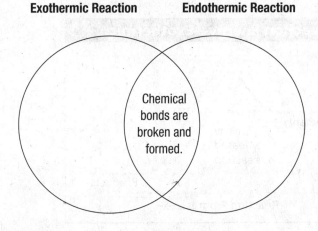

Exothermic Reaction   **Endothermic Reaction**

Chemical bonds are broken and formed.

Chemical Bonds and Energy (pages 206–207)

1. What is chemical energy? _____
   _____

2. Chemical reactions involve the breaking of chemical bonds in the reactants and the formation of chemical bonds in the _____.

3. Is the following sentence true or false? The formation of chemical bonds absorbs energy. _____

4. What role does the spark from the igniter play in the reaction that takes place when propane is burned in a gas grill? _____
   _____

5. Is the following sentence true or false? The heat and light given off by a propane stove result from the formation of new chemical bonds. _____

6. The combustion of one molecule of propane (C_3H_8) results in the formation of _____ C=O double bonds and _____ O−H single bonds.

Chapter 7   Chemical Reactions

Exothermic and Endothermic Reactions (pages 208–209)

7. During a chemical reaction, energy is either released or

_____.

8. Is the following sentence true or false? Physical and chemical changes can be either exothermic or endothermic changes.

_____

9. What is an exothermic reaction? _____

_____

10. Is the following sentence true or false? In exothermic reactions, the energy required to break the bonds in the reactants is greater than the energy released as the products form. _____

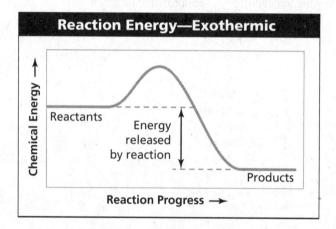

11. Circle the letter of each sentence that is correct for the graph above.

   a. The energy required to break the bonds in the reactants is greater than the energy released as the products form.

   b. The energy released as the products form is greater than the energy required to break the bonds in the reactants.

   c. The chemical energy of the reactants is greater than the chemical energy of the products.

   d. The chemical energy of the products is greater than the chemical energy of the reactants.

12. In an exothermic reaction, the difference between the chemical energy of the reactants and the chemical energy of the products equals

_____.

13. Where does the energy term appear in the equation for an endothermic reaction? _____

Conservation of Energy (page 209)

14. In an endothermic reaction, heat from the surroundings plus the chemical energy of the reactants is converted into the

_____.

Chapter 7   **Chemical Reactions**

Section 7.4 Reaction Rates
(pages 212–215)

This section discusses the factors that affect reaction rates.

Reading Strategy (page 212)

Building Vocabulary As you read, complete the web diagram below with key terms from this section. For more information on this Reading Strategy, see the **Reading and Study Skills** in the **Skills and Reference Handbook** at the end of your textbook.

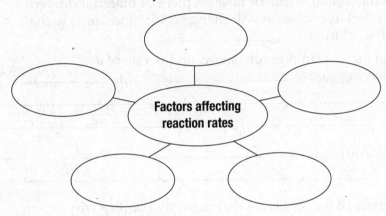

Reactions Over Time (page 212)

1. Any change that happens over time can be expressed as a(n) _____.

2. What is a reaction rate? _____

_____

Factors Affecting Reaction Rates (pages 213–215)

3. Is the following sentence true or false? One way to observe the rate of a reaction is to observe how fast products are being formed.

    _____

4. Is the following sentence true or false? The rate of any reaction is a constant that does not change when the reaction conditions change.

    _____

5. Generally, an increase in temperature will _____ the reaction rate.

6. Is the following sentence true or false? Storing milk in a refrigerator stops the reactions that would cause the milk to spoil.

    _____

7. How does an increase in surface area affect the exposure of reactants to one another? _____

_____

Chapter 7   Chemical Reactions

8. Why does increasing the surface area of a reactant tend to increase the reaction rate? _____

_____

9. Stirring the reactants in a reaction mixture will generally _____ the reaction rate.

10. Is the following sentence true or false? Increasing the concentration of the reactants will generally slow down a chemical reaction. _____

11. Is the following sentence true or false? A piece of material dipped in a concentrated dye solution will change color more quickly than in a dilute dye solution. _____

12. Why does an increase in pressure speed up the rate of a reaction involving gases? _____

_____

_____

13. What is a catalyst? _____

_____

14. Circle the letters of the sentences that correctly identify why chemists use catalysts.

   a. to speed up a reaction

   b. to enable a reaction to occur at a higher temperature

   c. to slow down a reaction

   d. to enable a reaction to occur at a lower temperature

15. Is the following sentence true or false? Because a catalyst is quickly consumed in a reaction, it must be added to the reaction mixture over and over again to keep the reaction going. _____

16. Identify where the catalyst V_2O_5 should go in the formula shown and write it in the correct location.

$$2SO_2 + O_2 \longrightarrow 2SO_3$$

17. Circle the letter of the correct answer. In the reaction represented by the equation $2H_2O_2 \xrightarrow{\text{Pt}} 2H_2O + O_2$, which substance acts as a catalyst?

   a. H_2O_2 b. Pt

   c. H_2O d. O_2

18. One way that a catalyst can lower the energy barrier of a reaction is by providing a surface on which the _____ can come together.

Chapter 7   Chemical Reactions

Section 7.5 Equilibrium
(pages 216–219)

This section explains physical and chemical equilibria, and describes the factors that affect chemical equilibrium.

Reading Strategy (page 216)

Outlining As you read, make an outline of the most important ideas from this section. For more information on this Reading Strategy, see the **Reading and Study Skills** in the **Skills and Reference Handbook** at the end of your textbook.

I. Equilibrium

   A. Types of Equilibria

      1.

      2.

   B.

      1. Temperature

      2. Pressure

      3.

Types of Equilibria (pages 216–217)

1. What is equilibrium? _____

_____

_____

2. Circle the letter of the correct answer. In the system described by the equation $H_2O(l) \rightleftharpoons H_2O(g)$, at room temperature, which of the following two physical changes are in equilibrium?

   a. sublimation and condensation

   b. evaporation and melting

   c. sublimation and deposition

   d. evaporation and condensation

3. What happens when a physical change does not go to completion?

_____

_____

4. What does the single arrow imply about the reaction described in the following equation?

   $CH_4(g) + 2O_2(g) \longrightarrow CO_2(g) + 2H_2O(g)$

_____

_____

Chapter 7   Chemical Reactions

5. Circle the letter of the correct answer. In the system described by the equation $2SO_2(g) + O_2(g) \rightleftharpoons 2SO_3(g)$, what two reaction types are in equilibrium?

a. synthesis and decomposition   b. single replacement and decomposition

c. synthesis and combustion   d. synthesis and double replacement

6. What happens when a chemical change does not go to completion?

_____

_____

Factors Affecting Chemical Equilibrium (pages 218–219)

7. Is the following sentence true or false? A change in reaction conditions does not affect a chemical equilibrium. _____

8. Circle the letter of each correct answer. The synthesis of ammonia is described by the equation $N_2(g) + 3H_2(g) \rightleftharpoons 2NH_3(g) + \text{heat}$. Which reaction is favored when the temperature is lowered?

a. the forward reaction

b. the reverse reaction

c. the reaction that removes heat from the system

d. the reaction that adds heat to the system

9. Circle the letter of each correct answer. During the synthesis of ammonia, which reaction is favored when hydrogen is added to the system?

a. the forward reaction

b. the reverse reaction

c. the reaction that removes hydrogen from the system

d. the reaction that adds hydrogen to the system

10. According to Le Châtelier's principle, how does lowering the concentration of a reaction product affect a chemical equilibrium? _____

_____

11. Use the equation $C(s) + H_2O(g) + \text{heat} \rightleftharpoons CO(g) + H_2(g)$ to complete the table below.

An Example of Le Châtelier's Principle		
An increase in	**Shifts the equilibrium so as to**	**Favoring the**
	Remove heat	Forward reaction
Pressure	Produce fewer gas molecules	
Concentration of H_2		Reverse reaction

Chapter 7   Chemical Reactions

WordWise

Answer the questions by writing the correct vocabulary term in the blanks.
Use the circled letter in each term to find the hidden vocabulary word. Then,
write a definition for the hidden word.

Clues

Describes a reaction that releases
energy to its surroundings

_ _ _ _ _ _ Ⓞ _ _ _

A state in which the forward and reverse
paths of a change take place at the
same rate

Ⓞ _ _ _ _ _ _ _ _ _ _

A substance that affects the reaction rate
without being used up in the reaction

_ Ⓞ _ _ _ _ _ _

A reaction in which a compound breaks
down into two or more simpler substances

_ _ Ⓞ _ _ _ _ _ _ _ _ _ _

A reaction in which two or more
substances react to form a single substance

_ _ _ Ⓞ _ _ _ _ _

The mass of one mole of a substance

_ _ _ Ⓞ _ _ _ _ _

A number that appears before a formula
in a chemical equation

_ _ _ _ _ _ _ _ _ _ Ⓞ _

A reaction in which a substance reacts
rapidly with oxygen, often producing
heat and light

_ _ _ _ _ _ Ⓞ _ _ _

The substances formed as the result
of a chemical change

_ _ _ _ _ _ _ Ⓞ

Vocabulary Terms

Hidden Term: _ _ _ _ _ _ _ _ _ _

Definition: _____

_____

Chapter 7   Chemical Reactions

Balancing Chemical Equations

Write a balanced equation for the reaction between potassium and water to produce hydrogen and potassium hydroxide, KOH.

Math Skill:
Formulas and
Equations

You may want to read more about this **Math Skill** in the **Skills and Reference Handbook** at the end of your textbook.

1. Read and Understand

What information are you given?

Reactants: K, H_2O
Products: H_2, KOH

2. Plan and Solve

Write a chemical equation with the reactants on the left side and the products on the right.

$K + H_2O \longrightarrow H_2 + KOH$

This equation is not balanced. The number of hydrogen atoms on the left does not equal the number of hydrogen atoms on the right. Change the coefficients of H_2O and KOH in order to balance the number of hydrogen atoms.

$K + 2H_2O \longrightarrow H_2 + 2KOH$

Change the coefficient of K in order to balance the number of potassium atoms.

$2K + 2H_2O \longrightarrow H_2 + 2KOH$

3. Look Back and Check

Is your answer reasonable?

The number of atoms on the left equals the number of atoms on the right.

Math Practice

On a separate sheet of paper, solve the following problems.

1. Magnesium burns in the presence of oxygen to form magnesium oxide, MgO. Write a balanced equation for this reaction.

2. Hydrogen peroxide, H_2O_2, decomposes to form water and oxygen. Write a balanced equation for this reaction.

3. Barium hydroxide, $Ba(OH)_2$, reacts with nitric acid, HNO_3, to form barium nitrate and water. Write a balanced equation for this reaction.

Chapter 8   Solutions, Acids, and Bases

Section 8.1 Formation of Solutions
(pages 228–234)

This section explains the parts of a solution, the processes that occur when compounds dissolve, and how the properties of a solution compare with those of its solvent and solute.

Reading Strategy (page 228)

Comparing and Contrasting Contrast dissociation and ionization by listing the ways they differ in the Venn diagram below. For more information on this reading strategy, see the **Reading and Study Skills** in the **Skills and Reference Handbook** at the end of your textbook.

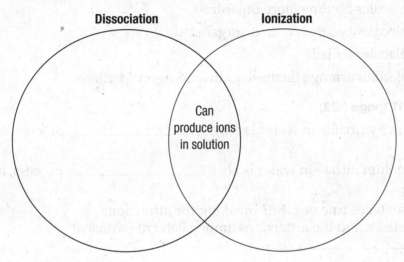

Dissolving (page 229)

1. Define a solution. _____
_____

2. Circle the letter that identifies a substance whose particles are dissolved in a solution.

   a. solvent   b. solute

   c. solid   d. ion

3. Circle the letter that identifies the solvent in air.

   a. oxygen   b. carbon dioxide

   c. nitrogen   d. argon

4. The process in which an ionic compound separates into ions as it dissolves is called _____.

5. The process in which particles dissolve by breaking apart and scattering is called _____.

6. A(n) _____ is transferred from each HCl molecule to a water molecule when hydrogen chloride gas dissolves in water.

7. Is the following sentence true or false? Dissolving by ionization is a physical change. _____

Chapter 8   Solutions, Acids, and Bases

Properties of Liquid Solutions (page 231)

8. What physical properties of a solution can differ from those of its solute and solvent?

   a. _____

   b. _____

   c. _____

9. Compare the conductivities of solid sodium chloride and saltwater. _____

   _____

10. Circle the letters that identify what happens to water as it freezes.

   a. The water molecules become more organized.

   b. The water molecules become more disorganized.

   c. The water molecules ionize.

   d. The water molecules arrange themselves in a hexagonal pattern.

Heat of Solution (page 232)

11. Dissolving sodium hydroxide in water is a(n) _____ process, as it releases heat.

12. Dissolving ammonium nitrate in water is a(n) _____ process, as it absorbs heat.

13. Is the following sentence true or false? Breaking the attractions among solute particles and the attractions among solvent particles releases energy. _____

14. Describe heat of solution. _____

   _____

   _____

Factors Affecting Rates of Dissolving (page 234)

15. How are rates of dissolving similar to rates of chemical reactions?

   _____

16. Why does powdered sugar dissolve in water faster than granulated sugar? _____

   _____

17. Heating a solvent _____ the energy of its particles, making them move faster on average, and _____ the rate at which a solid solute can dissolve in the solvent.

18. Explain how stirring or shaking a mixture of powdered detergent and water can affect the rate of dissolving. _____

   _____

   _____

Chapter 8   Solutions, Acids, and Bases

Section 8.2 Solubility and Concentration
(pages 235–239)

This section explains solubility, the factors affecting solubility, and different ways of expressing the concentration of a solution.

Reading Strategy (page 235)

Previewing Before you read the section, rewrite the topic headings as *how, why,* and *what* questions. As you read, write an answer to each question. For more information on this reading strategy, see the **Reading and Study Skills** in the **Skills and Reference Handbook** at the end of your textbook.

Question	Answer
What is solubility?	
	Solvent, temperature, and pressure

Solubility (pages 235–237)

1. Define solubility. _____

_____

2. List the following solutes in order from most soluble to least soluble in water: table salt, baking soda, table sugar.

   a. _____

   b. _____

   c. _____

3. Circle the letters that identify how solutions can be classified based on solubility.

   a. unsaturated   b. desaturated

   c. saturated   d. supersaturated

4. Describe a saturated solution. _____

_____

5. A solution that has less than the maximum amount of solute that can be dissolved is called a(n) _____.

6. Is the following sentence true or false? It is impossible for a solution to contain more solute than the solvent can hold at a given temperature. _____

Chapter 8   Solutions, Acids, and Bases

Factors Affecting Solubility (page 237)

7. Circle the letters of factors that affect the solubility of a solute.

   a. polarity of the solvent

   b. amount of solvent

   c. pressure

   d. temperature

8. What is a common guideline for predicting solubility?
   _____

9. Describe how soap cleans grease off your hands. _____
   _____
   _____

10. Is the following statement true or false? In general, the solubility of
    solids increases as the solvent temperature increases.
    _____

11. In general, the solubility of gases decreases as the solvent
    temperature _____.

12. In general, the solubility of a gas increases as pressure
    _____.

Concentration of Solutions (pages 238–239)

13. What does the concentration of a solution refer to? _____
    _____
    _____

14. Circle the letters that identify ways to express the concentration
    of a solution.

    a. density

    b. percent by volume

    c. percent by mass

    d. molarity

15. Complete the equation.

    Percent by volume =

    _____

16. Write the equation used to calculate percent by mass.

    _____

17. Is this sentence true or false? Molarity is the number of moles of a solvent per liter
    of solution. _____

18. How many grams of NaCl are needed to make 1.00 liter of a
    3.00 M NaCl solution? _____

Chapter 8   Solutions, Acids, and Bases

Section 8.3 Properties of Acids and Bases
(pages 240–245)

This section describes the general properties of acids and bases.

Reading Strategy (page 240)

Using Prior Knowledge Before you read, write your definition of each vocabulary term in the table below. After you read, write the scientific definition of each term and compare it with your original definition. For more information on this reading strategy, see the **Reading and Study Skills** in the **Skills and Reference Handbook** at the end of your textbook.

Term	Your Definition	Scientific Definition
Acid		
Base		
Salt		

Identifying Acids (pages 240–241)

1. Define an acid. _____

_____

Match these common acids to their uses.

Acids	Uses
_____ 2. acetic acid	a. Fertilizer production
_____ 3. sulfuric acid	b. Carbonated beverages
_____ 4. hydrochloric acid	c. Vinegar
_____ 5. carbonic acid	d. Car batteries
_____ 6. nitric acid	e. Digestive juices in stomach

7. Describe some general properties of acids. _____

_____

8. Place the following substances in the correct column in the table: lemons, vinegar, grapefruit, sour milk, tomatoes.

Foods Containing Acetic Acid	Foods Containing Citric Acid	Foods Containing Butyric Acid

9. The reaction between an acid and a metal can be classified as a(n)

_____ .

10. Explain why an indicator is useful. _____

_____

Identifying Bases (pages 242–243)

11. Define a base. _____

_____

12. Use the following compounds to complete the chart: aluminum
hydroxide, calcium hydroxide, magnesium hydroxide, and
sodium hydroxide.

Common Bases		
Name	Formula	Uses
	NaOH	Drain cleaner, soap production
	Mg(OH)$_2$	Antacid, laxative
	Ca(OH)$_2$	Concrete, plaster
	Al(OH)$_3$	Deodorant, antacid

13. What can a gardener add to the soil to change the flowers of a
hydrangea from pink to blue? _____

14. Circle the letter that describes how basic solutions generally taste.

   a. sweet   b. sour

   c. bitter   d. salty

15. Is the following sentence true or false? Bases turn red litmus paper
blue. _____

Neutralization and Salts (page 244)

16. The reaction between an acid and a base is called _____.

17. Describe how a salt can be produced by a chemical reaction. _____

_____

18. Write a chemical equation describing the neutralization reaction
between calcium hydroxide and hydrochloric acid.

_____

Proton Donors and Acceptors (page 245)

19. Acids can be described as proton _____; bases can
be described as proton _____.

20. When hydrogen chloride ionizes in water, which reactant is the
proton donor? Which reactant is the proton acceptor? _____

_____

Section 8.4 Strength of Acids and Bases

(pages 246–249)

This section explains how to describe acids and bases in terms of both concentration and strength.

Reading Strategy (page 246)

Comparing and Contrasting As you read, complete the diagram by comparing and contrasting acids and bases. For more information on this reading strategy, see the **Reading and Study Skills** in the **Skills and Reference Handbook** at the end of your textbook.

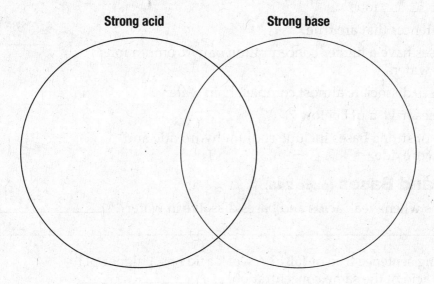

Strong acid   Strong base

The pH Scale (page 247)

1. What is the name of the number scale chemists use to describe the concentration of hydronium ions in a solution?
   _____

2. The pH scale ranges from _____ to _____.

3. Circle the letter that indicates the pH of a neutral solution.
   a. 0
   b. 3
   c. 7
   d. 12

4. Water is neutral because it contains small but equal concentrations of _____ and _____.

5. Is the following sentence true or false? The higher the pH value of a solution, the greater the H_3O^+ ion concentration is.
   _____

6. If you add acid to pure water, the concentration of H_3O^+ _____ and the concentration of OH _____.

Chapter 8   Solutions, Acids, and Bases

Strong Acids and Bases (pages 247–248)

7. What happens when strong acids and bases dissolve in water? _____

8. Is the following sentence true or false? A strong acid always has a lower pH than a weak acid. _____

9. Circle the letters that identify a strong acid.

   a. HCl   b. $Ca(OH)_2$

   c. H_2O d. HNO_3

10. When dissolved in water, sodium hydroxide almost completely dissociates into _____ and _____ ions.

11. Circle the sentences that are true.

   a. Strong bases have a higher concentration of hydronium ions than pure water.

   b. Strong bases dissociate almost completely in water.

   c. Strong bases have a pH below 7.

   d. Examples of strong bases include sodium hydroxide and calcium hydroxide.

Weak Acids and Bases (page 248)

12. What happens when weak acids and bases dissolve in water? _____

_____

13. Is the following sentence true or false? A weak acid has a higher pH than a strong acid of the same concentration. _____

14. Describe the difference between concentration and strength. _____

_____

_____

15. Describe a buffer. _____

_____

Electrolytes (page 249)

16. An electrolyte is _____

_____

17. Is the following sentence true or false? Strong acids and bases are weak electrolytes because they dissociate or ionize almost completely in water. _____

18. Is acetic acid an example of a weak electrolyte? Explain. _____

_____

Chapter 8   Solutions, Acids, and Bases

WordWise

Use the clues below to identify some of the vocabulary terms from Chapter 8.
Write the words on the line, putting one letter in each blank. When you finish,
the words enclosed in the circle will reveal an important term.

Clues

1. A(n) _____ solution is one in which you can dissolve more solute.

2. A substance in which other materials dissolve is called a(n) _____.

3. A(n) _____ is a substance that forms ions when dissolved in water.

4. A(n) _____ is a solution containing either a weak acid and its salt or a weak base and its salt.

5. A(n) _____ is a compound that produces hydroxide ions when dissolved in water.

6. The process in which a substance breaks up into smaller particles as it dissolves is called _____.

7. The reaction between an acid and a base is called _____.

8. A(n) _____ is a compound that produces hydronium ions when dissolved in water.

9. When neutral molecules gain or lose electrons, the process is known as _____.

10. The number of moles of solute that is dissolved in 1 liter of solution is _____.

Vocabulary Terms

1. _ _ _ _ _ _ _ _ _ _
2. _ _ _ _ _ _ _
3. _ _ _ _ _ _ _ _ _ _
4. _ _ _ _ _ _ _
5. _ _ _ _ _
6. _ _ _ _ _ _ _ _ _
7. _ _ _ _ _ _ _ _ _ _ _
8. _ _ _ _
9. _ _ _ _ _ _ _
10. _ _ _ _ _ _ _ _

Hidden Word: _ _ _ _ _ _ _ _ _

Definition: _____

_____

Chapter 8   Solutions, Acids, and Bases

Calculating the Molarity of a Solution

Suppose you dissolve 58.5 grams of sodium chloride into enough water to make exactly 1.00 liter of solution. What is the molarity of the solution?

Math Skill: Calculating with Significant Figures

You may want to read more about this **Math Skill** in the **Skills and Reference Handbook** at the end of your textbook.

1. Read and Understand

What information are you given?

Mass of solute = 58.5 g NaCl

Volume of solution = 1.00 L

2. Plan and Solve

What unknown are you trying to solve?

Molarity = ?

What equation can you use?

$$\text{Molarity} = \frac{\text{moles of solute}}{\text{liters of solution}}$$

Convert the mass of the solute into moles.

$$\text{Moles of solute} = \frac{\text{Mass of NaCl}}{\text{Molar mass of NaCl}}$$

$$= \frac{58.5 \text{ g NaCl}}{58.5 \text{ g NaCl/mol NaCl}} = 1.00 \text{ mol NaCl}$$

Solve the equation for molarity.

$$\text{Molarity} = \frac{1.00 \text{ mol NaCl}}{1.00 \text{ L}} = 1.00 \text{ M NaCl}$$

3. Look Back and Check

Is your answer reasonable?

A 1.00 M NaCl solution contains 1.00 mole of NaCl per liter of solution. The answer is reasonable.

Math Practice

On a separate sheet of paper, solve the following problems.

1. Suppose you had 4.0 moles of solute dissolved into 2.0 liters of solution. What is the molarity?

2. A saltwater solution containing 43.9 grams of NaCl has a total volume of 1.5 liters. What is the molarity?

3. Table sugar has a molar mass of 342 grams. How many grams of table sugar are needed to make 2.00 liters of a 0.500 M solution?

Chapter 9   Carbon Chemistry

Section 9.1 Carbon Compounds
(pages 262–269)

This section describes different forms of carbon that exist in nature. It also discusses saturated and unsaturated hydrocarbons. It explains the formation of fossil fuels and describes the products of their combustion.

Reading Strategy (page 262)

Previewing Before you read, use the models in Figure 2 to describe the arrangement of carbon atoms in each form of carbon. For more information on this Reading Strategy, see the **Reading and Study Skills** in the **Skills and Reference Handbook** at the end of your textbook.

Forms of Carbon	
Diamond	
Graphite	
Buckminsterfullerene	

1. The two elements that all organic compounds contain are

   _____.

2. Circle the letter of the approximate percentage of all known compounds that are organic compounds.

   a. 10 percent   b. 30 percent

   c. 60 percent   d. 90 percent

Forms of Carbon (page 263)

3. Circle the letter of each form of carbon.

   a. soot   b. diamond

   c. fullerenes   d. graphite

4. Describe a network solid. _____

   _____

5. Circle the letter of each property of graphite.

   a. soft   b. rigid

   c. compact   d. slippery

Saturated Hydrocarbons (pages 264–265)

6. Is the following sentence true or false? A hydrocarbon is an organic compound that contains carbon, hydrogen, and oxygen. _____

7. Is the following sentence true or false? A saturated hydrocarbon contains only single bonds. _____

8. Name the factors that determine the properties of a hydrocarbon.

   a. _____   b. _____

9. Name the three ways that carbon atoms can be arranged in hydrocarbon molecules.

   a. _____   b. _____   c. _____

10. Circle the letter of the correct answer. What does a structural formula show that a molecular formula does not?

   a. the type of atoms in the compound

   b. the number of atoms in a molecule of the compound

   c. the arrangement of atoms in the compound

   d. the state of the compound at room temperature

11. Describe isomers. _____
   _____

Unsaturated Hydrocarbons (page 266)

12. Circle the letter of each type of unsaturated hydrocarbon.

   a. alkene   b. alkane

   c. alkyne   d. aromatic hydrocarbon

13. Circle the letter of the most reactive type of hydrocarbon.

   a. alkanes   b. alkenes

   c. alkynes   d. aromatic hydrocarbons

Fossil Fuels (page 267–268)

14. Define fossil fuels. _____
   _____

15. Circle the letter of each fossil fuel.

   a. coal   b. natural gas

   c. ferns   d. petroleum

16. Is the following sentence true or false? In a distillation tower, compounds with lower boiling points condense first. _____

Combustion of Fossil Fuels (pages 268–269)

17. Circle the letter of each primary product of the complete combustion of fossil fuels.

   a. carbon dioxide   b. carbon monoxide

   c. sulfur dioxide   d. water

18. When an insufficient amount of oxygen is available for complete combustion of a fossil fuel, one product of the combustion reaction is the deadly gas _____.

19. Why is rain always slightly acidic? _____
   _____

Chapter 9   Carbon Chemistry

Section 9.2 Substituted Hydrocarbons
(pages 272–274)

This section discusses organic compounds that contain atoms of elements other than carbon and hydrogen. It also explains the relationship between the properties of organic compounds and functional groups.

Reading Strategy (page 272)

Monitoring Your Understanding As you read, complete the table by connecting each functional group with the type of compound that contains the functional group. For more information on this Reading Strategy, see the **Reading and Study Skills** in the **Skills and Reference Handbook** at the end of your textbook.

Connecting Functional Groups to Types of Compounds	
Functional Group	**Type of Compound**
–OH	
–COOH	
–NH$_2$	

1. Name the two main products when methane and chlorine react.

   a. _____

   b. _____

2. To which environmental problem have researchers connected halocarbons containing chlorine and fluorine? _____

   _____

   _____

3. Describe a substituted hydrocarbon. _____

   _____

   _____

4. Is the following sentence true or false? The functional group in a substituted hydrocarbon determines the properties of the compound. _____

Alcohols (page 273)

5. Methanol and ethanol are two examples of a class of organic compounds called _____.

6. The functional group in an alcohol is represented as –OH and is called a(n) _____ group.

7. Identify two ways a halocarbon can be produced.

   a. _____

   b. _____

Chapter 9   Carbon Chemistry

Organic Acids and Bases (pages 273–274)

8. What two physical properties do organic acids tend to have?

   a. _____

   b. _____

9. Is the following sentence true or false? Amines are organic bases. _____

10. Name three products where amines can be found.

    a. _____

    b. _____

    c. _____

11. Complete the following table.

Substituted Hydrocarbons		
Type of Compound	Name of Functional Group	Formula of Functional Group
	Hydroxyl	
Organic acid		–COOH
Organic base	Amino	

Esters (page 274)

12. What type of compound gives many flowers a pleasant odor?

    _____

13. Which two types of compounds can react and form esters?

    a. _____

    b. _____

14. Circle the letter of the other product of the reaction that forms an ester.

    a. an alcohol

    b. carbon dioxide

    c. a salt

    d. water

15. Is the following sentence true or false? Esters are used to make various fruit flavors in processed foods. _____

Chapter 9   Carbon Chemistry

Section 9.3 Polymers
(pages 275–280)

This section explains how polymers form. It also discusses examples of synthetic and natural polymers.

Reading Strategy (page 275)

Identifying Main Ideas As you read, complete the concept map to summarize two main ideas about polymers. For more information on this Reading Strategy, see the **Reading and Study Skills** in the **Skills and Reference Handbook** at the end of your textbook.

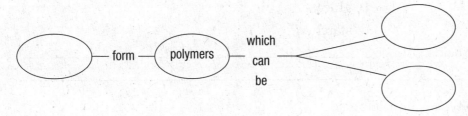

1. Describe a polymer. _____

_____

2. The smaller molecules that join together to form a polymer are called _____.

3. Is the following sentence true or false? More than one type of monomer can be present in some polymers. _____

4. Name the two general classifications of polymers.

   a. _____   b. _____

Synthetic Polymers (page 276)

5. Name three polymers that can be synthesized.

   a. _____   b. _____   c. _____

6. Is the following sentence true or false? The more carbon atoms there are in a polyethylene chain, the harder the polymer is.

   _____

Natural Polymers (pages 278–280)

7. Name four types of polymers that are produced in plant and animal cells.

   a. _____   b. _____

   c. _____   d. _____

8. Circle the letter of the molecular formula of a simple sugar.

   a. CH_2O b. $C_6H_{12}O_6$

   c. $C_{12}H_{22}O_{11}$ d. $C_{12}H_{24}O_{12}$

9. Circle the letter of the simple sugar glucose and fructose can react to form.

    a. glucose   b. fructose

    c. cellulose   d. sucrose

10. How are starches used in plants? _____

_____

11. Simple sugars, slightly more complex sugars, and polymers built from sugar monomers are classified as _____.

12. Circle the letter of the main component of cotton and wood.

    a. cellulose   b. glucose

    c. protein   d. starch

13. Define nucleic acids. _____

_____

14. Name the two types of nucleic acid.

    a. _____   b. _____

15. Name the three parts of a nucleotide in DNA.

    a. _____   b. _____   c. _____

16. Circle the letter of the term that best describes the structure of DNA.

    a. helix   b. double helix

    c. ring   d. chain

17. How does DNA store information? _____

_____

18. Is the following sentence true or false? The human body can manufacture all of the essential amino acids. _____

19. Amino acids are the monomers that cells use to build the polymers known as _____.

20. Complete the following concept map about amino acids.

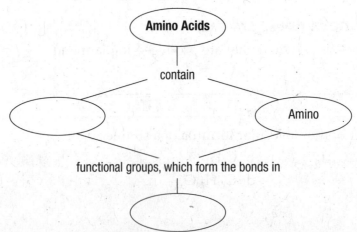

Chapter 9   Carbon Chemistry

Section 9.4 Reactions in Cells
(pages 282–284)

This section describes and compares photosynthesis and cellular respiration. It also discusses the roles of enzymes and vitamins.

Reading Strategy (page 282)

Summarizing As you read, complete the table by recording a main idea for each heading. For more information on this Reading Strategy, see the **Reading and Study Skills** in the **Skills and Reference Handbook** at the end of your textbook.

Heading	Main Idea
Photosynthesis	
Cellular Respiration	
Enzymes and Vitamins	

1. Two processes that allow organisms to meet their energy needs are _____ and _____.

Photosynthesis (page 282)

2. Describe what happens during photosynthesis. _____
_____
_____

3. Circle the letter of each requirement for photosynthesis to occur.
   a. chlorophyll   b. oxygen
   c. carbohydrates   d. light

4. Identify the energy conversion that takes place during photosynthesis. _____
_____

5. Circle the letter of each product of photosynthesis.
   a. carbon dioxide   b. carbohydrates
   c. oxygen   d. water

6. Is the following sentence true or false? When all the reactions in photosynthesis are complete, energy from sunlight has been stored in the covalent bonds of molecules. _____

Cellular Respiration (page 283)

7. During cellular respiration, the _____ stored in the products of photosynthesis is released.

Chapter 9   Carbon Chemistry

8. How is cellular respiration related to photosynthesis? _____

_____

9. Is the following sentence true or false? Carbohydrates produce more energy per gram than fats do. _____

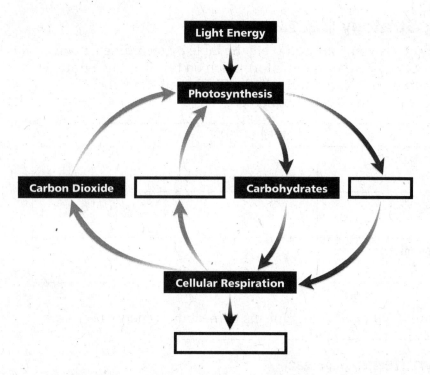

10. Complete the diagram relating photosynthesis to cellular respiration.

a. _____ b. _____ c. _____

Enzymes and Vitamins (page 284)

11. Describe what enzymes and vitamins have in common. _____

_____

12. Define enzymes. _____

_____

13. Is the following sentence true or false? Enzymes require high temperatures in order to function. _____

14. Is the following sentence true or false? Some enzymes require a co-enzyme in order to function. _____

15. Define vitamins. _____

_____

16. Is the following sentence true or false? All vitamins dissolve in water and must be replaced daily. _____

17. Identify the property of vitamin A that allows it to build up in body tissues over time. _____

Chapter 9   Carbon Chemistry

WordWise

Complete the following crossword puzzle, using the clues provided below.

Clues across:

1. A hydrocarbon in which all of the bonds are single bonds

2. A compound containing carbon and hydrogen, often combined with other elements such as oxygen and nitrogen

3. A small molecule that joins with other small molecules to form a polymer

4. _____ acid: a large nitrogen-containing polymer found mainly in the nuclei of cells

5. Organic compounds that contain only carbon and hydrogen

Clues down:

6. An organic compound that organisms need in small amounts, but cannot produce

7. Organic compounds that contain both carboxyl and amino functional groups

8. Compounds with the same molecular formula but different structural formulas

9. A polymer in which at least 100 amino acid monomers are linked through bonds between an amino group and a carboxyl group

10. _____ solid: a type of solid in which all of the atoms are linked by covalent bonds

Chapter 9   Carbon Chemistry

Balancing Equations for Organic Reactions

Math Skill:
Ratios and
Proportions

You may want to read more about this **Math Skill** in the **Skills and Reference Handbook** at the end of your textbook.

When propane, C_3H_8, combines with oxygen, the products are carbon dioxide and water. Write a balanced equation for the complete combustion of propane.

1. Read and Understand

What information are you given?

Reactants = propane (C_3H_8) and oxygen (O_2)

Products = carbon dioxide (CO_2) and water (H_2O)

2. Plan and Solve

What unknowns are you trying to determine?

The coefficients for the equation

What equation contains the given information?

$C_3H_8 + O_2 \longrightarrow CO_2 + H_2O$ (unbalanced equation)

First, balance the equation for carbon. Because there are 3 carbon atoms in C_3H_8, you need to place the coefficient 3 in front of CO_2.

$C_3H_8 + O_2 \longrightarrow 3CO_2 + H_2O$

Next, balance the equation for hydrogen. Because there are 8 hydrogen atoms in C_3H_8 and only 2 hydrogen atoms in H_2O, you need to place the coefficient 4 in front of H_2O.

$C_3H_8 + O_2 \longrightarrow 3CO_2 + 4H_2O$

Finally, balance the equation for oxygen. Because there are 6 oxygen atoms in 3 molecules of CO_2 and 4 oxygen atoms in 4 molecules of H_2O for a total of 10 oxygen atoms, you need to place the coefficient 5 in front of O_2.

$C_3H_8 + 5O_2 \longrightarrow 3CO_2 + 4H_2O$

3. Look Back and Check

Is your answer reasonable?

Each side of the equation has 3 carbon atoms, 8 hydrogen atoms, and 10 oxygen atoms. The equation is balanced.

Math Practice

On a separate sheet of paper, solve the following problems.

1. Balance the equation for the reaction of benzene and hydrogen to form cyclohexane.

$C_6H_6 + \underline{\hspace{1cm}} H_2 \xrightarrow{\text{Pt}} C_6H_{12}$

2. Write a balanced equation for the complete combustion of methane, CH_4.

3. Write a balanced equation for the combustion of glucose, $C_6H_{12}O_6$.

Chapter 10   Nuclear Chemistry

Section 10.1 Radioactivity
(pages 292–297)

This section discusses the different types of nuclear radiation and how they affect matter.

Reading Strategy (page 292)

Previewing Before you read the section, rewrite the topic headings in the table as *how, why,* and *what* questions. As you read, write an answer to each question. For more information on this Reading Strategy, see the **Reading and Study Skills** in the **Skills and Reference Handbook** at the end of your textbook.

Exploring Radioactivity	
Question	**Answer**
What is nuclear decay?	
	Alpha, beta, gamma

Nuclear Decay (pages 292–293)

1. Describe radioactivity. _____

_____

2. A radioisotope is any atom that contains an unstable _____.

3. Describe what happens to radioisotopes during nuclear decay. _____

_____

Types of Nuclear Radiation (pages 293–296)

4. Nuclear radiation is charged particles and energy that are emitted from the _____ of radioisotopes.

5. Circle the letters that identify each common type of nuclear radiation.
   a. X-rays   b. alpha particles
   c. beta particles   d. gamma rays

6. Circle the letters that identify which groups of particles make up an alpha particle.
   a. two electrons   b. two protons
   c. two neutrons   d. four neutrons

7. How is the product isotope different from the reactant isotope in alpha decay? _____

_____

8. Circle the letters that identify each event that takes place during beta decay.

   a. A proton decomposes into a neutron and an electron.

   b. A neutron decomposes into a proton and an electron.

   c. An electron is emitted from the nucleus.

   d. A neutron is emitted from the nucleus.

9. Why are beta particles more penetrating than alpha particles?

_____

10. Is the following sentence true or false? All nuclear radiation consists of charged particles. _____

11. What is a gamma ray? _____

_____

12. How fast do gamma rays travel through space?

_____

13. Complete the following table about nuclear radiation.

Characteristics of Nuclear Radiation			
Radiation Type	Charge	Mass (amu)	Usually Stopped By
	−1		
Beta particle		$\frac{1}{1836}$	Aluminum sheet
	0		Several meters of concrete

Effects of Nuclear Radiation (pages 296–297)

14. How does nuclear radiation affect atoms? _____

_____

15. Is the following sentence true or false? One potential danger of radon gas is that prolonged exposure to it can lead to lung cancer.

_____

Detecting Nuclear Radiation (page 297)

16. Name two devices that are used to detect nuclear radiation.

   a. _____   b. _____

Chapter 10   Nuclear Chemistry

Section 10.2 Rates of Nuclear Decay
(pages 298–301)

This section discusses half-lives and explains how nuclear decay can be used to estimate the age of objects.

Reading Strategy (page 298)

Identifying Details As you read, complete the concept map below to identify details about radiocarbon dating. For more information on this Reading Strategy, see the **Reading and Study Skills** in the **Skills and Reference Handbook** at the end of your textbook.

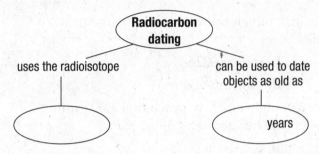

Half-life (pages 299–300)

1. A nuclear decay rate describes _____
_____.

2. Is the following sentence true or false? All radioisotopes decay at the same rate. _____

3. Describe a half-life. _____
_____

4. Circle the letter that describes a sample of a radioisotope after two half-lives.

   a. One eighth of the original sample is unchanged.

   b. One quarter of the original sample is unchanged.

   c. Half of the original sample is unchanged.

   d. Three quarters of the original sample is unchanged.

5. Circle the letter of the correct answer. Iodine-131 has a half-life of 8.07 days. What fraction of a sample of iodine-131 is left unchanged after 16.14 days?

   a. $\dfrac{1}{2}$ b. $\dfrac{1}{4}$

   c. $\dfrac{1}{8}$ d. $\dfrac{1}{16}$

6. Is the following sentence true or false? Like chemical reaction rates, nuclear decay rates vary with the conditions of reaction.

   _____

Chapter 10 Nuclear Chemistry

Use the following table to answer questions 7 and 8.

Half-Lives of Selected Radioisotopes	
Isotope	**Half-life**
Radon-222	3.82 days
Iodine-131	8.07 days
Thorium-234	24.1 days
Radium-226	1620 years
Carbon-14	5730 years

7. Circle the letter that identifies which sample would be the most unchanged after 100 years.

    a. iodine-131   b. radium-226

    c. radon-222   d. thorium-234

8. Circle the letter of the correct answer. How much of a 1.00 gram sample of radium-226 is left unchanged after 4860 years?

    a. 0.500 g   b. 0.250 g

    c. 0.125 g   d. 0.050 g

Radioactive Dating (pages 300–301)

9. How is carbon-14 formed in the upper atmosphere? _____

_____

10. Circle the letter that identifies the correct equation for the beta decay of carbon–14.

    a. $^{14}_{6}C \longrightarrow ^{14}_{7}N + ^{0}_{-1}e$ b. $^{14}_{6}C \longrightarrow ^{13}_{5}B + ^{1}_{1}p$

    c. $^{14}_{6}C \longrightarrow ^{14}_{5}B + ^{0}_{-1}e$ d. $^{14}_{6}C \longrightarrow ^{10}_{4}Be + ^{4}_{2}He$

11. Is the following sentence true or false? Plants and animals continue to absorb carbon from the atmosphere after they die. _____

12. How is the age of an object determined in radiocarbon dating? _____

_____

13. Circle the letter of each characteristic of radiocarbon dating.

    a. Carbon-14 levels in the atmosphere can change over time.

    b. Carbon-14 levels in the atmosphere stay constant.

    c. Scientists often use objects of known age in radiocarbon dating.

    d. Objects of known age are not useful in radiocarbon dating.

14. Is the following sentence true or false? Radiocarbon dating is highly accurate in dating objects that are more than 50,000 years old. _____

Chapter 10   Nuclear Chemistry

Section 10.3 Artificial Transmutation
(pages 303–305)

This section discusses transmutations, transuranium elements,
and particle accelerators.

Reading Strategy (page 303)

Monitoring Your Understanding Preview the Key Concepts, topic
headings, vocabulary, and figures in this section. List two things you
expect to learn. After reading, state what you learned about each item
you listed. For more information on this Reading Strategy, see the
Reading and Study Skills in the **Skills and Reference Handbook** at
the end of your textbook.

Understanding Artificial Transmutation	
What I Expect to Learn	**What I Learned**

Nuclear Reactions in the Laboratory (page 303)

1. Define transmutation. _____
_____

2. An example of a transmutation that occurs naturally is _____.

3. How do scientists perform artificial transmutations? _____
_____
_____

4. Circle the letter that identifies the scientist who performed the first
   artificial transmutation.
   a. Ernest Rutherford   b. Niels Bohr
   c. Enrico Fermi   d. Lise Meitner

5. The experiment that produced the first artificial transmutation also
   provided evidence that the nucleus contains _____.

Transuranium Elements (page 304)

6. Describe a transuranium element. _____
_____

7. Is the following sentence true or false? All transuranium elements
   are radioactive. _____

Chapter 10   Nuclear Chemistry

8. Scientists can synthesize a transuranium element by the artificial transmutation of a(n) _____ element.

9. Circle the letter of the first transuranium element to be synthesized.

    a. plutonium   b. americium

    c. technetium   d. neptunium

10. Circle the letter of the element that is used as a source of radiation in smoke detectors.

    a. uranium   b. americium

    c. technetium   d. plutonium

Particle Accelerators (page 305)

11. Why are particle accelerators needed for some transmutations? _____
_____

12. Is the following sentence true or false? A particle accelerator can accelerate charged particles to speeds very close to the speed of light. _____

13. Describe a quark. _____
_____

14. Circle the letter that identifies the number of quarks in each proton or neutron.

    a. zero   b. two

    c. three   d. six

15. Complete the following concept map about alpha particles.

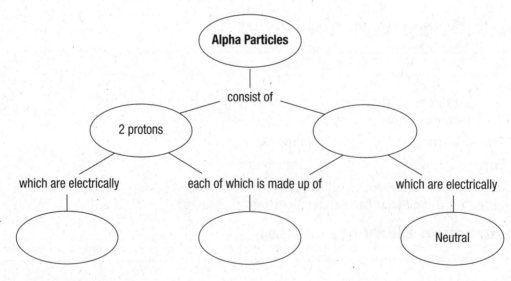

Chapter 10   Nuclear Chemistry

Section 10.4 Fission and Fusion
(pages 308–315)

This section discusses nuclear forces and the conversion of mass into energy. It also describes the nuclear processes of fission and fusion.

Reading Strategy (page 308)

Comparing and Contrasting As you read, contrast fission and fusion in the Venn diagram below by listing the ways they differ. For more information on this Reading Strategy, see the **Reading and Study Skills** in the **Skills and Reference Handbook** at the end of your textbook.

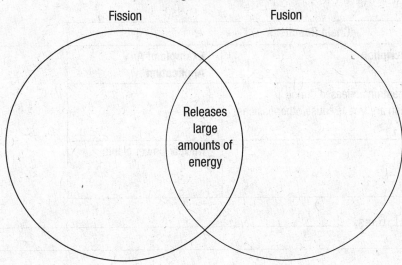

Contrasting Fission and Fusion

Nuclear Forces (pages 308–309)

1. Describe the strong nuclear force. _____

_____

2. Is the following sentence true or false? Over very short distances, the strong nuclear force is much greater than the electric forces among protons. _____

3. Electric forces in atomic nuclei depend on _____.

4. Is the following sentence true or false? The strong nuclear force on a proton or neutron is much greater in a large nucleus than in a small nucleus. _____

5. All nuclei with 83 or more protons are _____.

Fission (pages 309–313)

6. Describe fission. _____

_____

7. Fission can produce very large amounts of energy from very small amounts of _____.

8. Circle the letter that identifies what *c* represents in Einstein's mass-energy equation, $E = mc^2$.

   a. the charge on a proton   b. the speed of light

   c. the charge on an electron   d. the specific heat of the material

9. Is the following sentence true or false? During nuclear reactions mass is not conserved, but energy is conserved.

_____

10. Describe what can happen to a uranium-235 nucleus that absorbs a neutron. _____

_____

11. Complete the following table.

Chain Reactions		
Type of Chain Reaction	**Description**	**Example of An Application**
Uncontrolled	All neutrons released during fission are free to cause other fissions.	
		Nuclear power plants

12. Describe a critical mass. _____

_____

13. Is the following sentence true or false? Unlike power plants that burn fossil fuels, nuclear power plants do not emit air pollutants such as oxides of sulfur and nitrogen. _____

14. Describe what happens during a meltdown. _____

_____

Fusion (page 315)

15. The state of matter in which atoms have been stripped of their electrons is _____.

16. Circle the letter of each main problem that scientists must face in designing a fusion reactor.

   a. Extremely high temperatures are necessary for a fusion reaction to start.

   b. The plasma that results from the reaction conditions must be contained.

   c. The hydrogen needed as a starting material is extremely scarce.

   d. Fusion reactions produce large quantities of radioactive waste.

Chapter 10   Nuclear Chemistry

WordWise

Write the answer to each definition using one of the scrambled words below.

abte petalric
gnostr rauncel crefo
magma yar
pieatodorsoi

dorataivyicit
licticar sams
onisifs
ruqak

fonius
lunarce tiadorian
pahal claptrie
samlap

Definition	Term
A subatomic particle theorized to be among the basic units of matter	_____
Charged particles and energy that are emitted from the nuclei of radioisotopes	_____
A positively charged particle made up of two protons and two neutrons	_____
A state of matter in which atoms have been stripped of their electrons	_____
The process in which an unstable atomic nucleus emits charged particles and energy	_____
A penetrating ray of energy emitted by an unstable nucleus	_____
The attractive force that binds protons and neutrons together in the nucleus	_____
The splitting of an atomic nucleus into two smaller parts	_____
An electron emitted by an unstable nucleus	_____
The smallest possible mass of a fissionable material that can sustain a chain reaction	_____
A process in which the nuclei of two atoms combine to form a larger nucleus	_____
Any atom containing an unstable nucleus	_____

Nuclear Equations for Alpha Decay

Write a balanced nuclear equation for the alpha decay of polonium-218.

Math Skill:
Formulas and Equations

You may want to read more about this **Math Skill** in the **Skills and Reference Handbook** at the end of your textbook.

1. Read and Understand

What information are you given?

Reactant isotope = polonium-218

Radiation emitted = ^4_2He (alpha particle)

Use the periodic table to obtain the atomic number of polonium.

Reactant isotope = $^{218}_{84}Po$

2. Plan and Solve

What unknowns are you trying to calculate?

Atomic number of product isotope, Z = ?

Mass number of product isotope, A = ?

Chemical symbol of product isotope, X = ?

What equation contains the given information?

$$^{218}_{84}Po \longrightarrow ^A_ZX + ^4_2He$$

Write and solve equations for atomic mass and atomic number.

$218 = A + 4$	$84 = Z + 2$
$218 - 4 = A$	$84 - 2 = Z$
$214 = A$	$82 = Z$

On the periodic table, lead, Pb, has an atomic number of 82. So, X is Pb. The balanced nuclear equation is shown below.

$$^{218}_{84}Po \longrightarrow ^{214}_{82}Pb + ^4_2He$$

3. Look Back and Check

Is your answer reasonable?

The mass number on the left equals the sum of the mass numbers on the right. The atomic number on the left equals the sum of the atomic numbers on the right. The equation is balanced.

Math Practice

On separate sheet of paper, solve the following problems.

1. Write a balanced nuclear equation for the alpha decay of uranium-238.

2. Write a balanced nuclear equation for the alpha decay of thorium-230.

Chapter 11   Motion

Section 11.1 Distance and Displacement
(pages 328–331)

This section defines distance and displacement. Methods of describing motion are presented. Vector addition and subtraction are introduced.

Reading Strategy (page 328)

Predicting Write a definition for *frame of reference* in your own words in the left column of the table. After you read the section, compare your definition to the scientific definition and explain why a frame of reference is important. For more information on this Reading Strategy, see the **Reading and Study Skills** in the **Skills and Reference Handbook** at the end of your textbook.

Frame of Reference	
Frame of reference probably means	**Frame of reference actually means**

1. What two things must you know to describe the motion of an object?
_____

Choosing a Frame of Reference (pages 328–329)

2. Is the following sentence true or false? A frame of reference is not necessary to describe motion accurately and completely. _____

3. What is a frame of reference? _____
_____

4. Movement in relation to a frame of reference is called _____.

5. Imagine that you are a passenger in a car. Circle the letter of the best frame of reference you could use to determine how fast the car is moving relative to the ground.

   a. the people sitting next to you in the backseat

   b. the driver of the car

   c. a van traveling in the lane next to your car

   d. a sign post on the side of the road

Measuring Distance (page 329)

6. Distance is _____.

7. Circle the letter of the SI unit best suited for measuring the length of a room in your home.

   a. kilometers   b. meters

   c. centimeters   d. millimeters

Chapter 11 Motion

Measuring Displacements (page 330)

8. Is the following sentence true or false? Five blocks south is an example of a displacement. _____

9. Compare and contrast distance and displacement. _____

_____

_____

10. What would your total displacement be if you walked from your front door, around the block, and then stopped when you reached your front door again?

   a. one block   b. two blocks

   c. the entire distance of your trip   d. zero

Combining Displacements (pages 330–331)

11. A vector is a quantity that has both _____ and

   _____.

12. Circle the letter of each answer that could describe the magnitude of a vector.

   a. length   b. direction

   c. amount   d. size

13. To combine two displacements that are in opposite directions, the magnitudes _____ from one another.

For questions 14 and 15, refer to the figure below.

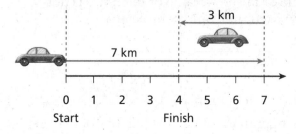

14. The magnitudes of the two displacement vectors are _____ and _____.

15. Because the two displacements are in opposite directions, the magnitude of the total displacement is _____.

16. Circle the letter that answers the question. What is the displacement of a cyclist who travels 1 mile north, then 1 mile east, and finally 1 mile south?

   a. 3 miles east   b. 1 mile north

   c. 3 miles south   d. 1 mile east

17. The vector sum of two or more other vectors is called the

   _____.

Chapter 11   Motion

Section 11.2 Speed and Velocity
(pages 332–337)

This section defines and compares speed and velocity. It also describes how to calculate average speed.

Reading Strategy (page 332)

Monitoring Your Understanding After you read this section, identify several things you have learned that are relevant to your life. Explain why they are relevant to you. For more information on this Reading Strategy, see the **Reading and Study Skills** in the **Skills and Reference Handbook** at the end of your textbook.

Facts About Speed and Velocity	
What Is Important	**Why It Is Important**

Speed (pages 332–334)

1. Define speed. _____

_____

2. The SI units for speed are _____.

3. How is instantaneous speed different from average speed? _____

_____

4. The equation used for calculating average speed is _____.

5. Is the following sentence true or false? You can determine how fast you were going at the midpoint of a trip by calculating average speed for the entire trip. _____

6. A student walked 1.5 km in 25 minutes, and then, realizing he was late, ran the remaining 0.5 km in 5 minutes. Calculate his average speed on the way to school.

_____

7. What type of speed does an automobile's speedometer display?

_____

Graphing Motion (page 334)

8. The slope of a line on a distance-time graph represents _____.

Chapter 11   Motion

For questions 9 through 11, refer to the graph below.

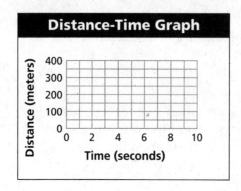

Distance-Time Graph

9. Draw a point on the graph that represents 200 m traveled in 4 seconds. Draw a line connecting this point with the origin (0,0). Label this as line A.

10. Draw a point on the graph that represents 100 m traveled in 10 seconds. Draw a line connecting this point with the origin (0,0). Label this as line B.

11. Calculate the average speed (slope) of lines A and B. Be sure to include units. _____

Velocity (page 336)

12. How do speed and velocity differ? _____

_____

13. Circle the letter of each sentence that describes a change in velocity.

    a. A moving object gains speed.

    b. A moving object changes direction.

    c. A moving object moves in a straight line at a constant speed.

    d. A moving object slows down.

14. Is the following sentence true or false? If a car travels around a gentle curve on a highway at 60 km/h, the velocity does not change. _____

Combining Velocities (page 337)

15. How do velocities combine? _____

16. A river flows at a velocity of 3 km/h relative to the riverbank. A boat moves upstream at a velocity of 15 km/h relative to the river. What is the velocity of the boat relative to the riverbank?

    a. 18 km/h downstream

    b. 15 km/h upstream

    c. 12 km/h upstream

    d. 12 km/h downstream

Chapter 11 Motion

Section 11.3 Acceleration
(pages 342–348)

This section describes the relationships among speed, velocity, and acceleration. Examples of these concepts are discussed. Sample calculations of acceleration and graphs representing accelerated motion are presented.

Reading Strategy (page 342)

Summarizing Read the section on acceleration. Then complete the concept map to organize what you know about acceleration. For more information on this Reading Strategy, see the **Reading and Study Skills** in the **Skills and Reference Handbook** at the end of your textbook.

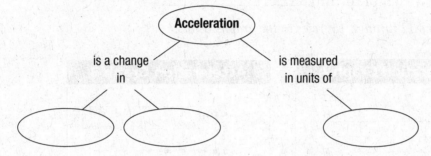

What Is Acceleration? (pages 342–345)

1. The rate at which velocity changes is called _____.

2. In terms of speed and direction, in what ways can an object accelerate? _____

   _____

3. Because acceleration is a quantity that has both magnitude and direction, it is a(n) _____.

4. Is the following sentence true or false? Acceleration is the result of increases or decreases in speed. _____

5. Ignoring air resistance, a rock in free fall will have a velocity of _____ after 4.0 seconds.

6. A horse on a carousel that is moving at a constant speed is accelerating because _____.

7. Describe constant acceleration. _____

   _____

Calculating Acceleration (pages 345–346)

8. Write the equation used to calculate the acceleration of an object.

   _____

9. Is the following sentence true or false? When the final velocity is less than the initial velocity of an object, the acceleration is negative. _____

10. A skateboarder begins down a ramp at a speed of 1.0 m/s. After 3 seconds, her speed has increased to 4.0 m/s. Calculate her acceleration.

    a. 1.0 m/s^2 b. 3.0 m/s^2

    c. 5.0 m/s^2 d. 9.8 m/s^2

Graphs of Accelerated Motion (pages 346–348)

11. A speed-time graph in which the displayed data forms a straight line is an example of a(n) _____.

For questions 12 through 15, refer to the graphs below.

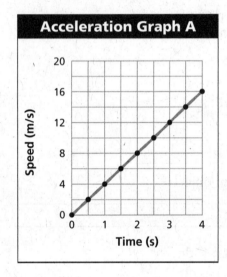

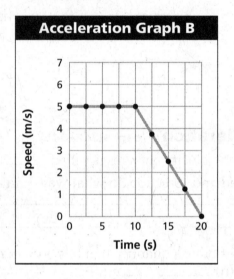

12. Graph A represents the motion of a downhill skier. How fast was the skier moving after traveling down the hill for 2.5 seconds? _____

13. In which graph does an object move at constant speed during the first 4 seconds? _____

14. Graph B represents the motion of a mountain biker. What is the biker's speed at times of 10 s and 20 s? _____

15. Determine the acceleration of the mountain biker during the 10 second to 20 second time period. Show your work.

_____

_____

16. The plotted data points representing acceleration in a distance-time graph form a(n) _____.

Instantaneous Acceleration (page 348)

17. The measure of how fast a velocity is changing at a specific instant is known as _____.

Chapter 11   Motion

WordWise

Complete the sentences by using one of the scrambled vocabulary words below.

vrlaeeit oinotm	mefar fo ecrneeefr	gvaeera dspee
levotciy	nerlia	centidsa
esdep	erfe lafl	aulsettrn crovet
atnicoelecar	rotcev	nnilraeon

An expression for _____ is $(v_f - v_i)/t$.

A quantity that has both magnitude and direction is called a(n)_____.

The total distance traveled divided by the total time is

_____.

A speed-time graph in which data points form a straight line is an example of a(n) _____ graph.

Common units for _____ include meters per second (m/s).

In order to accurately and completely describe the motion of an object, a(n) _____ is necessary.

You can determine _____ by measuring the length of the actual path between two points in space.

Two or more vectors combine to form a(n) _____.

Objects in _____ accelerate at 9.8 m/s^2.

A curve often connects data points on a(n) _____ graph.

Together, the speed and direction in which an object is moving are called _____.

Movement in relation to a frame of reference is _____.

Chapter 11   Motion

Interpreting a Distance-Time Graph

Math Skill:
Line Graphs and
Conversion Factors

The distance-time graph below illustrates the motion of a car whose speed varied with time during a trip. Calculate the average speed of the car during the first 8 seconds of the trip. Give your answer in km/h.

You may want to read more about this **Math Skill** in the **Skills and Reference Handbook** at the end of your textbook.

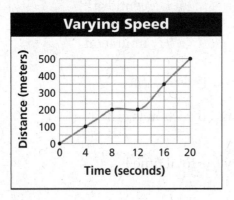

Varying Speed

1. **Read and Understand**

   What information are you given?

   A graph of distance versus time.

2. **Plan and Solve**

   How will you determine speed for the time interval referenced in the question?

   1. To determine the distance traveled in 8 s, move your finger up from the 8 s mark on the time axis to the plotted line.

   2. Now move your finger horizontally to the left to the distance axis. Read the value from the axis. (200 m)

   3. Calculate the average speed using the formula

   Speed = Distance/Time = 200 m/8 s = 25 m/s

   4. Convert from m/s to km/h:

   (25 m/s)(3600 s/h)(1 km/1000 m) = 90 km/h

3. **Look Back and Check**

   Is your answer reasonable?

   A quick calculation from the interval of constant speed shows that the car traveled 100 meters in 4 seconds—an average speed of 25 m/s.

Math Practice

On a separate sheet of paper, solve the following problems.

1. How long did it take the car to travel a distance of 350 m? _____

2. Determine the speed of the car in km/h during the interval 0 s to 12 s.

Chapter 12   Forces and Motion

Section 12.1 Forces
(pages 356–362)

This section describes what forces are and explains how forces affect the motion of various objects.

Reading Strategy (page 356)

Relating Text and Visuals As you read about forces, look carefully at Figures 2, 3, and 5 in your textbook. Then complete the table by describing the forces and motion shown in each figure. For more information on this Reading Strategy, see the **Reading and Study Skills** in the **Skills and Reference Handbook** at the end of your textbook.

Forces and Motion		
Figure	**Is Net Force 0?**	**Effect on Motion**
2A		
2B		
3		
5A		
5B		

What is a Force? (pages 356–357)

1. A force is defined as a(n) _____ or a(n) _____ that acts on an object.

2. Is the following sentence true or false? A force can act to cause an object at rest to move or it can accelerate an object that is already moving. _____

3. How can a force change the motion of an object that is already moving?
_____
_____

4. Circle the letter of the best answer. What force causes a 1-kg mass to accelerate at a rate of 1 meter per second each second?
    a. $1 \text{ kg/m} \cdot \text{s}^2$ b. 1 kg/s
    c. $1 \text{ kg} \cdot \text{m}$ d. 1 newton

Combining Forces (pages 357–358)

5. The overall force acting on an object after all the forces are combined is the _____.

6. How do balanced and unbalanced forces affect the motion of an object?
_____
_____
_____

Chapter 12 Forces and Motion

Friction (pages 359–360)

7. Is the following sentence true or false? Friction is a force that helps objects that are touching move past each other more easily. _____

8. Circle the letters that identify types of friction.
   a. rolling   b. gravity
   c. static   d. sliding

9. The friction force that acts on objects that are at rest is _____.

10. Why is less force needed to keep an object moving than to start the object in motion? _____

    _____

    _____

11. Complete the table below about friction forces.

Types of Friction Forces	
Friction Force	**Example**
Static	
	Pushing a book along your desk
Rolling	

12. Is the following sentence true or false? Fluid friction is a force that opposes the motion of an object through a fluid such as water. _____

Gravity (page 361)

13. Gravity is a(n) _____ force that pulls objects together.

14. Is the following sentence true or false? Earth's gravity acts downward toward the center of Earth. _____

15. Describe how gravity and air resistance affect the motion of a falling object. _____

    _____

16. Is the following sentence true or false? Terminal velocity is the constant velocity of a falling object when the force of air resistance equals the force of gravity. _____

Projectile Motion (page 362)

17. The curved path caused by the combination of an initial forward velocity and the downward force of gravity is known as _____ motion.

ter 12   Forces and Motion

12.2 Newton's First and
ws of Motion

*w force and mass affect acceleration. The acceleration
nd mass and weight are compared.*

age 363)

ng Vocabulary As you read this section, write a definition in
the table for each vocabulary word you encounter. Use your own
words in the definitions. For more information on this Reading
Strategy, see the **Reading and Study Skills** in the **Skills and
Reference Handbook** at the end of your textbook.

Matter and Motion	
Vocabulary	**Definition**
Inertia	

Aristotle, Galileo, and Newton (pages 363–364)

Match each scientist with his accomplishment.

Accomplishment

_____ **1.** Italian scientist who did experiments
that helped correct misconceptions
about force and motion

_____ **2.** Scientist who studied in England and
introduced several laws describing
force and motion

_____ **3.** An ancient Greek philosopher who
made many scientific discoveries
through observation and logical reasoning

Scientist

a. Aristotle

b. Galileo

c. Newton

Newton's First Law of Motion (pages 364–365)

4. Is the following sentence true or false? According to Newton's first
law of motion, an object's state of motion does not change as long as
the net force acting on it is zero. _____

5. What is inertia? _____

_____

6. Is the following sentence true or false? The law of inertia states that an object in motion will eventually slow down and come to a complete stop if it travels far enough in the same direction. _____

Newton's Second Law of Motion (pages 365–368)

7. According to Newton's second law of motion, acceleration of an object depends upon the _____ of the object and the _____ acting on it.

Match each term with its description.

Description	Term
_____ 8. A measure of the inertia of an object	a. mass
_____ 9. Net force/Mass	b. net force
_____ 10. Causes an object's velocity to change	c. acceleration

11. Is the following sentence true or false? The acceleration of an object is always in the same direction as the net force acting on the object. _____

12. Is the following sentence true or false? If the same force acts upon two objects with different masses, the acceleration will be greater for the object with greater mass. _____

Weight and Mass (pages 368–369)

13. What is weight? _____

_____

14. Write the formula used to calculate the weight of an object.

_____

15. Is the following sentence true or false? Because the weight formula shows that mass and weight are proportional, doubling the mass of an object will not affect its weight. _____

16. Complete the table below by describing the difference between mass and weight.

Mass and Weight	
Mass	**Weight**

17. On the moon, the acceleration due to gravity is only about one sixth that on Earth. Thus, an object will weigh _____ on the moon than it weighs on Earth.

Chapter 12   Forces and Motion

Section 12.3 Newton's Third Law of Motion and Momentum
(pages 372–377)

This section describes action-reaction forces and how the momentum of objects is determined.

Reading Strategy (page 372)

Summarizing As you read about momentum in this section, complete the concept map to organize what you learn. For more information on this Reading Strategy, see the **Reading and Study Skills in the Skills and Reference Handbook** at the end of your textbook.

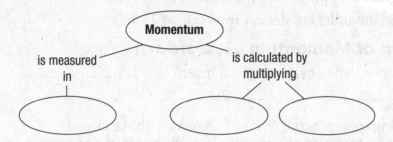

Newton's Third Law (page 373)

1. According to Newton's third law of motion, what happens whenever one object exerts a force on a second object? _____

_____

2. The equal and opposite forces described by Newton's third law are called _____ and _____ forces.

3. Circle the letters that identify each sentence that is true about action-reaction forces.

   a. Newton's second law describes action-reaction forces.

   b. Forces always exist in pairs.

   c. Action-reaction forces never cancel.

   d. All action-reaction forces produce motion.

4. Is the following statement true or false? Action-reaction forces do not cancel each other because the action force is always greater than the reaction force. _____

Momentum (pages 374–375)

5. Circle the letter of each factor that affects the momentum of a moving object.

   a. mass   b. volume   c. shape   d. velocity

6. If two identical objects are moving at different velocities, the object that is moving faster will have _____ momentum.

ay of 2.0 m/s

₀₁ain car traveling at 5 m/s

c. a 40-kilogram shopping cart rolling along at 0.5 m/s

d. a 300-kilogram roller coaster car traveling at 25 m/s

Conservation of Momentum (pages 376–377)

11. What does conservation of momentum mean? _____

_____

12. Is the following sentence true or false? Objects within a closed
system can exert forces on one another, but other objects and forces
cannot leave or enter the system. _____

13. According to the law of conservation of momentum, what happens
to the total momentum of a system if no net force acts on the system?

_____

14. Is the following sentence true or false? In a closed system with two
objects, the loss of momentum of one object equals the gain in
momentum of the other object. _____

For questions 15 and 16, refer to the graph below.

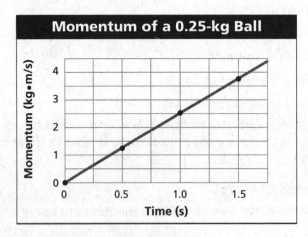

15. The momentum of the ball at one second is _____.

16. What is the speed of the ball at 0.5 seconds? Show your
calculation. *Hint:* Solve the momentum formula for velocity.

Chapter 12   Forces and Motion

8. Circle the letter of the best answer. Over extremely short distances, approximately how many times stronger is the strong nuclear force than the electric force of repulsion?

   a. 10   b. 100   c. 1000   d. 10,000

9. Compare and contrast the strong and weak nuclear forces. _____

   _____

   _____

Gravitational Force (pages 380–382)

10. State Newton's law of universal gravitation. _____

    _____

11. Circle the letter of each sentence that is true about gravitational force.

    a. The closer two objects are to one another, the weaker the gravitational force.

    b. The farther apart two objects are, the weaker the gravitational force.

    c. The greater the mass of an object, the stronger its gravitational force.

    d. Earth's gravitational force is stronger than the gravitational force of the sun.

12. The gravitational force of attraction between two objects depends on _____ and _____.

13. Is the following sentence true or false? Gravity is the weakest universal force, but it is the most effective force over long distances. _____

14. The sun's mass is much greater than the mass of Earth, so the sun's gravitational force is much _____ than that of Earth.

15. Why does the moon orbit Earth in a nearly circular path? _____

    _____

16. Is the following sentence true or false? The gravitational pull of the moon is the primary cause of Earth's ocean tides.

    _____

17. Is the following sentence true or false? An artificial satellite in a high orbit will slow down and lose altitude due to the pull of Earth's gravity. _____

18. List four uses of artificial satellites. _____

    _____

    _____

    _____

Chapter 12   Forces and Motion

WordWise

Complete the sentences using one of the scrambled words below.

nicofirt	vtiyagr	aecmleorntcgeti corfe
ssma	raeeaclnocit	hwgeti
ten eofrc	lirnetcptae refco	swonten
lfudi tnfcriio	kewa cnuarel	teianri
mtnmoemu		

A measure of an object's inertia is its _____.

The _____ force affects all particles in a nucleus and acts only over a short range.

A sky diver experiences _____, which opposes the force of gravity.

A change in an object's speed or direction of motion is called _____.

The product of an object's mass and its velocity is _____.

A measure of the force of gravity acting on an object is its _____.

A center-directed _____ continuously changes the direction of an object to make it move in a circle.

A force associated with charged particles is _____.

Mass is the measure of the _____ of an object.

A force that opposes the motion of objects that touch as they move past each other is called _____.

The universal force that causes every object to attract every other object is _____.

A person's weight on Mars, measured in _____, is 0.38 times the weight on Earth.

Acceleration equals _____ divided by mass.

Chapter 12   Forces and Motion

Calculating Acceleration

A car with a mass of 1300 kg accelerates as it leaves a parking lot. If the net force on the car is 3900 newtons, what is the car's *acceleration*?

Math Skill:
Formulas and Equations

You may want to read more about this **Math Skill** in the **Skills and Reference Handbook** at the end of your textbook.

1. Read and Understand

What information are you given?

Mass , m = 1300 kg

Force, F = 3900 N (in the forward direction)

2. Plan and Solve

What unknown are you trying to calculate?

Acceleration, a = ?

What formula contains the given quantities and the unknown?

$$a = \frac{F}{m}$$

Replace each variable with its known value and solve.

$$a = \frac{3900 \text{ N}}{1300 \text{ kg}} = 3 \ \frac{\text{N}}{\text{kg}} = 3 \ \frac{\text{kg} \bullet \text{m/s}^2}{\text{kg}} = 3 \text{ m/s}^2$$

a = 3 m/s² in the forward direction

3. Look Back and Check

Is your answer reasonable?

Powerful sports cars can accelerate at 6 m/s², so a smaller acceleration of 3 m/s² seems reasonable.

Math Practice

On a separate sheet of paper, solve the following problems.

1. A construction worker pushes a wheelbarrow with a total mass of 50.0 kg. What is the acceleration of the wheelbarrow if the net force on it is 75 N?

2. A van with a mass of 1500 kg accelerates at a rate of 3.5 m/s² in the forward direction. What is the net force acting on the van? (*Hint:* Solve the acceleration formula for force.)

3. A 6.0×10^3 N force accelerates a truck entering a highway at 2.5 m/s². What is the mass of the truck? (*Hint:* Solve the acceleration formula for mass.)

Chapter 13   Forces in Fluids

Section 13.1 Fluid Pressure
(pages 390–393)

This section defines pressure and describes factors that determine fluid pressure. The atmosphere as a fluid is discussed, including how air pressure changes with altitude.

Reading Strategy (page 390)

Using Prior Knowledge Before reading the section, write a common definition of the word *pressure*. After you have read the section, write the scientific definition of *pressure* and contrast it to your original definition. For more information on this Reading Strategy, see the **Reading and Study Skills** in the **Skills and Reference Handbook** at the end of your textbook.

Meanings of *Pressure*	
Common definition	
Scientific definition	

Pressure (pages 390–391)

1. Pressure is the result of a(n) _____ distributed over a(n) _____.

2. The same force is exerted by each of the following. Which exerts the most pressure?

   a. a foot   b. a large book

   c. a fingertip   d. the tip of a ball-point pen

3. How is pressure calculated? _____

   _____

4. A wooden crate that measures 2.0 m long and 0.40 m wide rests on the floor. If the crate has a weight of 600.0 N, what pressure does it exert on the floor?

   a. 0.80 m^2 b. 480 Pa

   c. 3.0 × 10^3 N/m^2 d. 750 Pa

Pressure in Fluids (pages 391–392)

5. A substance that assumes the shape of its container is called a(n) _____.

6. List four examples of fluids.

   a. _____   b. _____

   c. _____   d. _____

Chapter 13   Forces in Fluids

7. Circle the letter of each sentence that is true about fluid pressure.

   a. Water pressure decreases as depth decreases.

   b. Fluid pressure is exerted only at the base of the container holding the fluid.

   c. The pressure in a fluid at any given depth is constant, and it is exerted equally in all directions.

   d. The two factors that determine the pressure a fluid exerts are type of the fluid and its depth.

8. Is the following sentence true or false? The pressure at a depth of 2 feet in a large lake is greater than the pressure at the same depth in a swimming pool. _____

Air Pressure and the Atmosphere (pages 392–393)

9. Instead of referring to their depth in the atmosphere, people refer to their _____ above sea level.

For questions 10 through 13, refer to the air pressure table below.

Changes in Air Pressure with Altitude		
Altitude Above Sea Level (m)	Air Pressure (bars)	Air Pressure (kPa)
0	1.000	
200	0.9971	
400		96.68
600		94.42
800	0.9103	92.21
1000	0.8888	
1200	0.8677	87.89

10. Complete the air pressure columns in the table by converting between units of air pressure. *Hint:* 1 bar = 101.3 kPa.

11. How does air pressure change as a function of altitude?

    _____

12. Suppose a hiker is on a mountain ridge 1200 meters above sea level. Approximately what air pressure will she experience?

    _____

13. By how much does the air pressure decrease, in bars, from sea level to an altitude of 1200 meters? _____

14. Is the following sentence true or false? Air exerts a force of more than 1000 N on top of your head. _____

15. What keeps a person from being crushed by air pressure? _____

    _____

Chapter 13   Forces in Fluids

Section 13.2 Forces and Pressure in Fluids
(pages 394–397)

This section presents Pascal's and Bernoulli's principles. Examples of each principle from nature and industry are discussed.

Reading Strategy (pages 394)

Predicting Imagine two small foam balls hanging from strings at the same height with about three centimeters of space between them. Before you read the section, write a prediction about what will happen to the balls when you blow air through the space between them. Identify your reasons. After you have read the section, check the accuracy of your prediction. For more information on this Reading Strategy, see the **Reading and Study Skills** in the **Skills and Reference Handbook** at the end of your textbook.

Predicting Forces and Pressure in Fluids	
Prediction	
Reason for Prediction	

Transmitting Pressure in a Fluid (pages 394–395)

1. In a fluid-filled container, why is the pressure greater at the base of the container? _____

_____

2. Is the following sentence true or false? If you squeeze a container filled with fluid, the pressure within the fluid increases equally throughout the fluid. _____

3. According to Pascal's principle, what happens when there is a change in pressure at any point in a fluid? _____

_____

4. The science of applying Pascal's principle is called _____.

5. In a hydraulic lift system, an increased output force is produced because constant _____ is exerted on the larger area of the output piston.

6. Is the following sentence true or false? In a hydraulic system, the output force is greater than the input force because the pressure acting on the output piston is greater than the pressure acting on the input piston. _____

Chapter 13   Forces in Fluids

Bernoulli's Principle (pages 396–397)

7. Circle the letter of the sentence that correctly states Bernoulli's principle.

    a. As the speed of a fluid decreases, the pressure within the fluid decreases.

    b. As the speed of a fluid increases, the pressure within the fluid increases.

    c. As the speed of a fluid increases, the pressure within the fluid decreases.

    d. Fluid motion has no effect on pressure within the fluid.

8. Because the air traveling over the top of an airplane wing moves faster than the air passing underneath the wing, the pressure above the wings is _____ than the pressure below the wing.

9. What is lift, and how does it relate to an airplane's flight? _____

    _____

    _____

10. What is a spoiler on a racecar designed to do? _____

    _____

For questions 11 through 14, refer to the figure below. Place the correct letter after each phrase.

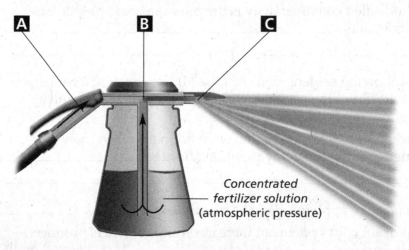

Spray Bottle with Fertilizer

Concentrated fertilizer solution (atmospheric pressure)

11. Location where the water and fertilizer solution mix. _____

12. Location where water enters the sprayer at high speed. _____

13. Location where the water-fertilizer mixture exits the sprayer. _____

14. Use Bernoulli's principle to explain why the fertilizer solution moves up the tube.

    _____

    _____

    _____

Chapter 13   Forces in Fluids

Section 13.3 Buoyancy
(pages 400–404)

*This section discusses buoyancy and Archimedes' principle of factors that
determine whether an object will sink or float in a fluid.*

Reading Strategy (page 400)

Summarizing As you read about buoyancy, write a brief summary of
the text following each green heading. Your summary should include
only the most important information. For more information on this
Reading Strategy, see the **Reading and Study Skills** in the **Skills and
Reference Handbook** at the end of your textbook.

Buoyant Force	Buoyant force is the apparent loss of weight of an object submerged in a fluid.

Buoyant Force (page 400)

1. What is buoyancy? _____
_____

2. Circle the letter of the correct answer. In which direction does a
buoyant force act?

   a. in the direction of gravity   b. perpendicular to gravity

   c. in the direction opposite of gravity   d. from above the fluid

3. Is the following sentence true or false? The greater a fluid's density,
the greater its buoyant force. _____

4. Buoyancy causes an apparent _____ of weight of an
object immersed in a fluid.

5. Circle the letter of each sentence that is true about buoyancy.

   a. Forces pushing up on a submerged object are greater than the
forces pushing down on it.

   b. Forces acting on the sides of a submerged object cancel each
other out.

   c. Gravitational forces work together with buoyant forces.

   d. The net buoyant force is non-vertical.

Chapter 13   Forces in Fluids

Archimedes' Principle (page 401)

6. According to Archimedes' principle, the weight of fluid displaced by a floating object is equal to the _____ acting on that object.

7. Is the following sentence true or false? When an object floats partially submerged in a fluid, it displaces a volume of fluid equal to its own volume. _____

Density and Buoyancy (pages 401–404)

Match each description with the correct property. Properties may be used more than once.

Description

_____ 8. This property is the ratio of an object's mass to its volume, often expressed in g/cm³.

_____ 9. This force is equal to the force of gravity that acts on a floating object.

_____ 10. When this property is greater for an object than for the fluid it is in, the object sinks.

_____ 11. These two forces act on every object in a fluid.

_____ 12. An object will either float or be suspended when the buoyant force is equal to this.

Property

a. weight

b. buoyant force

c. density

13. Use what you know about density and buoyancy to predict whether each of the substances listed in the table will float or sink in water. The density of water is 1.0 g/cm³.

Will It Float or Sink?		
Substance	Density (g/cm³)	Float or Sink?
Gold	19.3	
Balsa Wood	0.15	
Ice	0.92	
Brick	1.84	
Milk	1.03	
Gasoline	0.70	

14. How is a heavy steel ship able to float?

a. Because the density of steel is 7.8 g/cm³.

b. The ship's shape enables it to displace a large volume of water.

c. Because the density of water is 1 g/cm³.

d. The ship's effective density is greater than that of water.

Chapter 13   Forces in Fluids

WordWise

Solve the clues to determine which vocabulary words from Chapter 13 are hidden in the puzzle. Then find and circle the terms in the puzzle. The terms may occur vertically, horizontally, or diagonally.

```
h   y   d   r   a   u   l   i   c   s   y   s   t   e   m
v   a   h   u   s   p   i   a   c   f   r   h   y   e   b
s   r   q   a   z   f   f   r   e   r   f   v   d   c   q
p   c   i   u   y   t   t   p   r   e   s   s   u   r   e
t   h   d   f   r   g   s   f   l   u   t   m   a   o   e
k   i   u   b   p   l   o   e   k   j   h   t   u   f   z
k   m   t   y   u   i   r   f   l   u   i   d   l   t   d
v   e   k   p   o   o   p   f   v   b   n   m   i   n   m
o   d   k   a   r   p   y   o   i   m   q   c   c   a   f
p   e   g   s   y   h   z   a   v   b   n   h   s   y   b
p   s   e   c   u   h   n   j   n   m   l   o   m   o   q
l   r   i   a   j   u   e   r   t   c   v   f   d   u   a
p   o   i   l   m   j   g   b   h   f   y   u   j   b   o
```

Clues	**Hidden Words**
Mathematician who discovered that the buoyant force on an object equals the weight of the fluid displaced by the object	_____
The result of a force distributed over an area	_____
Type of substance that assumes the shape of its container	_____
Ability of a fluid to exert an upward force on an object within it	_____
SI-unit of measure used to express pressure	_____
Upward force that keeps an aircraft aloft	_____
Device that uses pressurized fluids acting on pistons of different sizes to change a force	_____
Force that opposes the weight of an object floating in a fluid	_____

Chapter 13   Forces in Fluids

Calculating Pressure

Each tile on the bottom of a swimming pool has an area of 0.50 m². The water above each tile exerts a force of 11,000 N on each tile. How much pressure does the water exert on each tile?

Math Skill:
Formulas and Equations

You may want to read more about this **Math Skill** in the **Skills and Reference Handbook** at the end of your textbook.

1. Read and Understand

What information are you given?

   Force = 11,000 N

   Area = 0.50 m²

2. Plan and Solve

What formula contains the given quantities and the unknown?

$$\text{Pressure} = \frac{\text{Force}}{\text{Area}}$$

Replace each variable with its known value and solve.

$$\text{Pressure} = \frac{11,000 \text{ N}}{0.50 \text{ m}^2} = 22,000 \text{ N/m}^2 = 22,000 \text{ Pa} = 22 \text{ kPa}$$

3. Look Back and Check

Is your answer reasonable?

Because the area of each tile is a half square meter and pressure is defined as force per square meter, the pressure exerted will be double the magnitude of the force. Thus, an 11,000 N force will produce 22,000 Pa of pressure on the tiles. The calculation verifies this result.

Math Practice

On a separate sheet of paper, answer the following questions.

1. The weight of the gasoline in a 55-gallon drum creates a force of 1456 newtons. The area of the bottom of the drum is 0.80 m². How much pressure does the gasoline exert on the bottom of the drum?

2. The weight of a gallon of milk is about 38 N. If you pour 3.0 gallons of milk into a container whose bottom has an area of 0.60 m², how much pressure will the milk exert on the bottom of the container?

3. A company makes garden statues by pouring concrete into a mold. The amount of concrete used to make a statue of a deer weighs 3600 N. If the base of the deer statue is 0.60 meters long and 0.40 meters wide, how much pressure will the statue exert on the ground? (*Hint:* Area is equal to length times width.)

Section 14.1 Work and Power
(pages 412–416)

This section defines work and power, describes how they are related, and explains how to calculate their values.

Reading Strategy (page 412)

Relating Text and Visuals As you read, look carefully at Figures 1 and 2 and read their captions. Complete the table by describing the work shown in each figure. For more information on this Reading Strategy, see the **Reading and Study Skills** in the **Skills and Reference Handbook** at the end of your textbook.

Figure	Direction of Force	Direction of Motion	Is Work Done?
1			
2A			
2B			
2C			

What Is Work? (pages 412–413)

1. In science, work is done when a(n) _____ acts on an object in the direction the object moves.

2. Why isn't work being done on a barbell when a weight lifter is holding the barbell over his head? _____

_____

3. Describe what conditions of force and motion result in maximum work done on an object. _____

_____

4. Is the following sentence true or false? A vertical force does work on an object that is moving in a horizontal direction. _____

Calculating Work (pages 413–414)

5. In science, work that is done on an object can be described as the force acting on the object multiplied by the _____ the object moves.

6. Circle the letter of the correct form of the work equation to use when determining the distance an object moves as a result of a force applied to it.

   a. Distance = Force × Work

   b. Distance = $\dfrac{\text{Force}}{\text{Work}}$

   c. Distance = $(\text{Force})^2$

   d. Distance = $\dfrac{\text{Work}}{\text{Force}}$

Chapter 14   Work, Power, and Machines

7. The SI unit of work is the _____.

8. Circle the letter of the amount of work done when a 1 newton force moves an object 1 meter.

    a. 1 newton per second   b. 1 joule

    c. 1 watt   d. 1 newton per meter

What Is Power? (page 414)

9. Is the following sentence true or false? Power is the rate of doing work. _____

10. In order to do work faster, more _____ is required.

11. Circle the letter of each sentence that is true about power.

    a. Power and work are always equal.

    b. You can increase power by doing a given amount of work in a shorter period of time.

    c. When you decrease the force acting on an object, the power increases.

    d. When you do less work in a given time period, the power decreases.

Calculating Power (page 415)

12. Write a word equation describing how to calculate power. _____

13. The SI unit of power is the _____.

14. Circle the letter of the expression that is equivalent to one watt.

    a. one newton per meter

    b. one joule per meter

    c. one newton per second

    d. one joule per second

15. How much work does a 100-watt light bulb do when it is lit for 30 seconds? _____

James Watt and Horsepower (page 416)

16. Circle the letter of the quantity that is approximately equal to one horsepower.

    a. 746 J   b. 746 W

    c. 7460 N/m   d. 7460 J

17. Why did James Watt use the power output of a horse to compare the power outputs of steam engines he designed? _____

Chapter 14   Work, Power, and Machines

Section 14.2 Work and Machines
(pages 417–420)

This section describes how machines change forces to make work easier to do. Input forces exerted on and output forces exerted by machines are identified and input work and output work are discussed.

Reading Strategy (page 417)

Summarizing As you read, complete the table for each machine. After you read, write a sentence summarizing the idea that your table illustrates. For more information on this Reading Strategy, see the **Reading and Study Skills** in the **Skills and Reference Handbook** at the end of your textbook.

Machine	Increases or Decreases Input Force	Increases or Decreases Input Distance
Tire jack		
Lug wrench		
Rowing oar		
Summary: As input force decreases, the input distance increases.		

Machines Do Work (pages 417–418)

1. Describe what a machine is able to do. _____
_____

2. Is the following sentence true or false? A machine can make work easier to do by changing the size of the force needed, the direction of a force, or the distance over which a force acts.
_____

3. Consider the equation Work = Force × Distance. If a machine increases the distance over which a force is exerted, the force required to do a given amount of work _____.

4. Give an example of a machine that changes the direction of an applied force. _____

5. When you make several trips to unload a few heavy items from a car instead of moving them all at once, the total distance over which you exert yourself _____.

Work Input and Work Output (pages 419–420)

6. The work done by a machine is always less than the work done on a machine because of _____.

Chapter 14   Work, Power, and Machines

7. Circle the letter of the definition for input force.

   a. the amount of force exerted by a machine

   b. the amount of friction slowing the speed of a machine

   c. the amount of work done by a machine

   d. the amount of force exerted on a machine

8. Write a word equation that describes work input.

   _____

9. Is the following sentence true or false? Every machine uses some of its work input to overcome friction. _____

10. The force exerted by a machine is called the _____ force.

11. Circle the letter of the expression that equals the work output of a machine.

   a. $\dfrac{\text{Input distance}}{\text{Output distance}}$ b. Output distance × Input distance

   c. $\dfrac{\text{Output distance}}{\text{friction}}$ d. Output distance × Output force

12. Is the following sentence true or false? Output work always is less than input work. _____

For questions 13 through 15, refer to the figure below.

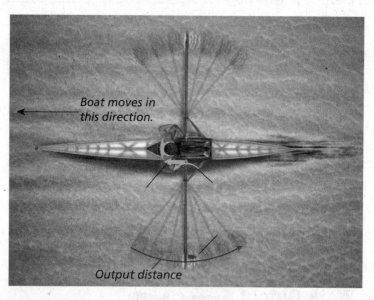

Boat moves in this direction.

Output distance

13. Which arrow represents the input force? Label it on the figure.

14. Which arrow represents the input distance? Label it on the figure.

15. Which arrow represents the output force? Label it on the figure.

16. How can you increase a machine's work output? _____

   _____

Chapter 14   Work, Power, and Machines

Section 14.3 Mechanical Advantage and Efficiency
(pages 421–426)

This section describes mechanical advantage and efficiency and how to calculate these values. Ways to maximize mechanical advantage and efficiency are discussed.

Reading Strategy (page 421)

Building Vocabulary As you read the section, write a definition in the table for each vocabulary term in your own words. For more information on this Reading Strategy, see the **Reading and Study Skills** in the **Skills and Reference Handbook** at the end of your textbook.

Mechanical Advantage	
Vocabulary	**Definition**
Mechanical advantage	

Mechanical Advantage (pages 421–423)

1. The number of times that a machine increases an input force is the _____ of the machine.

2. For a given input force, what affects the output force that a nutcracker can exert on a nut? _____
   _____

3. Mechanical advantage describes the relationship between input force and _____ force.

4. How is the actual mechanical advantage of a machine determined?
   _____

5. Greater input force is required to move an object along a ramp with a rough surface, compared to a ramp with a smooth surface, because a greater force is needed to overcome _____.

6. Is the following sentence true or false? A loading ramp with a rough surface has a greater mechanical advantage than one with a smooth surface. _____

7. Because friction is always present, the actual mechanical advantage of a machine is never _____ than its ideal mechanical advantage (IMA).

8. A machine's _____ is the mechanical advantage in the absence of friction.

9. What type of materials do engineers use to increase the mechanical advantage of a machine?

Calculating Mechanical Advantage (pages 424–425)

10. Is the following sentence true or false? To calculate ideal mechanical advantage, divide input distance by output distance, and then divide the result by the force of friction. _____

11. Is the following sentence true or false? An inclined plane is an example of a machine. _____

12. Calculate the IMA of a ramp for the distances given in the table.

Ideal Mechanical Advantages of Ramps		
Horizontal Distance	Vertical Rise	IMA
1.5 meters	0.5 meters	
12 meters	1.5 meters	
3.6 meters	0.3 meters	

13. Is the following sentence true or false? If the input distance of a machine is greater than the output distance, then the IMA for that machine is greater than one. _____

Efficiency (pages 425–426)

14. Why is the efficiency of a machine always less than 100 percent? _____

15. Is the following sentence true or false? To calculate the efficiency of a machine, divide the work output by work input, and then multiply by 100. _____

16. What is a significant factor affecting a car's fuel efficiency? _____

17. Calculate the efficiency of a machine with a work output of 120 J and a work input of 500 J. _____

18. Circle the letter of the work input for a machine with a work output of 240 J and an efficiency of 80 percent.

    a. 300 J   b. 200 J

    c. 320 J   d. 200 W

19. Reducing friction _____ the efficiency of a machine.

Chapter 14   Work, Power, and Machines

Section 14.4 Simple Machines
(pages 427–435)

This section presents the six types of simple machines. A discussion of how each type works and how to determine its mechanical advantage is given. Common uses of simple machines are also described.

Reading Strategy (page 427)

Summarizing After reading the section on levers, complete the concept map to organize what you know about first-class levers. On a separate sheet of paper, construct and complete similar concept maps for second- and third-class levers. For more information on this Reading Strategy, see the **Reading and Study Skills** in the **Skills and Reference Handbook** at the end of your textbook.

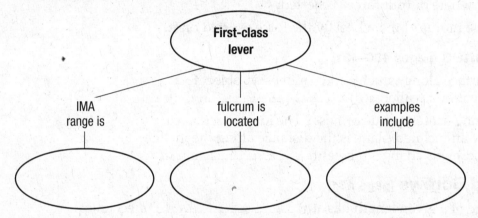

1. List the six types of simple machines.

   a. _____   b. _____

   c. _____   d. _____

   e. _____   f. _____

Levers (pages 428–429)

2. A screwdriver used to pry the lid off a paint can is an example of a(n) _____.

3. The fixed point that a lever rotates around is called the

   _____.

4. To calculate the ideal mechanical advantage of any lever, divide the input arm by the _____.

5. What characteristics distinguish levers as first-class, second-class, or third-class?

   _____

   _____

6. Is the following sentence true or false? First-class levers always have a mechanical advantage that is greater than one.

   _____

Chapter 14   Work, Power, and Machines

7. Is the following sentence true or false? All second-class levers have a mechanical advantage greater than one because the input arm is longer than the output arm. _____

Wheel and Axle (page 430)

8. Describe a wheel and axle. _____

_____

9. Circle the letter of the sentence that describes how to calculate the IMA of a wheel and axle.

   a. Multiply the area of the wheel by the area of the axle.

   b. Divide input force by output force.

   c. Divide the diameter where input force is exerted by the diameter where output force is exerted.

   d. Divide the radius of the wheel by the force exerted on it.

Inclined Planes (pages 430–431)

10. A slanted surface along which a force moves an object to a different elevation is called a(n) _____.

11. Is the following sentence true or false? The ideal mechanical advantage of an inclined plane is the distance along the incline plane divided by its change in height. _____

Wedges and Screws (page 431)

12. A thin wedge of a given length has a(n) _____ mechanical advantage than a thick wedge of the same length.

13. Screws with threads that are close together have a greater

_____.

Pulleys (pages 432–433)

14. A simple machine consisting of a rope fitted into a groove in a wheel is a(n) _____.

15. What determines the ideal mechanical advantage of a pulley or pulley system?

_____

Compound Machines (page 435)

16. Is the following sentence true or false? A compound machine is a combination of two or more simple machines that operate together. _____

17. Circle each letter that identifies a compound machine.

   a. a car   b. a handheld screwdriver

   c. a washing machine   d. a watch

Chapter 14   Work, Power, and Machines

WordWise

*Answer the question or identify the clue by writing the correct vocabulary
term in the blanks. Use the circled letter(s) in each term to find the hidden
vocabulary word. Then, write a definition for the hidden word.*

Clues	**Vocabulary Terms**
$\dfrac{\text{Work output}}{\text{Work input}} \times 100\%$	_ _ _ O _ _ _ _ _ _
A mechanical watch is an example of this.	_ _ _ _ _ _ O _ _ _ _ _ _ _ _
One way to determine this is to divide output work by output force.	_ _ _ O _ _ , _ _ _ _ _ _ _ _ _
This is the SI unit of work.	_ _ O _ _ _
On a lever, it is the distance between the fulcrum and the input force.	_ _ _ _ O _ _ _ _
The IMA of this machine increases as its thickness decreases relative to its length.	_ _ O _ _
This is exerted on a jack handle to lift a car.	O _ _ _ _ _ _ _ _ _ _
This unit equals about 746 joules.	_ _ _ O _ _ _ _ _ _ _
This is the distance between the output force and the fulcrum.	_ _ O _ _ _ _ _ _ _
This SI unit of power is used to describe light bulbs.	_ O _ _
The IMA of this machine is the distance along its surface divided by the change in height.	_ _ _ _ _ O _ _ _ _ _ _ _ _
A device that can change the size of the force required to do work.	_ _ O _ _ _
This quantity is equal to Work/Time.	_ _ _ O _

Hidden words: _ _ _ _ _ _   _ _ _ _ _ _ _ _

Definition: _____

_____

Chapter 14   Work, Power, and Machines

Calculating Work and Power

Calculate the power of a machine that exerts a force of 800.0 N over a distance of 6.0 m in 2.0 s.

Math Skill:
Formulas and
Equations

You may want to read more about this **Math Skill** in the **Skills and Reference Handbook** at the end of your textbook.

1. Read and Understand

What information are you given?

Force = 800.0 N

Distance = 6.0 m

Time = 2.0 s

2. Plan and Solve

What variable are you trying to determine?

Power =?

What formula contains the given quantities and the unknown?

$$\text{Power} = \frac{\text{Work}}{\text{Time}} = \frac{\text{Force} \times \text{Distance}}{\text{Time}}$$

$$\text{Power} = \frac{800.0 \text{ N} \times 6.0 \text{ m}}{2.0 \text{ s}}$$

$$\text{Power} = \frac{4800 \text{ J}}{2.0 \text{ s}} = 2400 \text{ J/s} = 2400 \text{ W}$$

3. Look Back and Check

Is your answer reasonable?

Work = (2400 J/s) × 2.0 s = 4800 J

This is a reasonable answer. Substituting power and time back into the power equation yields the original value for work.

Math Practice

On a separate sheet of paper, solve the following problems.

1. Suppose 900.0 J of work are done by a light bulb in 15.0 s. What is the power of the light bulb?

2. What is the power of a machine if an output force of 500.0 N is exerted over an output distance of 8.0 m in 4.0 s?

3. The power of a machine is 6.0×10^3 J/s. This machine is scheduled for design improvements. What would its power be if the same work could be done in half the time?

Chapter 15   Energy

Section 15.1 Energy and Its Forms
(pages 446–452)

This section describes how energy and work are related. Kinetic energy and potential energy are defined, and examples are shown for calculating these forms of energy. Examples of various types of energy are discussed.

Reading Strategy (page 446)

Building Vocabulary As you read, complete the concept map with vocabulary terms and definitions from this section. For more information on this Reading Strategy, see the **Reading and Study Skills** in the **Skills and Reference Handbook** at the end of your textbook.

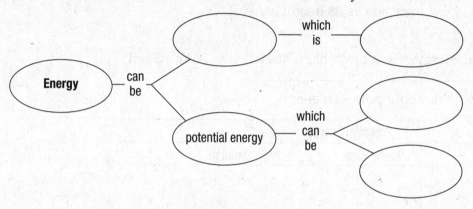

Energy and Work (page 447)

1. What is energy? _____

2. When work is done on an object, _____ is transferred to that object.

3. Circle the letter of each sentence that is true about work and energy.

   a. Energy in food is converted into muscle movement.

   b. Energy is transferred when work is done.

   c. Both work and energy are usually measured in joules.

   d. One joule equals one meter per newton.

Kinetic Energy (pages 447–448)

4. The energy of motion is called _____.

5. Is the following sentence true or false? You can determine the kinetic energy of an object if you know its mass and its volume.

   _____

6. Write the formula used to calculate an object's kinetic energy.

   _____

7. Calculate the kinetic energy of a 0.25-kg toy car traveling at a constant velocity of 2 m/s. _____

   _____

Chapter 15   Energy

Potential Energy (pages 448–450)

8. What is potential energy? _____

_____

9. Is the following sentence true or false? The work done by a rock climber going up a cliff decreases her potential energy.

_____

10. An object's gravitational potential energy depends on its _____, its _____, and the acceleration due to gravity.

11. Is the following sentence true or false? Gravitational potential energy of an object increases as its height increases.

_____

12. The potential energy of an object that is stretched or compressed is known as _____.

13. Complete the table about potential energy.

Potential Energy		
Type	Description	Example
Gravitational		
	Stretched or compressed objects	

Forms of Energy (pages 450–452)

For numbers 14 through 19, write the letter of the form of energy that best matches the description.

Descriptions	Forms of Energy
_____ 14. Energy stored in gasoline, coal, and wood	a. mechanical energy
_____ 15. The sum of an object's potential energy and kinetic energy, excluding atomic-scale movements	b. chemical energy
	c. electrical energy
_____ 16. Produces the sun's heat and light	d. thermal energy
_____ 17. Travels through space in the form of waves	e. nuclear energy
_____ 18. Produces lightning bolts	f. electromagnetic energy
_____ 19. Increases as atoms within an object move faster	

Chapter 15   Energy

Section 15.2 Energy Conversion and Conservation
(pages 453–459)

This section describes how energy is converted from one form to another. The law of conservation of energy also is presented.

Reading Strategy (page 453)

Relating Cause and Effect As you read, complete the flowchart to explain an energy conversion used by some gulls to obtain food. For more information on this Reading Strategy, see the **Reading and Study Skills** in the **Skills and Reference Handbook** at the end of your textbook.

How Gulls Use Energy Conversions

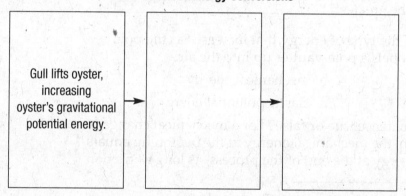

Gull lifts oyster, increasing oyster's gravitational potential energy.

Energy Conversion (page 454)

1. Is the following sentence true or false? Energy can be converted from one form to another. _____

2. When a wind-up toy is set in motion, elastic potential energy that was stored in a compressed spring is converted into the _____ of the toy's moving parts.

3. Is the following sentence true or false? The action of striking a match shows that stored chemical energy in the match can be converted into thermal energy and electromagnetic energy of the flame in a single step. _____

Conservation of Energy (page 455)

4. What does the law of conservation of energy state? _____

_____

5. Is the following sentence true or false? When an object slows down because of frictional force acting on it, an amount of energy is destroyed that is equivalent to the decrease in kinetic energy of the object. _____

6. A moving object slows down because friction causes a continual conversion of kinetic energy into _____.

Chapter 15 Energy

Energy Conversions (pages 456–458)

7. As an object falls, the gravitational potential energy of the object is converted into _____.

8. Circle the letter of each sentence that is true about pendulums.

  a. A pendulum consists of a weight suspended from a string that swings back and forth.

  b. The weight at the end of a pendulum reaches maximum kinetic energy at the highest point in the pendulum's swing.

  c. Potential energy and kinetic energy undergo constant conversion as a pendulum swings.

  d. Frictional forces enable a pendulum to continue swinging without slowing down.

9. At what point during a pole-vaulter's jump is his gravitational potential energy the greatest? _____

10. Circle the letter of the type of energy that increases as the pole bends before it propels a pole-vaulter up into the air.

  a. kinetic energy   b. mechanical energy

  c. frictional force   d. elastic potential energy

11. Is the following sentence true or false? For a mechanical change in an isolated system, the mechanical energy at the beginning equals the mechanical energy at the end of the process, as long as friction is negligible. _____

12. Tell whether the following situations illustrate *kinetic energy, potential energy,* or *both.*

What Type of Energy Is It?	
Situation	**Form of Energy**
A stationary wind-up toy with a compressed spring	
A descending roller coaster car	
A skier poised to take off at the top of a hill	
A car driving on a flat road	
A vibrating guitar string	

Energy and Mass (page 459)

13. What does Einstein's equation imply about mass and energy? _____

_____

14. Is the following sentence true or false? Einstein's equation, $E = mc^2$, suggests that mass and energy together are conserved.

_____

Chapter 15   Energy

Section 15.3 Energy Resources
(pages 462–466)

This section describes types of energy resources and ways to conserve them.

Reading Strategy (page 462)

Identifying Main Ideas As you read the section, write the main idea for each heading in the table. For more information on this Reading Strategy, see the **Reading and Study Skills** in the **Skills and Reference Handbook** at the end of your textbook.

Heading	Main Idea
Nonrenewable energy resources	
Renewable energy resources	
Conserving energy resources	

Nonrenewable Energy Resources (page 462)

1. What are nonrenewable energy resources? _____
_____

2. List four examples of nonrenewable energy resources.

   a. _____   b. _____

   c. _____   d. _____

3. Circle the letter of each resource that is considered to be a fossil fuel.

   a. tree

   b. uranium

   c. oil

   d. coal

4. Is the following sentence true or false? Although fossil fuels are evenly distributed throughout Earth, they only represent ten percent of total energy consumed. _____

5. What are some advantages and disadvantages of using fossil fuels as a source of energy? _____
_____

Renewable Energy Resources (pages 463–464)

6. An energy resource that can be replaced in a reasonably short period of time is called a(n) _____ resource.

Chapter 15   Energy

7. Circle the letter of each sentence that is true about renewable energy resources.

   a. Wind and solar energy are both renewable energy resources.

   b. Renewable energy resources are always more efficient than nonrenewable resources.

   c. Renewable energy resources can be used to generate electricity and to heat homes.

   d. Magma generates most renewable energy, either directly or indirectly.

8. Describe one energy conversion that takes place during the generation of hydroelectric power. _____

   _____

9. Is the following sentence true or false? One disadvantage of hydroelectric power is that it is among the most expensive energy sources. _____

For numbers 10 through 15, match the letter of each renewable energy source to its description.

Description	Renewable Energy Sources
_____ **10.** Water pumped below ground is converted to steam.	a. hydroelectric
_____ **11.** The most likely raw material is hydrogen.	b. solar
_____ **12.** Mirrors concentrate sunlight to produce electricity.	c. geothermal
_____ **13.** Kinetic energy of moving air is converted into rotational energy of a turbine.	d. wind
_____ **14.** Energy is obtained from flowing water.	e. biomass
_____ **15.** Chemical energy stored in wood, peat, and agricultural waste can be converted into thermal energy.	f. nuclear fusion

16. Is the following sentence true or false? Hydrogen fuel cells generate electricity by combining hydrogen with oxygen.

   _____

Conserving Energy Resources (page 466)

17. What are two ways that energy resources can be conserved? _____

   _____

18. Name two practical ways in which people can conserve energy. _____

   _____

   _____

Chapter 15 Energy

WordWise

Complete the sentences by using one of the scrambled vocabulary words below.

absoism reegny   ynrege vnsnoorctaie   slisfo sluef
rslao eeyngr   neegyr seonoscvri   caurnle rygnee
mrelhta eeryng   loptnieat nygeer   gyreen
mcelhaci reeyng   ctniiek yenrge   rvtnatgialoai

When an object is raised to a higher level, its _____
potential energy increases.

The motion of microscopic particles in matter partly determines the
amount of _____ within it.

As a pole-vaulter springs higher into the air, her kinetic energy
decreases as her gravitational potential energy increases. This is an
example of _____.

Atomic fission and fusion produce _____.

When your muscles move, _____ from the cereal you
ate for breakfast is converted into _____.

The _____ of a 100-kg boulder perched high on a cliff
is greater than that of a 50-kg boulder at the same height.

You can recognize _____ by the changes it causes, such
as motion and sound.

Formed from the remains of once-living organisms,
_____ are nonrenewable energy resources.

Photovoltaic cells convert _____ into electrical energy.

Methods of _____ include ways to reduce
energy needs.

When you sit around a campfire, you are enjoying energy stored in
wood—a type of _____.

Chapter 15   Energy

Calculating Potential Energy

A 60.0-kg person is standing on the edge of a pier that is 2.5 m above the surface of a lake. How much higher would the pier have to be to raise the gravitational potential energy of this person by 10 percent?

Math Skill: Percents and Decimals

You may want to read more about this **Math Skill** in the **Skills and Reference Handbook** at the end of your textbook.

1. Read and Understand

What information are you given?

Mass of person = m = 60.0 kg

Height above lake level = h = 2.5 m

Acceleration due to gravity = g = 9.8 m/s^2

2. Plan and Solve

What variable are you trying to determine?

Gravitational potential energy = ?

What formula contains the given variables?

Gravitational potential energy (PE) = mgh

Initial PE = (60.0 kg)(9.8 m/s^2)(2.5 m) = 1500 J

Determine the 10-percent increase of PE.

(1500 J)(0.10) = 150 J

Final PE = 1500 J + 150 J = 1650 J

Rearrange the equation to determine the final height.

h = PE/mg = 1650 J/(60.0 kg)(9.8 m/s^2) = 2.8 m

The height increase for the pier would be 2.8 m − 2.5 m = 0.3 m.

3. Look Back and Check

Is your answer reasonable?

This is a reasonable answer because 0.3 m is about 10 percent of 2.5 m. A 10-percent increase in h should result in a 10-percent increase in the gravitational PE.

Math Practice

On a separate sheet of paper, solve the following problems.

1. A 300-gram toy car and a 500-gram toy car are sitting on a shelf that is 2 meters higher than the floor. By what percent is the PE of the 500-g car greater than the PE of the 300-g car?

2. An 80-kg rock climber is standing on a cliff so that his gravitational PE = 10,000 J. What percent increase in height is required to raise his PE by 3500 J?

Chapter 16   Thermal Energy and Heat

Section 16.1 Thermal Energy and Matter
(pages 474–478)

This section defines heat and describes how work, temperature, and thermal energy are related to heat. Thermal expansion and contraction of materials is discussed, and uses of a calorimeter are explained.

Reading Strategy (page 474)

Previewing Before you read, preview the figures in this section and add two more questions in the table. As you read, write answers to your questions. For more information on this Reading Strategy, see the **Reading and Study Skills** in the **Skills and Reference Handbook** at the end of your textbook.

Thermal Energy and Matter	
Questions About Thermal Energy and Matter	**Answers**
Which has more thermal energy, a cup of tea or a pitcher of juice?	

Work and Heat (page 474)

1. Heat is the transfer of thermal energy from one object to another as the result of a difference in _____.

2. Circle the letter of each sentence that is true about heat.

    a. Heat is a fluid that flows between particles of matter.

    b. Heat flows spontaneously from hot objects to cold objects.

    c. Friction produces heat.

    d. The transfer of thermal energy from one object to another is heat.

Temperature (page 475)

3. What is temperature? _____

_____

4. Is the following sentence true or false? On the Celsius scale, the reference points for temperature are the freezing and boiling points of water. _____

Chapter 16   Thermal Energy and Heat

5. Circle the letter of each sentence that explains what happens when an object heats up.

a. Its particles move faster, on average.

b. The average kinetic energy of its particles decreases.

c. Its mass increases.

d. Its temperature increases.

Thermal Energy (page 475)

6. What is thermal energy? _____

_____

7. Thermal energy depends upon the _____,
_____, and _____ of an object.

8. Is the following sentence true or false? Two substances can be the same temperature and have different thermal energies.
_____

Thermal Expansion and Contraction (page 476)

9. Is the following sentence true or false? Thermal contraction occurs when matter is heated, because particles of matter tend to move closer together as temperature increases. _____

10. Describe thermal expansion and contraction by completing the table below.

Thermal Expansion and Contraction			
Condition	Temperature	Space Between Particles	Volume
	Increases		
			Decreases

Specific Heat (pages 476–477)

11. The amount of heat needed to raise the temperature of one gram of material by one degree Celsius is called _____.

12. Why are you more likely to burn yourself on a metal toy than on a plastic toy if both have been sitting in the sun? _____

_____

_____

Measuring Heat Changes (page 478)

13. What device is used to measure changes in thermal energy?
_____

14. Is the following sentence true or false? A calorimeter uses the principle that heat flows from a hotter object to a colder object until both reach the same temperature. _____

Chapter 16   Thermal Energy and Heat

Section 16.2 Heat and Thermodynamics
(pages 479–483)

This section discusses three kinds of thermal energy transfer and introduces the first, second, and third laws of thermodynamics.

Reading Strategy (page 479)

Build Vocabulary As you read this section, add definitions and examples to complete the table. For more information on this Reading Strategy, see the **Reading and Study Skills** in the **Skills and Reference Handbook** at the end of your textbook.

Transfer of Thermal Energy	
Definitions	**Examples**
Conduction: transfer of thermal energy with no net transfer of matter	Frying pan handle heats up
Convection:	
Radiation:	

Conduction (pages 479–480)

1. The transfer of thermal energy with no overall transfer of matter is called _____.

2. Why is conduction slower in gases than in liquids and solids? _____
_____
_____

3. Is the following sentence true or false? Conduction is faster in metals than in other solids because metals have free electrons that transfer thermal energy. _____

4. Circle the letter of each sentence that is true about conduction.

   a. Thermal energy is transferred without transfer of matter.

   b. Matter is transferred great distances during conduction.

   c. Conduction can occur between materials that are not touching.

   d. In most solids, conduction takes place as particles vibrate in place.

5. Complete the table about conduction.

Conduction		
Type of Material	**Quality of Conduction**	**Two Examples**
	Conducts thermal energy well	Copper;
Thermal insulator		Wood;

Chapter 16   Thermal Energy and Heat

Convection (pages 480–481)

6. The transfer of thermal energy when particles of a fluid move from one place to another is called _____.

7. Why is temperature higher at the bottom of an oven? _____

_____

_____

8. When a fluid circulates in a loop as it alternately heats up and cools down, a(n) _____ occurs.

9. Give three examples of convection currents in nature. _____

_____

Radiation (page 481)

10. The transfer of energy by waves moving through space is called

_____.

11. Circle the letter of each sentence that is true about radiation.

a. Energy is transferred by waves.

b. All objects radiate energy.

c. The amount of energy radiated from an object decreases as its temperature increases.

d. The farther away you are from a radiating object, the less radiation you receive.

Thermodynamics (pages 482–483)

12. Thermodynamics is the study of conversions between _____ and other forms of energy.

13. Is the following sentence true or false? Energy cannot be created or destroyed, but it can be converted into different forms.

_____

14. Thermal energy flows spontaneously from _____ objects to _____ ones.

15. According to the second law of thermodynamics, what must happen for thermal energy to flow from a colder object to a hotter object? _____

_____

16. Thermal energy that is not converted into work is called

_____.

17. Is the following sentence true or false? Scientists have created a heat engine with 100 percent efficiency by reducing the temperature of the outside environment to absolute zero.

_____

18. Is the following sentence true or false? Matter can be cooled to absolute zero. _____

Chapter 16 Thermal Energy and Heat

Section 16.3 Using Heat
(pages 486–492)

*This section describes ways in which humans benefit from heat engines,
heating systems, and cooling systems. It also discusses how each of these
systems works.*

Reading Strategy (page 486)

Sequencing As you read, complete the cycle diagram to show the
sequence of events in a gasoline engine. For more information on this
Reading Strategy, see the **Reading and Study Skills** in the **Skills and
Reference Handbook** at the end of your textbook.

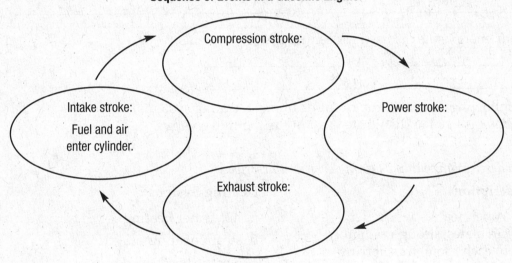

Sequence of Events in a Gasoline Engine

Heat Engines (pages 486–487)

1. The two main types of heat engines are the _____
   and the _____ .

2. A steam engine is an external combustion engine because it burns
   fuel _____ the engine.

3. Who developed the first practical steam engine?

   a. James Prescott Joule

   b. Thomas Newcomen

   c. James Watt

   d. Benjamin Thompson

4. How is heat converted into work in a steam engine? _____

   _____

5. A heat engine used by most cars in which fuel burns inside the
   engine is called a(n) _____ .

6. Each upward or downward motion of a piston in an internal
   combustion engine is called a(n) _____ .

Chapter 16   Thermal Energy and Heat

7. Is the following sentence true or false? In a typical car, the crankshaft produces a linear motion that turns the wheels. _____

8. Why is it important for an internal combustion engine to have a cooling system? _____

_____

9. Is the following sentence true or false? Gasoline engines operate very efficiently in converting fuel energy to work. _____

Heating Systems (pages 489–490)

10. What is a central heating system? _____

_____

11. List four energy sources used for central heating systems.

   a. _____   b. _____

   c. _____   d. _____

12. Is the following sentence true or false? In most heating systems, conduction is used to distribute most of the thermal energy. _____

Match each description with the heating system it describes.

Description	Heating System
_____ 13. Water heated by a boiler circulates through radiators in each room, transferring thermal energy.	a. hot-water heating
_____ 14. Fans are used to circulate warm air through ducts to the rooms in a building.	b. steam heating
_____ 15. A hot coil heats air by conduction and radiation.	c. electric baseboard heating
_____ 16. This system is often used in older buildings or to heat many buildings from a single location.	d. forced-air heating

Cooling Systems (pages 490–492)

17. Is the following sentence true or false? Most cooling systems, such as air conditioners and refrigerators, are heat pumps. _____

18. A fluid that vaporizes and condenses inside the tubing of a heat pump is called a(n) _____.

19. How does a heat pump reverse the normal flow of thermal energy? _____

_____

_____

Chapter 16   Thermal Energy and Heat

WordWise

Answer the questions by writing the correct vocabulary term in the blanks.
Use the circled letter(s) in each term to find the hidden vocabulary word.
Then, write a definition for the hidden word.

Clues	Vocabulary Terms
This flows spontaneously from hot objects to cold objects.	_ _ _ ◯
Any device that converts heat into work	◯ ◯ _ _ _ _ _ _ _ _
A heat pump does work on this so you can keep your veggies cold.	_ _ _ ◯ _ _ _ _ _ _
The Kelvin scale is used to measure this.	_ _ ◯ _ _ _ _ _ _ _
A device used to determine the specific heat of a material	_ ◯ ◯ _ _ _ _ _ _
The transfer of thermal energy when particles of a fluid move from place to place	_ _ _ _ _ _ _ ◯ _ ◯
The amount of heat needed to raise the temperature of one gram of a material by one degree Celsius	◯ _ _ _ _ _ _ _ _ _ _ _
The transfer of thermal energy with no overall transfer of matter	_ _ _ _ ◯ _ _ _ _
The total potential and kinetic energy of all the particles in an object	_ _ _ _ _ ◯ _ _ _ _ _ _
The transfer of energy by waves moving through space	_ ◯ _ _ ◯ _ ◯ _
According to the first law of thermodynamics, this is conserved.	_ _ _ ◯ _ _

Hidden words: _ _ _ _ _ _ _ _ _ _ _ _ _ _

Definition: _____

_____

Chapter 16   Thermal Energy and Heat

Calculating with Specific Heat

How much heat is required to raise the temperature of a
gold earring from 25.0°C to 30.0°C? The earring weighs
25 grams, and the specific heat of gold is 0.128 J/g•°C.

**Math Skill:
Formulas and
Equations**

You may want to read
more about this **Math
Skill** in the **Skills and
Reference Handbook**
at the end of your
textbook.

1. Read and Understand

What information are you given?

Specific heat = c = 0.128 J/g•°C

Mass = m = 25.0 grams

Change in Temperature = ΔT = (30.0°C − 25.0°C) = 5.0°C

2. Plan and Solve

What unknown are you trying to calculate?

Amount of heat needed = Q = ?

What formula contains the given quantities and the unknown?

Q = Mass × Specific heat × Change in Temperature

$Q = m \times c \times \Delta T$

Replace each variable with its known value.

Q = 25.0 g × 0.128 J/g•°C × 5.0°C = 16 J

3. Look Back and Check

Is your answer reasonable?

$$\frac{\text{Heat absorbed}}{(m \times c)} = 16 \text{ J}/(25.0 \text{ g} \times 0.128 \text{ J/g•°C}) = 5.0°C$$

This is a reasonable answer for the heat required to raise the
temperature of the earring.

Math Practice

On a separate sheet of paper, solve the following problems.

1. How much heat is required to raise the temperature of 25 grams
   of water from 25.0°C to 30.0°C? The specific heat of water is
   4.18 J/g•°C.

2. Determine the mass of a sample of silver if 705 J of heat are required
   to raise its temperature from 25°C to 35°C. The specific heat of silver
   is 0.235 J/g•°C.

3. An iron skillet has a mass of 500.0 g. The specific heat of iron is
   0.449 J/g•°C. The pan is heated by adding 19,082.5 J of heat. How
   much does the temperature of the pan increase?

Chapter 17   Mechanical Waves and Sound

Section 17.1 Mechanical Waves
(pages 500–503)

This section explains what mechanical waves are, how they form, and how they travel. Three main types of mechanical waves—transverse, longitudinal, and surface waves—are discussed and examples are given for each type.

Reading Strategy (page 500)

Previewing As you read this section, use Figure 2 on page 501 to complete the web diagram. Then use Figures 3 and 4 to make similar diagrams for longitudinal waves and surface waves on a separate sheet of paper. For more information on this Reading Strategy, see the **Reading and Study Skills** in the **Skills and Reference Handbook** at the end of your textbook.

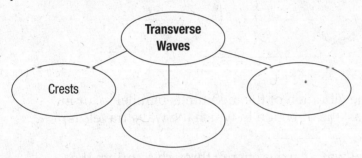

What Are Mechanical Waves? (page 500)

1. A disturbance in matter that carries energy from one place to another is called a(n) _____.

2. Is the following sentence true or false? Mechanical waves can travel through empty space. _____

3. The material through which a wave travels is called a(n) _____.

4. Is the following sentence true or false? Solids, liquids, and gases all can act as mediums for waves. _____

5. What creates a mechanical wave? _____
_____

Types of Mechanical Waves (pages 501–503)

6. Is the following sentence true or false? The three main types of mechanical waves are water waves, longitudinal waves, and surface waves. _____

7. Circle the letter of the characteristic used to classify a mechanical wave.

   a. the height of its crest

   b. the depth of its trough

   c. the way it travels through a medium

   d. the type of medium through which it travels

Chapter 17   Mechanical Waves and Sound

  8. The highest point of a wave above the rest position is the
     _____ and the lowest point below the rest position
     is the _____.

  9. What is a transverse wave? _____
     _____

 10. Look at the figure below. Label the missing aspects of the wave in
     the rope.

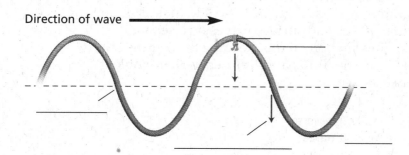

Direction of wave ⟶

 11. A wave in which the vibration of the medium is parallel to, or in
     the same direction as, the direction in which the wave travels is
     called a(n) _____.

 12. When a longitudinal wave carries energy through a spring, the
     area where the coils of a spring are closer together than they would
     be in the rest position is called a(n) _____.

 13. Is the following sentence true or false? A rarefaction is a region in a
     longitudinal wave where particles of a medium spread out.
     _____

 14. Why is an ocean wave classified as a surface wave? _____
     _____

 15. Why do ocean waves transport objects on the surface of the water as they
     approach shore? _____
     _____

*Match the type of wave to each description below. The type of wave may be
used more than once.*

Description	Type of Wave
_____ 16. P wave	a. transverse wave
_____ 17. Direction of travel is perpendicular to vibration direction	b. longitudinal wave
_____ 18. Rarefactions with particles that are spread out	c. surface wave
_____ 19. A wave that travels along a boundary separating two mediums	
_____ 20. An ocean wave	

Section 17.2 Properties of Mechanical Waves
(pages 504–507)

This section introduces measurable properties used to describe mechanical waves, including frequency, period, wavelength, speed, and amplitude.

Reading Strategy (page 504)

Build Vocabulary As you read, write a definition in your own words for each term in the table below. For more information on this Reading Strategy, see the **Reading and Study Skills** in the **Skills and Reference Handbook** at the end of your textbook.

Properties of Waves	
Vocabulary Term	**Definition**
Period	
Frequency	
Wavelength	
Amplitude	

Frequency and Period (page 504)

1. Is the following sentence true or false? A periodic motion repeats at regular time intervals. _____

2. The time required for one cycle, a complete motion that returns to its starting point, is called the _____.

3. The number of complete cycles in a given period of time is the _____ of a periodic motion.

4. Circle the letter of each sentence that is true about frequency.

   a. Frequency is measured in cycles per second, or hertz.

   b. A wave's frequency equals the frequency of the vibrating source producing it.

   c. Five cycles per minute is a frequency of five hertz.

   d. Any periodic motion has a frequency.

Wavelength (page 505)

5. The distance between a point on one wave and the same point on the next cycle of the wave is called _____.

6. How is wavelength determined for a longitudinal wave?

_____

Chapter 17   Mechanical Waves and Sound

Wave Speed (pages 505–506)

7. Write a formula you can use to determine the speed of a wave.

_____

8. Is the following sentence true or false? The speed of a wave equals its wavelength divided by its period. _____

9. What variables can cause the speed of a wave to change? _____

_____

10. Circle the letter of the sentence that tells how wavelength is related to frequency for a wave traveling at a constant speed.

   a. Wavelength is equal to frequency.

   b. Wavelength is directly proportional to frequency.

   c. Wavelength is inversely proportional to frequency.

   d. A wave with a higher frequency will have a longer wavelength.

Amplitude (page 507)

11. What is the amplitude of a wave? _____

_____

12. It takes more energy to produce a wave with higher crests and deeper troughs, so the more energy a wave has, the
   _____ its amplitude.

Questions 13 through 17 refer to the figure below.

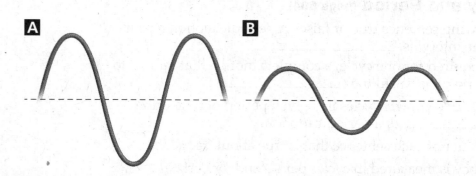

13. The type of waves shown are _____.

14. Label the rest position for waves A and B.

15. Add arrows to the figure to indicate the amplitude of each wave. Which wave has the greater amplitude? _____

16. Which wave shown has more energy? _____

17. Add an arrow to indicate one wavelength on wave B.

Chapter 17   Mechanical Waves and Sound

Section 17.3 Behavior of Waves
(pages 508–512)

This section describes different interactions that can occur when a mechanical wave encounters an obstacle, a change in medium, or another wave. These interactions include reflection, refraction, diffraction, and interference.

Reading Strategy (page 508)

Identifying Main Ideas Complete the table below. As you read, write the main idea of each topic. For more information on this Reading Strategy, see the **Reading and Study Skills** in the **Skills and Reference Handbook** at the end of your textbook.

Wave Interactions	
Topic	**Main Idea**
Reflection	
Refraction	
Diffraction	
Interference	
Standing waves	

Reflection (page 508)

1. Is the following sentence true or false? Reflection occurs when a wave bounces off a surface that it cannot pass through. _____

2. Circle the letter of the results that occur when a wave reflects off a fixed boundary.

   a. The reflected wave will be turned upside down.

   b. The amplitude will double as it strikes the surface.

   c. The speed of the wave will decrease.

   d. The frequency of the wave will decrease.

Refraction (page 509)

3. Why does refraction occur when a wave enters a new medium at an angle? _____

   _____

4. Is the following sentence true or false? Refraction always involves a change in the speed and direction of a wave. _____

Chapter 17   Mechanical Waves and Sound

Diffraction (page 510)

5. What is required in order for diffraction to occur? _____
_____

6. Is the following sentence true or false? A wave diffracts more if its wavelength is small compared to the size of an opening or obstacle. _____

Interference (pages 510–511)

7. What causes wave interference? _____
_____

8. Complete the table about interference.

Interference		
Type	Alignment	Displacement Change
Constructive	Crests align with crests; troughs align with troughs	
		Displacements combine to produce a reduced amplitude.

9. Is the following sentence true or false? Destructive interference can result in wave displacements that are above the rest position.
_____

10. How can an increased depth of a trough be considered constructive interference? _____
_____

Standing Waves (page 512)

11. At certain frequencies, interference between a wave and its reflection can produce a(n) _____.

12. Circle each letter of a sentence that is true about standing waves.

   a. A node is a point that has no displacement from the rest position.

   b. Standing waves appear to move through a medium, such as a string.

   c. Complete destructive interference occurs at antinodes.

   d. A standing wave will form for any wavelength, as long as two ends of a rope or string are stretched tightly between two points.

13. Is the following sentence true or false? If a standing wave occurs in a medium at a given frequency, another standing wave will occur if this frequency is doubled. _____

14. Give an example of a common standing wave. _____
_____

Chapter 17   Mechanical Waves and Sound

Section 17.4 Sound and Hearing
(pages 514–521)

This section discusses properties of sound waves, how they are produced, and how the ear perceives sound. A description of how music is produced and recorded also is presented.

Reading Strategy (page 514)

Using Prior Knowledge Before you read, add properties you already know about sound waves to the diagram below. Then add details about each property as you read the section. For more information on this Reading Strategy, see the **Reading and Study Skills** in the **Skills and Reference Handbook** at the end of your textbook.

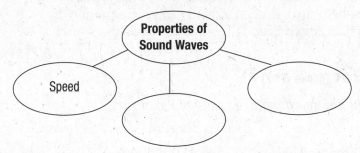

Properties of Sound Waves (pages 514–515)

1. Circle the letter of each sentence that is true about sound.

   a. Many behaviors of sound can be explained using a few properties.

   b. Sound waves are compressions and rarefactions that travel through a medium.

   c. Sound waves usually travel more slowly in solids than in gases.

   d. The speed of sound in air is about 30 meters per second.

Match each description with one or more sound properties.

Description	Property
_____ 2. This property is measured in units called decibels.	a. loudness
_____ 3. These properties are affected by the length of tubing in a musical instrument.	b. pitch
_____ 4. This property is the frequency of a sound as your ears perceive it.	c. intensity
_____ 5. These properties depend on factors such as your age and the health of your ears.	d. frequency
_____ 6. This property is a physical response to the intensity of sound.	

Chapter 17   Mechanical Waves and Sound

Ultrasound (page 516)

7. Is the following sentence true or false? Ultrasound is sound at frequencies that are lower than most people are capable of hearing.
_____

8. Describe some applications of ultrasound. _____
_____

The Doppler Effect (page 516)

9. Is the following sentence true or false? The Doppler effect is a change in sound frequency caused by motion of the sound source, motion of the listener, or both. _____

10. For a stationary observer, as a moving sound source approaches, the observer will first hear a(n) _____ frequency of sound and then a(n) _____ frequency as the source moves away.

Hearing and the Ear (page 517)

Match each description with the appropriate region(s) of the ear.

Description	Region
_____ 11. Sound is gathered and focused here.	a. outer ear
_____ 12. Nerve endings send signals to the brain.	b. middle ear
_____ 13. The eardrum is located at the boundary between these two regions of the ear.	c. inner ear
_____ 14. Hammer, anvil, and stirrup are located here.	
_____ 15. Sound vibrations are amplified.	

How Sound Is Reproduced (pages 518–519)

16. How is sound recorded? _____
_____

17. Sound is reproduced by converting _____ back into sound waves.

Music (page 521)

18. Is the following sentence true or false? Many musical instruments vary pitch by changing the frequency of standing waves.
_____

19. Theaters are designed to prevent "dead spots" where the volume is reduced by _____ of reflected sound waves.

20. The response of a standing wave to another wave of the same frequency is called _____.

Chapter 17   Mechanical Waves and Sound

WordWise

Test your knowledge of vocabulary terms from Chapter 17 by completing this crossword puzzle.

Clues across:

1. Maximum displacement of a wave

3. The time required for one complete wave cycle

6. An apparent change in frequency of a sound source that moves relative to an observer

8. A point of no displacement in a standing wave

9. Area where particles in a medium are spread out as a longitudinal wave travels through it

10. Distance from one point to the next identical point on a wave

Clues down:

2. Type of mechanical wave whose direction of vibration is perpendicular to its direction of travel

4. A unit used to compare sound intensity levels

5. Occurs when waves overlap

6. Occurs when a wave encounters an object or opening that is close in size to its wavelength

7. Lowest point of a wave below the rest position

Chapter 17 Mechanical Waves and Sound

Calculating Wave Properties

A transverse wave in a rope is traveling at a speed of 3.0 m/s. The period of this mechanical wave is 0.25 s. What is the wavelength?

Math Skill:
Formulas and
Equations

You may want to read more about this **Math Skill** in the **Skills and Reference Handbook** at the end of your textbook.

1. Read and Understand

What information are you given?
Speed = 3.0 m/s

Period = 0.25 s

2. Plan and Solve

What unknown are you trying to calculate?
Wavelength = ?

What formula contains the given quantities and the unknown?

$$\text{Speed} = \text{Wavelength} \times \text{Frequency} = \frac{\text{Wavelength}}{\text{Period}}$$

Wavelength = Period × Speed

Replace each variable with its known value.
Speed = 3.0 m/s

Period = 0.25 s

Wavelength = 0.25 s × 3.0 m/s = 0.75 m

3. Look Back and Check

Is your answer reasonable?

$$\text{Speed} = \text{Wavelength} \times \text{Frequency} = \text{Wavelength} \times \frac{1}{\text{Period}}$$

$$\text{Speed} = 0.75 \text{ m} \times \frac{1}{0.25 \text{ s}} = 3.0 \text{ m/s}.$$

Substituting the calculated wavelength into the equation yields the original speed of 3.0 m/s.

Math Practice

On a separate sheet of paper, solve the following problems.

1. What is the speed, in m/s, of a wave on a cord if it has a wavelength of 4 m and a period of 0.5 s?

2. What is the period of a wave traveling 5 m/s if its wavelength is 20 m?

3. Calculate the frequency, in Hz, of a wave in a string traveling 1.25 m/s, with a wavelength of 0.50 m.

Chapter 18   The Electromagnetic Spectrum and Light

Section 18.1 Electromagnetic Waves
(pages 532–538)

This section describes the characteristics of electromagnetic waves.

Reading Strategy (page 532)

Comparing and Contrasting As you read about electromagnetic waves, fill in the table below. If the characteristic listed in the table describes electromagnetic waves, write E in the column for Wave Type. Write M for mechanical waves and B for both. For more information on this Reading Strategy, see the **Reading and Study Skills** in the **Skills and Reference Handbook** at the end of your textbook.

Electromagnetic and Mechanical Waves	
Travels through a vacuum	E
Travels though medium	
Fits wave model	B
Fits particle model	
Transverse wave	
Longitudinal wave	

What Are Electromagnetic Waves? (page 533)

1. What are electromagnetic waves? _____

_____

2. Electric fields are produced by electrically charged particles and by changing _____.

3. Magnetic fields are produced by magnets, by changing _____, and by vibrating charges.

4. Electromagnetic waves are produced when a(n) _____ vibrates or accelerates.

5. Circle the letter of each sentence that is true about electric and magnetic fields.

   a. An electromagnetic wave occurs when electric and magnetic fields vibrate at right angles to each other.

   b. A magnetic field is surrounded by an electric current.

   c. Changing electric and magnetic fields regenerate each other.

   d. Electromagnetic waves are produced when an electric charge vibrates.

6. Is the following sentence true or false? Electromagnetic waves need a medium to travel through. _____

7. The transfer of energy by electromagnetic waves traveling through matter or across space is called _____.

Chapter 18   The Electromagnetic Spectrum and Light

The Speed of Electromagnetic Waves (page 534)

8. As a thunderstorm approaches, you see the lightning before you hear the thunder, because light travels _____ than sound.

9. Is the following sentence true or false? All electromagnetic waves travel at the same speed through a vacuum. _____

10. Circle the letter that gives the correct speed of light in a vacuum.

   a. 3.00×10^8 kilometers per second

   b. 3.00×10^8 meters per hour

   c. 3.00×10^8 meters per second

   d. 3.00×10^8 kilometers per hour

Wavelength and Frequency (page 535)

11. Circle the letter of each sentence that is true about electromagnetic waves.

   a. Different electromagnetic waves can have different frequencies.

   b. Wavelength is directly proportional to frequency.

   c. Electromagnetic waves always travel at the speed of light.

   d. All electromagnetic waves travel at the same speed in a vacuum.

12. As the wavelengths of electromagnetic waves increase, the frequencies _____, for waves moving in a(n) _____.

Wave or Particle? (pages 536–537)

13. Electromagnetic radiation behaves sometimes like a(n) _____ and sometimes like a stream of _____.

14. Interference only occurs when two or more waves overlap, so _____ experiment showed that light behaves like a _____.

15. The emission of electrons from a metal caused by light striking the metal is called the _____ effect.

16. Blue light has a higher frequency than red light, so photons of blue light have _____ energy than photons of red light.

Intensity (page 538)

17. The closer you get to a source of light, the _____ the light appears.

18. Intensity is the _____ at which a wave's energy flows through a given unit of area.

19. As photons travel farther from the source, the _____ of light decreases.

Chapter 18   The Electromagnetic Spectrum and Light

Section 18.2 The Electromagnetic Spectrum
(pages 539–545)

This section identifies the waves in the electromagnetic spectrum and describes their uses.

Reading Strategy (page 539)

Summarizing Complete the table for the electromagnetic spectrum. List at least two uses for each kind of wave. For more information on this Reading Strategy, see the **Reading and Study Skills** in the **Skills and Reference Handbook** at the end of your textbook.

The Electromagnetic Spectrum		
Type of Waves	**Uses**	
Radio Waves	Communications	
Infrared Rays		Keeping food warm

The Waves of the Spectrum (pages 539–540)

1. Is the following sentence true or false? William Herschel determined that the temperature of colors of light was higher at the blue end and lower at the red end. _____

2. Herschel's curiosity led him to conclude there must be invisible _____ beyond the red end of the color band.

3. Is the following sentence true or false? The full range of frequencies of electromagnetic radiation is called the electromagnetic spectrum. _____

4. Name each kind of wave in the electromagnetic spectrum, from the longest to shortest wavelength.

   a. _____   b. _____

   c. _____   d. _____

   e. _____   f. _____

Chapter 18   The Electromagnetic Spectrum and Light

Radio Waves (pages 540–542)

5. Circle the letter of each way that radio waves might be used.

   a. x-ray machines

   b. microwave ovens

   c. radio technology

   d. television technology

6. What is the difference between amplitude modulation (AM) and frequency modulation (FM)? _____

   _____

   _____

7. How far do microwaves generally penetrate food? _____

   _____

8. How is the Doppler effect used to detect the speed of a vehicle? ____

   _____

   _____

Infrared Rays (page 543)

9. Circle the letter of each way infrared rays are used.

   a. source of light

   b. to discover areas of heat differences

   c. source of heat

   d. to discover areas of depth differences

10. Thermograms show variations in _____ and are used to find places where a building loses heat to the environment.

Visible Light (page 543)

11. Is the following sentence true or false? One use for visible light is to help people communicate with one another. _____

Ultraviolet Rays (page 544)

12. Ultraviolet radiation has applications in _____ and _____.

13. Is the following sentence true or false? Ultraviolet radiation helps your skin produce vitamin D. _____

X-rays (page 544)

14. Is the following sentence true or false? X-rays have higher frequencies than ultraviolet rays. _____

15. Why are X-rays helpful? _____

   _____

Gamma Rays (page 545)

16. Gamma rays have the highest _____ and therefore the most _____ and the greatest penetrating ability of all the electromagnetic waves.

17. How is gamma radiation used in medicine? _____

   _____

Chapter 18   The Electromagnetic Spectrum and Light

Section 18.3 Behavior of Light
(pages 546-549)

This section discusses the behavior of light when it strikes different types of materials.

Reading Strategy (page 546)

Monitoring Your Understanding As you read, complete the flowchart to show how different materials affect light. For more information on this Reading Strategy, see the **Reading and Study Skills** in the **Skills and Reference Handbook** at the end of your textbook.

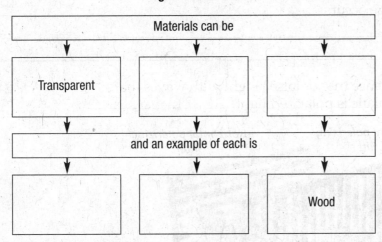

Light and Materials

Materials can be

Transparent

and an example of each is

Wood

Light and Materials (pages 546–547)

1. Is the following sentence true or false? Without light, nothing is visible. _____

Match each term to its definition.

Term	Definition
_____ **2.** transparent	a. Material that absorbs or reflects all of the light that strikes it
_____ **3.** opaque	b. Material that transmits light
_____ **4.** translucent	c. Material that scatters light

Interactions of Light (pages 547–549)

5. Is the following sentence true or false? Just as light can affect matter, matter can affect light. _____

6. When light strikes a new medium, it can be _____, _____, or _____.

Chapter 18   The Electromagnetic Spectrum and Light

7. When light is transmitted, it can be refracted, polarized, or
_____.

8. A copy of an object formed by reflected or refracted light waves is
known as a(n) _____.

9. When parallel light waves strike an uneven surface and reflect off
it in the same direction, _____ reflection occurs.

10. When parallel light waves strike a rough, uneven surface and
reflect in many different directions, _____
reflection occurs.

11. Light bends, or _____, when it passes at an angle
from one type of medium into another.

12. Explain why a mirage occurs. _____
_____
_____

13. Is the following sentence true or false? Light with waves that
vibrate in only one plane is polarized light. _____

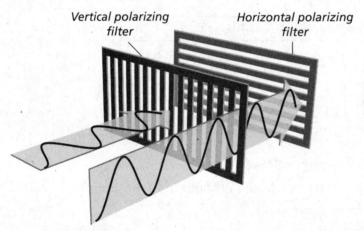

Vertical polarizing filter   Horizontal polarizing filter

14. Refer to the drawing and complete the table on polarizing filters.

Polarizing Filters		
Direction of Light Vibration	**Filter Type**	**Action**
Horizontal wave	Vertically polarizing filter	
	Vertically polarizing filter	Light passes through.

15. How do sunglasses block glare? _____
_____

16. The effect when light is redirected as it passes through a medium
is called _____.

17. Explain why the sun looks red at sunset and sunrise. _____
_____

Chapter 18   The Electromagnetic Spectrum and Light

Section 18.4 Color
(pages 550–553)

*This section explains how a prism separates white light. It also discusses
factors that influence the various properties of color.*

Reading Strategy (page 550)

Venn Diagram As you read, label the Venn diagram for mixing
primary colors of light. For more information on this Reading
Strategy, see the **Reading and Study Skills** in the **Skills and
Reference Handbook** at the end of your textbook.

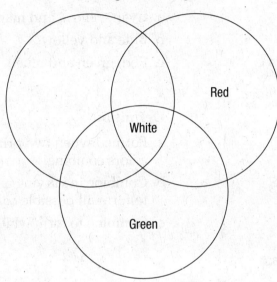

Mixing Colors of Light

Red

White

Green

Separating White Light Into Colors (page 551)

1. What did Isaac Newton's experiments with a prism in 1666 show?

_____

_____

2. What happens when white light passes through a prism? _____

_____

3. Circle the letter of the process in which white light is separated
into the colors of the rainbow.

   a. reflection   b. dispersion

   c. absorption   d. polarization

4. How does a rainbow form? _____

_____

Chapter 18   The Electromagnetic Spectrum and Light

The Colors of Objects (pages 551–552)

5. List two factors that determine the color of an object seen by reflected light.

a. _____

b. _____

6. Is the following sentence true or false? I see a red car in sunlight because the color of light reaching my eyes is mostly red light. _____

Mixing Colors of Light (page 552)

Match the colors of light with the correct type of color.

Type of Color	Colors of Light
_____ 7. primary colors	a. Cyan, yellow, and magenta
_____ 8. secondary colors	b. Blue and yellow
_____ 9. complementary colors	c. Red, green and blue

Match each color of light to its definition.

Type of Color	Definition
_____ 10. primary colors	a. Formed when two primary colors combine
_____ 11. secondary colors	b. Combine in varying amounts to form all possible colors
_____ 12. complementary colors	c. Combine to form white light

Mixing Pigments (page 553)

13. What is a pigment? _____

_____

14. List four natural sources of pigments.

a. _____   b. _____

c. _____   d. _____

15. The primary colors of pigments are _____, _____, and magenta.

Match the primary colors of pigment to the color they produce when combined.

Primary Colors	Color Produced
_____ 16. Cyan and magenta	a. green
_____ 17. Cyan and yellow	b. red
_____ 18. Yellow and magenta	c. blue

19. Any two colors of pigments that combine to make black pigment are _____ colors of pigments.

Chapter 18   The Electromagnetic Spectrum and Light

Section 18.5 Sources of Light
(pages 558–562)

This section discusses the major sources of light and their uses.

Reading Strategy (page 558)

Flowchart Complete the incandescent bulb flowchart. For more information on this Reading Strategy, see the **Reading and Study Skills in the Skills and Reference Handbook** at the end of your textbook.

Incandescent Bulb

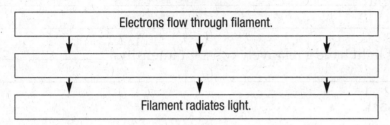

1. Objects that give off their own light are _____.

2. List six common sources of light.

   a. _____   b. _____

   c. _____   d. _____

   e. _____   f. _____

Incandescent Light (page 558)

3. The light produced when an object gets hot enough to glow is
   _____.

4. As electrons flow through an incandescent light bulb, the
   _____ heats up.

5. Is the following sentence true or false? To increase the life of the
   filament, incandescent light bulbs contain oxygen at very low
   pressure. _____

6. Most of the energy given off by incandescent bulbs is in the form
   of _____.

Fluorescent Light (page 559)

7. What happens in the process of fluorescence? _____

   _____

8. A solid material that can emit light by fluorescence is called a(n)
   _____.

9. Fluorescent bulbs emit most of their energy in the form of
   _____.

10. Is the following sentence true or false? Incandescent bulbs are
    more energy efficient than fluorescent bulbs. _____

Chapter 18   The Electromagnetic Spectrum and Light

Laser Light (page 560)

11. A laser is a device that generates _____.

12. The letters in the word *laser* stand for

l _____

a _____

s _____

e _____

r _____ .

13. What is coherent light? _____

_____

14. Why does coherent light have a relatively constant intensity? _____

_____

Neon Light (page 561)

15. How is neon light emitted? _____

_____

16. List three gases used to produce neon light.

a. _____

b. _____

c. _____

17. Why do different types of neon light glow in different colors? _____

_____

_____

_____

Sodium-Vapor Light (page 562)

18. Sodium-vapor lights contain a mixture of _____ and a small amount of solid _____ .

19. Explain what happens when an electric current passes through a sodium-vapor bulb. _____

_____

_____

Tungsten-Halogen Light (page 562)

20. Explain how a tungsten-halogen light bulb works. _____

_____

_____

Chapter 18   The Electromagnetic Spectrum and Light

WordWise

Complete the sentences using one of the scrambled words below.

nrcteleos	tarfes	qucreynef
treclefs	rigehh	kabcl
mefailnt	riotrafecn	ratenemypocml
yrecurm	snohpot	dairo
sifdel	culstantren	otehcern

Electromagnetic waves consist of changing electric and changing magnetic _____.

You hear thunder from a distant lightning bolt a few seconds after you see the lightning because light travels much _____ than sound.

If you know the wavelength of an electromagnetic wave in a vacuum, you can calculate its _____.

Although light behaves as a wave, the photoelectric effect shows that light also consists of bundles of energy called _____.

Antennas use _____ waves to send signals to television receivers.

Ultraviolet rays have a _____ frequency than waves of violet light.

If you can look through a material but what you see is not clear or distinct, then the material is said to be _____.

When a beam of light enters a new medium at an angle, it changes direction, and _____ occurs.

A truck appears red in the sunlight because its paint _____ mainly red light.

A color of light mixed equally with its _____ color of light yields white light.

Complementary colors of pigments combine to form _____ pigment.

An incandescent bulb produces light by using an electric current to heat a(n) _____.

Inside a fluorescent bulb, an electric current passes through _____ vapor and produces ultraviolet light.

Light that consists of a single wavelength of light with its crests and troughs lined up is called _____ light.

Neon lights emit light when _____ flow through gas in a tube.

Chapter 18   The Electromagnetic Spectrum and Light

Calculating Wavelength and Frequency

**Math Skill:
Multiplication
and Division
of Exponents**

You may want to read
more about this **Math
Skill** in the **Skills and
Reference Handbook**
at the end of your
textbook.

A particular AM radio station broadcasts at a frequency of
1030 MHz. What is the wavelength of the transmitted radio
wave assuming it travels in a vacuum?

1. Read and Understand

What information are you given?

Speed = c = 3.00×10^8 m/s

Frequency = 1030 kHz = 1030×10^3 Hz

2. Plan and Solve

What unknown are you trying to calculate?

Wavelength = ?

What formula contains the given quantities and the unknown?

Speed = Wavelength × Frequency

$$\text{Wavelength} = \frac{\text{Speed}}{\text{Frequency}}$$

Replace each variable with its known value.

$$\text{Wavelength} = \frac{3.00 \times 10^8 \text{ m/s}}{1030 \text{ Hz} \times 10^8 \text{ Hz}}$$

$$= \frac{3.00 \times 10^8 \text{ m/s}}{1.030 \times 10^6 \text{ 1/s}} = 291 \text{ m}$$

3. Look Back and Check

Is your answer reasonable?

Radio waves have frequencies greater that 1 mm, so 291 m is a
reasonable wavelength for a radio wave.

Math Practice

On a separate sheet of paper, solve the following problems.

1. In a vacuum, the wavelength of light from a laser is 630 nm
   (630×10^{-9} m). What is the frequency of the light?

2. If a radio wave vibrates at 80.0 MHz, what is its wavelength?

3. A radio station broadcasts at 780 kHz. The wavelength of its
   radio waves is 385 m. Verify that the radio wave travels at the
   speed of light.

Chapter 19   Optics

Section 19.1 Mirrors
(pages 570–573)

This section describes the law of reflection and explains how images are formed by plane, concave, and convex mirrors. Uses of mirrors are also described.

Reading Strategy (page 570)

Comparing and Contrasting After reading this section, compare mirror types by completing the table. For more information on this Reading Strategy, see the **Reading and Study Skills** in the **Skills and Reference Handbook** at the end of your textbook.

Mirror Types		
Mirror	**Shape of Surface**	**Image (virtual, real, or both)**
Plane	Flat	Virtual
Concave		
Convex		

The Law of Reflection (pages 570–571)

1. A ray diagram shows how rays _____ when they strike mirrors and pass through lenses.

2. Is the following sentence true or false? On a ray diagram, the angle of incidence is the angle that a reflected ray makes with a line drawn perpendicular to the surface of a mirror. _____

3. Circle the letter of the sentence that best answers the following question. What does a ray diagram of the law of reflection show?

   a. The angle of incidence is greater than the angle of reflection.

   b. The angle of reflection is greater than the angle of incidence.

   c. The angle of incidence is equal to the angle of reflection.

   d. The angle of incidence increases as the angle of reflection decreases.

Plane Mirrors (page 571)

4. A mirror with a flat surface is known as a(n) _____.

5. Circle the letter of each sentence that is true about plane mirrors.

   a. Plane mirrors always produce virtual images.

   b. Plane mirrors produce right-left reversed images of objects.

   c. Light rays reflect from a mirror at an angle that is twice as large as the angle of incidence.

   d. Your image appears to be the same distance behind a mirror as you are in front of it.

Chapter 19   Optics

6. What type of image is a copy of an object formed at the location from which the light rays appear to come?

   a. reversed image   b. virtual image

   c. real image   d. reflected image

Concave and Convex Mirrors (pages 572–573)

7. Circle the letter of the object that is most like the shape of a concave mirror.

   a. the inside of a shallow bowl   b. the bottom of a bucket

   c. the outside surface of a ball   d. a glass window pane

8. What is the focal point? _____

   _____

9. Is the following sentence true or false? A real image is a copy of an object formed at the point where light rays actually meet.

   _____

For questions 10 through 12, refer to the diagrams below.

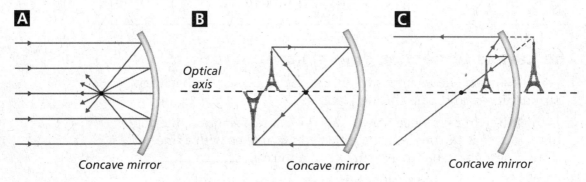

10. Label the focal point on each diagram.

11. In B and C, label the object and image locations and identify the image as real or virtual. *Hint:* The object is always right-side up and in front of the reflecting surface of the mirror.

12. What determines whether a concave mirror produces a real image or a virtual image?

   a. the size of the object

   b. the shape of the object

   c. the position of the object relative to the focal point

   d. the location of the optical axis

13. A curved mirror whose outside surface is the reflecting surface is called a(n) _____ mirror.

14. Why do convex mirrors always form virtual images? _____

   _____

15. Is the following sentence true or false? The image formed by a convex lens is always upright and smaller than the object.

   _____

Section 19.2 Lenses
(pages 574–578)

This section defines index of refraction and discusses how it is related to the way light behaves upon entering different materials. Image formation in concave and convex lenses are presented.

Reading Strategy (page 574)

Building Vocabulary As you read the section, define in your own words each vocabulary word listed in the table. For more information on this Reading Strategy, see the **Reading and Study Skills** in the **Skills and Reference Handbook** at the end of your textbook.

Refraction and Reflection	
Vocabulary Term	**Definition**
Index of refraction	
Critical angle	
Total internal reflection	

Index of Refraction of Light (pages 574–575)

1. Circle the letter of the sentence about the speed of light through media that is true.

   a. Once light passes from a vacuum into any medium, it speeds up.

   b. Compared to other media, air slows the speed of light only slightly.

   c. The speed of light is greater in water than in air.

   d. The speed of light in a new medium depends on the size of the new medium.

2. What determines how much a light ray bends when it passes from one medium to another? _____

   _____

3. The ratio of the speed of light in a vacuum to the speed of light in a particular material is known as the _____ of that material.

Concave and Convex Lenses (pages 576–577)

4. An object made of transparent material that has one or two curved surfaces that can refract light is called a(n) _____.

5. Two properties of a lens that affect the way it refracts light are _____ and _____.

6. A lens that is curved inward at the center and is thickest at the outside edges is called a(n) _____ lens.

Chapter 19   Optics

7. Concave lenses always cause light rays to _____.

8. Circle the letter of each sentence that is true about convex lenses.

   a. Convex lenses are diverging lenses.

   b. Fly eyes have many facets shaped like the surface of convex lenses.

   c. Convex lenses can form either real or virtual images.

   d. Convex lenses are shaped somewhat like the inside of a bowl.

9. What determines whether a convex lens will form a real image or a virtual image? _____

_____

For questions 10 and 11, refer to the diagrams below.

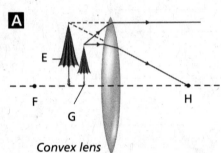

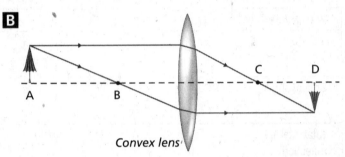

10. In each diagram identify the labeled items as the object, focal point, or image. Also, identify the image as virtual or real.

   A. _____   B. _____

   C. _____   D. _____

   E. _____   F. _____

   G. _____   H. _____

11. Which diagram shows the formation of a virtual image?

   _____

Total Internal Reflection (page 578)

12. Circle each letter of a sentence that is true about the critical angle.

   a. At the critical angle, light refracts along the surface between two media.

   b. All the light is reflected back into the first medium at the critical angle.

   c. Only concave lenses have critical angles.

   d. All the light is reflected back into the second, denser medium when the critical angle is exceeded.

13. Is the following sentence true or false? Materials that have small critical angles, such as the glass used in fiber optics, cause most of the light entering them to be totally internally reflected. _____

Chapter 19   Optics

Section 19.3 Optical Instruments
(pages 580–585)

This section describes optical instruments, including telescopes, cameras, and microscopes. The basic principles of image formation by these instruments are explained.

Reading Strategy (page 580)

Using Prior Knowledge Add the names and descriptions of other optical instruments you know to the diagram. Revise the diagram after you read the section. For more information on this Reading Strategy, see the **Reading and Study Skills** in the **Skills and Reference Handbook** at the end of your textbook.

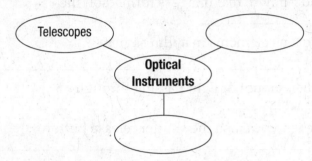

Telescopes (pages 580–581)

1. Circle the letter that best describes the amount of time it takes light from the most distant stars to reach Earth.

   a. seconds   b. hours

   c. millions of years   d. billions of years

2. An instrument that uses lenses or mirrors to collect and focus light from distant objects is called a(n) _____.

3. Complete the table about telescopes.

Telescopes		
Type	**Parts That Collect and Focus Light**	**Description of How Image Is Formed**
Reflecting telescope		
	Convex lenses	

Chapter 19   Optics

Cameras (pages 582–584)

4. Describe what a camera does. _____

_____

5. Circle the letter of each sentence that describes how cameras form or record images.

   a. An image is recorded on film or by a sensor.

   b. Light rays are focused to form virtual images.

   c. Light rays enter through an opening.

   d. Light rays are focused by the opening or lens.

6. Is the following sentence true or false? In a simple pinhole camera made from a box, an upside-down, real image is formed on the back wall of the box. _____

7. What is the purpose of the lens elements in a film camera?

_____

8. The device that controls the amount of light passing through a camera is the _____.

9. Describe what happens when you push the shutter release button on a modern film camera. _____

_____

10. How is the position of the lens of a modern film camera used to bring an object into focus? _____

_____

Microscopes (page 584)

11. An optical instrument that uses two convex lenses to magnify small objects is called a(n) _____.

12. Circle the letter that describes the path light rays follow through a compound microscope.

   a. Light rays from the objective lens pass through the object and then pass through the light source.

   b. Light rays from above pass up through the object and then pass through the objective lens.

   c. Light rays from below pass up through the object, the objective lens, and the eyepiece lens.

   d. Light rays from below pass up through the object, the concave lens, and the objective lens.

13. Is the following sentence true or false? When you look through the eyepiece of a compound microscope you see an enlarged, virtual image of the object. _____

Chapter 19   Optics

Section 19.4 The Eye and Vision
(pages 588–592)

This section describes the eye as an optical instrument. Parts of the eye and their functions are defined. Vision problems and how they can be corrected are also described.

Reading Strategy (page 588)

Outlining As you read, make an outline of the important ideas in this section. Use the green headings as the main topics and the blue headings as subtopics. For more information on this Reading Strategy, see the **Reading and Study Skills** in the **Skills and Reference Handbook** at the end of your textbook.

Section 19.4 Outline

I. The Eye and Vision

  A. Structure of the Eye

    1. _____

    2. _____

    3. _____

    4. _____

    5. _____

  B. _____

    1. _____

    2. _____

    3. _____

Structure of the Eye (pages 588–590)

Write the letter of the part of the eye that best matches each description.

Description	Part of Eye
_____ **1.** Its curved surface helps to focus light entering the eye.	a. pupil
_____ **2.** It focuses light onto sensor cells at the back of the eye.	b. retina
_____ **3.** This opening allows light to pass through the eye.	c. cornea
_____ **4.** This expands and contracts to control the amount of light entering the eye.	d. iris
_____ **5.** This is the transparent outer coating of the eye.	e. lens
_____ **6.** Its surface has rods and cones.	

Chapter 19   Optics

7. Is the following sentence true or false? Nerve endings called rods and cones convert light into electrical signals that are sent to the brain through the optic nerve. _____

8. Where on the retina does a blind spot occur? _____
_____

Correcting Vision Problems (pages 590–592)

For questions 9 and 10, refer to the figures below.

Problem: Nearsightedness (Eyeball is too long.)

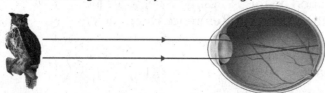

Correction:

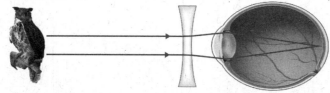

9. Circle the letter of the location where the image forms when nearsightedness occurs.

   a. on the retina   b. behind the retina

   c. before it reaches the retina   d. on the lens

10. Nearsightedness can be corrected by placing a(n) _____ lens in front of the eye.

Match each type of vision problem to its definition.

    Vision Problem   **Definition**

_____ 11. astigmatism

_____ 12. farsightedness

_____ 13. nearsightedness

a. A condition that causes distant objects to appear blurry because the cornea is too curved or the eyeball is too long

b. A condition that causes objects at any distance to appear blurry because the cornea or lens is misshapen

c. A condition that causes nearby objects to appear blurry because the cornea is not curved enough or the eyeball is too short

Chapter 19   Optics

WordWise

Use the clues below to identify vocabulary terms from Chapter 19. Write the terms below, putting one letter in each blank. When you finish, the term enclosed in the diagonal will reveal a term that is important in the study of optics.

Clues

1. Shows how the paths of light rays change when they strike mirrors or pass through lenses

2. Transparent material with one or two curved surfaces that can refract light

3. A mirror with a flat surface

4. An instrument that uses lenses or mirrors to collect and focus light from distant objects

5. Expands and contracts to control the amount of light entering the eye

6. An optical instrument that records an image of an object

7. Transparent outer layer of the eye

8. When the cornea is misshapen, this vision problem can result.

9. Type of lens that causes light rays to diverge

1. _ _ _ _ _ _ _ _ _ _ _

2. _ _ _ _

3. _ _ _ _ _ _ _ _ _ _

4. _ _ _ _ _ _ _ _ _

5. _ _ _

6. _ _ _ _ _

7. _ _ _ _ _ _

8. _ _ _ _ _ _ _ _ _ _ _

9. _ _ _ _ _ _ _ _ _ _ _ _

Hidden Word: _ _ _ _ _ _ _ _ _

Definition: _____

_____

Chapter 19   Optics

Calculating Index of Refraction

The speed of light in the mineral halite, NaCl, is approximately 1.95×10^8 m/s. Calculate the index of refraction for halite. (Recall that the speed of light in a vacuum is 3.00×10^8 m/s.)

Math Skill:
Ratios and
Proportions

You may want to read more about this **Math Skill** in the **Skills and Reference Handbook** at the end of your textbook.

1. Read and Understand

What information are you given?

Speed of light in halite = 1.95×10^8 m/s

Speed of light in vacuum = 3.00×10^8 m/s

2. Plan and Solve

What variable are you trying to determine?

Index of refraction = ?

What formulas contain the given variables?

Index of refraction = $\dfrac{\text{Speed of light}_{\text{vacuum}}}{\text{Speed of light}_{\text{material}}} = \dfrac{(3.00 \times 10^8 \text{ m/s})}{(1.95 \times 10^8 \text{ m/s})} = 1.54$

3. Look Back and Check

Is your answer reasonable?

Speed of light in vacuum = $(1.95 \times 10^8 \text{ m/s})(1.54) = 3.00 \times 10^8$ m/s

Yes, the answer is reasonable. Substituting the calculated index of refraction for halite back into the equation yields the value of the speed of light in a vacuum.

Math Practice

On a separate sheet of paper, solve the following problems.

1. The mineral uvarovite has an index of refraction of 1.86. Calculate the speed of light in this sample of uvarovite.

2. What is the index of refraction of a sample of opal, if the speed of light passing through it is 2.05×10^8 m/s?

3. Because its atomic structure varies with direction, a sample of the mineral calcite has an index of refraction of 1.486 along one direction in the crystal, while another direction has an index of refraction of 1.658. Which index represents the faster speed of light through the calcite? Explain your answer.

Section 20.1 Electric Charge and Static Electricity
(pages 600–603)

This section explains how electric charge is created and how positive and negative charges affect each other. It also discusses the different ways that electric charge can be transferred.

Reading Strategy (page 600)

Identifying Main Ideas Copy the table on a separate sheet of paper. As you read, write the main ideas. For more information on this Reading Strategy, see the **Reading and Study Skills** in the **Skills and Reference Handbook** at the end of your textbook.

Characteristics of Electric Charge	
Topic	**Main Idea**
Electric Charge	An excess or shortage of electrons produces a net electric charge.
Electric Forces	
Electric Fields	
Static Electricity	

Electric Charge (pages 600–601)

1. What are the two types of electric charge?

   a. _____   b. _____

2. Is the following sentence true or false? In an atom, negatively charged electrons surround a positively charged nucleus.

   _____

3. Is the following sentence true or false? If a neutral atom gains one or more electrons, it becomes a positively charged ion.

   _____

4. What is the SI unit of electric charge? _____

Electric Forces (page 601)

5. Circle the letter of each sentence that is true about electric force.

   a. Like charges attract and opposite charges repel.

   b. Electric force is the attraction or repulsion between electrically charged objects.

   c. Electric force is inversely proportional to the amount of charge.

   d. Electric force is inversely proportional to the square of the distance between two charges.

6. Which are stronger inside an atom, electric forces or gravitational forces? _____

7. Is the following sentence true or false? Electric forces cause friction and other contact forces. _____

Electric Fields (page 602)

8. A charge's electric field is the effect the charge has on _____ in the space around it.

9. Circle the letters of the factors that the strength of an electric field depends on.

    a. the direction of the field

    b. whether the charge is positive or negative

    c. the amount of charge that produces the field

    d. the distance from the charge

10. Is the following sentence true or false? The field of a negative charge points away from the charge. _____

Static Electricity and Charging (pages 602–603)

11. Static electricity is the study of the _____.

12. Is the following sentence true or false? Charge can be transferred by friction, by contact, and by induction. _____

13. What is the law of conservation of charge? _____

_____

14. Rubbing a balloon on your hair is an example of charging by

_____.

15. A charge transfer between objects that touch each other is called

_____.

16. Circle the letter of each sentence that is true about charging.

    a. When you rub a balloon on your hair, your hair loses electrons and becomes positively charged.

    b. The sphere of a Van de Graaff generator transfers all of its charge to you when you touch it.

    c. Induction occurs when charge is transferred without contact between materials.

    d. Static charges cannot move.

Static Discharge (page 603)

17. Is the following sentence true or false? Static discharge occurs when a pathway through which charges can move forms suddenly. _____

18. How does lightning occur? _____

_____

_____

Chapter 20   Electricity

Section 20.2 Electric Current and Ohm's Law
(pages 604–607)

This section discusses electric current, resistance, and voltage. It also uses Ohm's Law to explain how voltage, current, and resistance are related.

Reading Strategy (page 604)

Predicting Before you read, write a prediction of what electric current is in the table below. After you read, if your prediction was incorrect or incomplete, write what electric current actually is. For more information on this Reading Strategy, see the **Reading and Study Skills** in the **Skills and Reference Handbook** at the end of your textbook.

Electric Current	
Electric Current Probably Means	**Electric Current Actually Means**

Electric Current (page 604)

1. What is electric current? _____

_____

2. Complete the following table about electric current.

Electric Current		
Type of Current	**How Charge Flows**	**Examples**
Direct		
Alternating	Two directions	

3. Electrons flow in the wire from a(n) _____ terminal to a(n) _____ terminal.

Conductors and Insulators (page 605)

4. What is an electrical conductor? _____

_____

5. What is an electrical insulator? _____

_____

6. Is the following sentence true or false? Metals are good conductors because they do not have freely moving electrons.

_____

Chapter 20 Electricity

Match each material to the category of a conductor or insulator.

Material	Category
_____ **7.** Copper	a. conductor
_____ **8.** Plastic	b. insulator
_____ **9.** Rubber	
_____ **10.** Silver	
_____ **11.** Wood	

Resistance (page 605)

12. Explain why the current is reduced as electrons move through a conductor. _____

_____

_____

13. Circle the letter of each factor that affects a material's resistance.

a. its length   b. its temperature

c. its velocity   d. its thickness

14. What is a superconductor? _____

_____

Voltage (page 606)

Match each term to its definition.

Definition	Term
_____ **15.** A device that converts chemical energy to electrical energy	a. flow of charge
_____ **16.** Requires a complete loop	b. voltage
_____ **17.** The difference in electrical potential energy between two places in an electric field	c. battery

18. Is the following sentence true or false? Three common voltage sources are batteries, solar cells, and generators. _____

Ohm's Law (page 607)

19. Is the following sentence true or false? According to Ohm's law, the voltage in a circuit equals the product of the energy and the resistance. _____

20. Doubling the voltage in a circuit doubles the current if _____ is held constant.

21. Is the following sentence true or false? Doubling the resistance in a circuit will halve the current if voltage is held constant.

_____

Chapter 20   Electricity

Section 20.3 Electric Circuits
(pages 609–613)

This section describes circuit diagrams and types of circuits. It also explains calculation of electric power and electric energy and discusses electrical safety.

Reading Strategy (page 609)

Relating Text and Visuals As you read about household circuits, complete the table by listing three things the diagram in Figure 13 helps you understand about circuits. For more information on this Reading Strategy, see the **Reading and Study Skills** in the **Skills and Reference Handbook** at the end of your textbook.

Understanding a Circuit Diagram
What Can Be Seen in the Circuit Diagram?
Wire bringing current from outside

Circuit Diagrams (pages 609–610)

1. Circuit diagrams use _____ to represent parts of a circuit, including a source of electrical energy and devices that are run by the electrical energy.

Match each symbol to what it indicates on a circuit diagram.

	Symbol	What Symbol Indicates
_____	2. +	a. The direction of current
_____	3. −	b. A negative terminal
_____	4. →	c. A positive terminal

Series Circuits (page 610)

5. Is the following sentence true or false? In a series circuit, if one element stops functioning, then none of the elements can operate.

_____

6. Explain why the bulbs shine less brightly when more bulbs are added to a series circuit. _____

_____

Parallel Circuits (page 610)

7. Is the following sentence true or false? Circuits in a home are rarely wired in parallel. _____

8. If one element stops functioning in a parallel circuit, the rest of the elements _____.

Chapter 20   Electricity

Power and Energy Calculations (pages 611–612)

9. The rate at which electrical energy is converted to another form of energy is called _____.

10. The SI unit of electric power is the joule per second, or _____, which is abbreviated _____.

11. Is the following sentence true or false? Electric power is calculated by multiplying current times voltage. _____

12. Write the formula for calculating electrical energy.

    _____

13. The unit of energy usually used by electric power companies is the

    _____.

Electrical Safety (pages 612–613)

14. Circle the letters of what could happen if the current in a wire exceeds the circuit's safety limit.

    a. The wire could overheat.   b. The wire could get cooler.

    c. A fire could start.   d. A fuse could blow.

15. Explain how a fuse prevents current overload in a circuit. _____

    _____

16. A switch that opens to prevent overloads when current in a circuit is too high is called a(n) _____.

17. Explain why touching an electrical device with wet hands is dangerous. _____

    _____

18. Is the following sentence true or false? A ground-fault circuit interrupter shuts down the circuit if the current flowing through the circuit and current returning to ground are equal.

    _____

19. The transfer of excess charge through a conductor to Earth is called

    _____.

20. Complete the following table about equipment used to prevent electrical accidents.

Equipment to Prevent Current Overload	Equipment to Protect People from Shock	Equipment to Prevent Short Circuits
a. Circuit breaker	b. c. Grounding wire d.	e.

Chapter 20   Electricity

Section 20.4 Electronic Devices
(pages 618–622)

This section discusses how various electronic devices operate and what they are used for.

Reading Strategy (page 618)

Summarizing Copy the table on a separate sheet of paper. As you read, complete the table to summarize what you learned about solid-state components. For more information on this Reading Strategy, see the **Reading and Study Skills** in the **Skills and Reference Handbook** at the end of your textbook.

Solid–State Components		
Solid-State Component	**Description**	**Uses**
Diode		
Transistor		
Integrated Circuit		

Electronic Signals (pages 618–619)

Match each term to its definition.

Definition

_____ **1.** Information sent as patterns in the controlled flow of electrons through a circuit

_____ **2.** The science of using electric current to process or transmit information

_____ **3.** A smoothly varying signal produced by continuously changing the voltage or current in a circuit

_____ **4.** A signal that encodes information as a string of 1's and 0's

Term

a. electronics

b. analog signal

c. electronic signal

d. digital signal

5. Which type of signal is usually used by an AM radio station?

_____

6. Is the following sentence true or false? Analog signals are more reliable than digital signals. _____

Chapter 20   Electricity

Vacuum Tubes (page 619)

7. Circle the letter of each item that is a true about vacuum tubes.

   a. can change alternating current to direct current

   b. never burn out

   c. can increase the strength of a signal

   d. can turn a current on or off

8. Is the following sentence true or false? An image is produced in a CRT when phosphors glow red, green, and blue in response to electron beams. _____

Semiconductors (page 621)

9. What is a semiconductor? _____

   _____

10. Name the two types of semiconductors.

    a. _____   b. _____

11. Circle the letter of each sentence that is true about a p-type semiconductor.

    a. It can be made by adding a trace amount of boron to a silicon.

    b. Electrons are attracted to positively charged holes at each boron atom.

    c. As the electrons jump from hole to hole, it looks like a flow of positive charge.

    d. Boron atoms provide weakly bound electrons that can flow.

12. Is the following sentence true or false? In an n-type semiconductor, weakly bound electrons can conduct a current. _____

Solid-State Components (pages 621–622)

Match each term to its definition.

Term	Definition
_____ 13. diode	a. A solid-state component with three layers of semiconductors
_____ 14. transistor	b. A thin slice of silicon that contains many solid-state components
_____ 15. integrated circuit	c. A solid-state component that combines an n-type and p-type semiconductor

16. A chip or microchip is another name for a(n) _____.

Communications Technology (page 622)

17. Why is it useful for communication devices to use microchips? _____

    _____

18. A mobile phone can store data such as phone numbers because

    _____

Chapter 20   Electricity

WordWise

*Match each definition with the correct term in the grid and then write its
number under the appropriate term. When you have filled in all the boxes,
add up the numbers in each column, row, and the two diagonals.
What is surprising about the sums?* _____

Definitions

1. A property that causes subatomic particles such as protons and
   electrons to attract or repel other matter

2. The attraction or repulsion between electrically charged objects

3. Charge transfer without contact between materials

4. Law that total charge in an isolated system is constant

5. A continuous flow of electric charge

6. Material through which charge can easily flow

7. Material through which a charge cannot easily flow

8. The opposition to the flow of charges in a material

9. A circuit in which the charge has only one path through which it can flow

10. An electric circuit with two or more paths through which charge can flow

11. A switch that opens when current in a circuit is too high

12. Information sent as patterns in the controlled flow of electrons through a circuit

13. A smoothly varying signal produced by continuously changing the
    voltage or current in a circuit

14. A complete path through which a charge can flow

15. A solid-state component with three layers of semiconductors

16. A thin slice of silicon that contains many solid-state components

				Diagonal = _____
integrated circuit ____	induction ____	electric force ____	analog signal ____	= _____
electric current ____	parallel circuit ____	circuit breaker ____	resistance ____	= _____
series circuit ____	electrical conductor ____	electrical insulator ____	electronic signal ____	= _____
law of conservation of charge ____	transistor ____	electric circuit ____	electric charge ____	= _____
= _____	= _____	= _____	= _____	Diagonal = _____

Chapter 20   Electricity

Power, Voltage, and Current

The power rating on an electric soldering iron is 40.0 watts. If the soldering iron is connected to a 120-volt line, how much current does it use?

1. Read and Understand

What information are you given in the problem?
   Power = P = 40.0 watts

   Voltage = V = 120 volts

2. Plan and Solve

What unknown are you trying to calculate?
   Current = I =?

What formula contains the given quantities and the unknown?

$$P = I \times V; I = \frac{P}{V}$$

Replace each variable with its known value.

$$I = \frac{40.0 \text{ watts}}{120 \text{ volts}} = 0.33 \text{ amps}$$

3. Look Back and Check

Is your answer reasonable?
   The answer is reasonable because a soldering iron needs a relatively low current to generate heat.

Math Practice

On a separate sheet of paper, solve the following problems.

1. A steam cleaner has a power rating of 1100 watts. If the cleaner is connected to a 120-volt line, what current does it use?

2. A coffee maker uses 10.0 amps of current from a 120-volt line. How much power does it use?

3. A power mixer uses 3.0 amps of current and has a power rating of 360 watts. What voltage does this appliance require?

Math Skill:
Formulas and Equations

You may want to read more about this **Math Skill** in the **Skills and Reference Handbook** at the end of your textbook.

Chapter 21   Magnetism

Section 21.1 Magnets and Magnetic Fields
(pages 630–633)

This section describes magnetic forces and magnetic fields. Characteristics of magnetic materials also are discussed.

Reading Strategy (page 630)

Using Prior Knowledge Before you read, copy the diagram below and add what you already know about magnets to the diagram. After you read, revise the diagram based on what you learned. For more information on this Reading Strategy, see the **Reading and Study Skills** in the **Skills and Reference Handbook** at the end of your textbook.

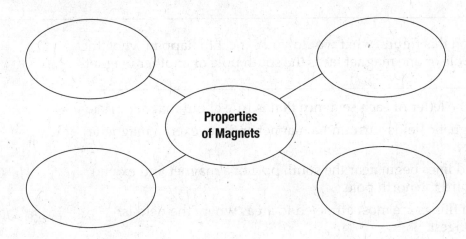

Properties of Magnets

1. In the year 1600, William Gilbert published a book explaining the properties of _____.

Magnetic Forces (page 630)

2. Is the following sentence true or false? Magnetic force can be exerted on moving charges, as well as on iron or on another magnet.

_____

3. What did William Gilbert discover when he used a compass to map forces around a magnetic sphere? _____

_____

4. Circle the letter of each sentence that is true about magnetic force.

   a. Two magnets that approach each other may attract or repel.

   b. Magnetic forces do not vary with distance.

   c. Opposite magnetic poles repel one another.

   d. Magnetic forces act over a distance.

Chapter 21   Magnetism

Magnetic Fields (pages 631–632)

For questions 5 and 6, refer to the figure below.

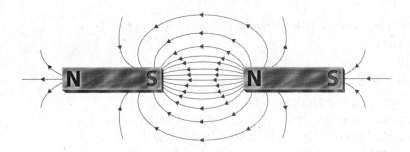

5. Where is the magnetic field the strongest? _____

_____

6. Based on this figure, what would you expect to happen when the north pole of one magnet faces the south pole of another magnet?

_____

7. Circle the letter of each sentence that is true about magnetic fields.

 a. Magnetic fields surround a magnet and can exert a magnetic force.

 b. Field lines begin near the south pole of a magnet and extend toward the north pole.

 c. Iron filings are most attracted to areas where the field is strongest.

 d. A magnetic field is strongest near the north and south poles of a magnet.

8. The area that is influenced by the magnetic field surrounding Earth is called the _____.

Magnetic Materials (pages 632–633)

Match each term with its description.

Description	Term
_____ 9. Can be magnetized because it has many domains	a. ferromagnetic material
_____ 10. Has randomly oriented domains	b. magnetic domain
_____ 11. Region that has many atoms with aligned magnetic fields	c. nonmagnetized material

12. What can cause the realignment of magnetic domains in a material?

_____

_____

Chapter 21   Magnetism

Section 21.2 Electromagnetism
(pages 635–639)

This section describes how electricity and magnetism are related. Uses of solenoids and electromagnetic devices are discussed, and a description of how these devices work is presented.

Reading Strategy (page 635)

Identifying Main Ideas Copy the table on a separate sheet of paper. As you read, write the main idea of the text that follows each topic in the table. For more information on this Reading Strategy, see the **Reading and Study Skills** in the **Skills and Reference Handbook** at the end of your textbook.

Electromagnetism	
Topic	**Main Idea**
Electricity and magnetism	
Direction of magnetic fields	
Direction of electric currents	
Solenoids and electromagnets	
Electromagnetic devices	

1. In 1820 Hans Oersted discovered a connection between electricity and _____.

Electricity and Magnetism (pages 635–636)

2. Electricity and magnetism are different aspects of a single force known as the _____ force.

3. Both aspects of the electromagnetic force are caused by

   _____.

4. Is the following sentence true or false? Moving electric charges create a magnetic field. _____

5. Is the following sentence true or false? The vibrating charges that produce an electromagnetic wave also create a magnetic field.

   _____

6. A charge moving in a magnetic field will be deflected in a direction that is _____ to both the magnetic field and to the velocity of the charge.

Chapter 21   Magnetism

Solenoids and Electromagnets (pages 637–638)

7. Is the following sentence true or false? The strength of the magnetic field through the center of a coil of current-carrying wire is calculated by adding together the fields from each turn of the coil. _____

8. A coil of current-carrying wire that produces a magnetic field is called a(n) _____.

9. What is an electromagnet? _____

_____

10. Circle the letter of each sentence that is true about electromagnets.

   a. Placing an iron rod in a solenoid reduces the strength of its magnetic field.

   b. Devices that utilize electromagnets include doorbells and telephones.

   c. A magnetic field can be turned on and off with an electromagnet.

   d. An electromagnet can control the direction of a magnetic field.

11. List three factors that determine the strength of an electromagnet.

   a. _____

   b. _____

   c. _____

12. Is the following sentence true or false? Decreasing the current in the solenoid decreases the strength of an electromagnet.

_____

13. What types of solenoid cores make stronger electromagnets? _____

_____

Electromagnetic Devices (pages 638–639)

14. Electromagnetic devices change _____ energy into _____ energy.

15. Complete the following table about electromagnetic devices.

Description	Device
Uses electromagnets to convert electrical signals into sound waves	
	Electric motor
Uses an electromagnet to measure small amounts of current	

Chapter 21   Magnetism

Section 21.3 Electrical Energy Generation and Transmission
(pages 642–647)

This section describes how electricity is generated and transmitted for human use. A description of how generators and transformers function is given.

Reading Strategy (page 642)

Sequencing As you read the section, complete the flowchart to show how a step-up transformer works. Then make a similar flowchart for a step-down transformer. For more information on this Reading Strategy, see the **Reading and Study Skills** in the **Skills and Reference Handbook** at the end of your textbook.

Step-up Transformers

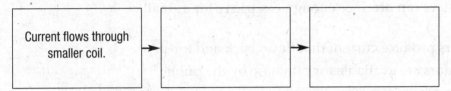

Generating Electric Current (pages 642–643)

1. Is the following sentence true or false? A magnetic field can be used to produce an electric current. _____

2. Circle the letter for the name of the process of generating a current by moving an electrical conductor relative to a magnetic field.

   a. electromagnetic force

   b. electromagnetic field

   c. electromagnetic induction

   d. electromagnetic conduction

3. Electrical charges can easily flow through materials known as _____.

4. Why is the discovery of electromagnetic induction significant? _____

   _____

5. According to Faraday's law, electric current can be induced in a conductor by _____.

6. Is the following sentence true or false? Moving a magnet relative to a coil of wire induces a current in the wire if the coil is part of a complete circuit. _____

Chapter 21   Magnetism

Generators (pages 643–644)

7. A generator converts _____ energy into _____ energy.

8. Circle the letter that best describes how most of the electrical energy used in homes and businesses is produced.

   a. with DC generators

   b. using AC generators at large power plants

   c. with small magnets moving inside coils

   d. by rotating a magnetic field around a coil of wire

9. Is the following sentence true or false? In an alternating current produced by an AC generator, the flow direction of charges switches back and forth. _____

10. Circle the letter of each sentence that is true about generators.

    a. Small generators can produce enough electricity for a small business.

    b. DC generators produce current that flows back and forth.

    c. Small generators are available for purchase by the public.

    d. Most modern power plants use DC generators.

Transformers (pages 644–645)

11. A device that increases or decreases voltage and current of two linked AC circuits is called a(n) _____.

12. How does a transformer change voltage and current? _____
_____

13. Why are transformers necessary for home electrical service? _____
_____

14. Is the following sentence true or false? To prevent overheating wires, voltage is decreased for long-distance transmission.
_____

15. How is voltage calculated in a transformer? _____
_____

16. Is the following sentence true or false? A step-down transformer decreases voltage and increases current. _____

Electrical Energy for Your Home (pages 646–647)

17. Name at least three sources used to produce electrical energy in the United States. _____
_____

18. A device with fanlike blades that can convert energy from various sources into electrical energy is called a(n) _____.

Chapter 21 Magnetism

WordWise

*Solve the clues to determine which vocabulary words from Chapter 21
are hidden in the puzzle. Then find and circle the terms in the puzzle.
The terms may occur vertically, horizontally, or diagonally. Some terms
may be spelled backwards.*

```
f  g  d  e  l  o  p  c  i  t  e  n  g  a  m
e  a  a  t  s  o  r  m  e  v  r  p  e  a  b
r  r  q  l  z  f  f  r  e  r  e  v  g  c  t
r  c  i  u  v  t  t  c  h  n  g  n  r  r  r
o  s  d  o  m  a  i  n  i  u  e  t  a  o  a
m  o  u  b  p  l  n  b  k  t  n  u  u  f  n
a  l  t  y  o  i  r  o  o  n  e  r  m  t  s
g  e  k  p  o  u  d  s  m  a  r  b  i  n  f
n  n  k  a  t  p  p  o  i  e  a  i  c  a  o
e  o  g  o  y  h  z  a  v  b  t  n  s  y  r
t  i  e  e  e  h  n  j  n  m  o  e  m  o  m
i  d  i  r  j  u  e  r  t  c  r  f  r  u  e
c  t  e  z  z  w  y  n  r  p  e  r  j  b  r
```

Clues	Hidden Words
Region where a magnetic field is strongest	_____
Nickel is a(n) _____ material.	_____
Current-carrying wire with a loop in it	_____
Uses an electromagnet to measure small amounts of current	_____
Device with fanlike blades that converts energy from various sources to electrical energy	_____
Area influenced by Earth's magnetic field	_____
Converts mechanical energy into electrical energy	_____
Aligned magnetic fields	_____
Step-down or step-up	_____

Chapter 21 Magnetism

Calculating Voltage

A step-down transformer has a primary coil with 500 turns of wire, and a secondary coil with 50 turns. If the input voltage is 120 V, what is the output voltage?

**Math Skill:
Ratios and
Proportions**

You may want to read more about this **Math Skill** in the **Skills and Reference Handbook** at the end of your textbook.

1. Read and Understand

What information are you given?

Input Voltage = 120 V

Primary Coil: 500 turns

Secondary Coil: 50 turns

2. Plan and Solve

What unknown are you trying to calculate?

Output Voltage = ?

What formula contains the given quantities and the unknown?

$$\frac{\text{Secondary Coil turns}}{\text{Primary Coil turns}} = \frac{\text{Output Voltage}}{\text{Input Voltage}}$$

Replace each variable with its known value.

$$\frac{50 \text{ turns}}{500 \text{ turns}} = \frac{\text{Output Voltage}}{120 \text{ V}}$$

$$\text{Output Voltage} = \frac{50 \text{ turns}}{500 \text{ turns}} \times 120 \text{ V} = 12 \text{ V}$$

3. Look Back and Check

Is your answer reasonable?

The ratio of secondary to primary turns is 1 : 10. 12 V is one tenth of 120 V, so the answer is reasonable.

Math Practice

On a separate sheet of paper, solve the following problems.

1. What is the ratio of turns for the secondary to primary coils in a step-down transformer, if the input voltage from a substation is 7200 V, and the output voltage to a home is 240 V?

2. The input voltage from a generating plant to a transformer is 11,000 V. If the output voltage from the transformer to high-voltage transmission lines is 240,000 V, what is the ratio of secondary to primary turns in this step-up transformer?

3. A step-down transformer has 200 turns of wire in its primary coil. How many turns are in the secondary coil if the input voltage = 120 V, and the output voltage = 6 V?

Chapter 22   Earth's Interior

Section 22.1 Earth's Structure
(pages 660–663)

This section explains what geologists study. It describes the main layers of Earth.

Reading Strategy (page 660)

Building Vocabulary Copy the table on a separate sheet of paper and add more rows as needed. As you read the section, define each vocabulary term in your own words. For more information on this Reading Strategy, see the **Reading and Study Skills** in the **Skills and Reference Handbook** at the end of your textbook.

Earth's Structure	
Vocabulary Term	**Definition**
Geologist	
Uniformitarianism	
Crust	

The Science of Geology (pages 660–661)

1. The study of planet Earth, including its composition and structure is called _____.

2. Is the following sentence true or false? People who study Earth and the processes that have shaped Earth over time are called geologists.

_____

3. What is uniformitarianism? _____

_____

_____

A Cross Section of Earth (pages 661–663)

4. Circle the letters of the major layers of Earth's interior.

   a. crust

   b. atmosphere

   c. mantle

   d. core

5. Scientists divide Earth's interior into the crust, mantle, and core based on the _____.

6. Much of the Earth's crust is made up of _____.

Chapter 22   Earth's Interior

Match each type of crust to its characteristics. Each type of crust will have more than one characteristic.

Crust	**Characteristic**
_____ **7.** oceanic crust	a. Averages about 7 kilometers thick
_____ **8.** continental crust	b. Consists mainly of less-dense rocks
	c. Averages 40 kilometers in thickness
	d. Composed mostly of dense rocks
	e. Makes up the ocean floor
	f. Makes up the continents

9. The layer of Earth called the _____ is found directly below the crust.

10. Circle the letters of each sentence that is true about Earth's mantle.

    a. It is the thickest layer of Earth.

    b. It is divided into layers based on the physical properties of rock.

    c. It is less dense than the crust.

    d. It is made mainly of silicates.

11. The lithosphere includes the uppermost part of Earth's mantle and Earth's _____.

12. Is the following sentence true or false? Rock flows slowly in the asthenosphere. _____

13. The stronger, lower part of the mantle is called the _____.

14. The sphere of metal inside Earth is called the _____.

15. Is the following sentence true or false? The outer core of Earth is liquid. _____

16. Label the main layers of Earth's interior in the diagram below.

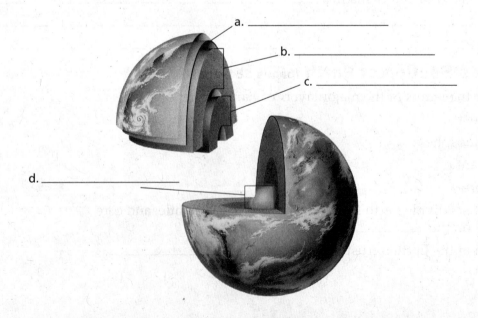

a. _____

b. _____

c. _____

d. _____

Chapter 22   Earth's Interior

Section 22.2 Minerals
(pages 664–669)

This section describes minerals and rocks found on Earth and their different properties.

Reading Strategy (page 664)

Outlining Copy the outline on a separate sheet of paper and add more lines as needed. Before you read, make an outline of this section. Use the green headings as main topics and the blue headings as subtopics. As you read, add supporting details. For more information on this Reading Strategy, see the **Reading and Study Skills** in the **Skills and Reference Handbook** at the end of your textbook.

Minerals

I. Minerals and Rocks

II. The Properties of Minerals

  A. Crystal Structure

  B. _____

  C. _____

  D. _____

Minerals and Rocks (page 665)

1. A solid combination of minerals or mineral materials is a(n) _____ .

2. Is the following sentence true or false? A mineral is a naturally occurring, inorganic solid with a crystal structure and a characteristic chemical composition. _____

3. A material is called _____ if it is not produced from a living thing.

4. Circle the letters of sentences that are true about minerals.

  a. Within each mineral, chemical composition is nearly constant.

  b. Minerals are organic.

  c. There are about 4000 known minerals.

  d. Minerals are the building blocks of rocks.

The Properties of Minerals (pages 666–669)

5. Is the following sentence true or false? Minerals such as sulfur can sometimes be identified by color. _____

6. What could cause two samples of the same mineral to have different colors?

_____

_____

7. Is the following sentence true or false? The color of a mineral's streak is not always the same color as the mineral. _____

8. How is a mineral's streak found? _____

_____

9. The density of a mineral depends on its _____

10. Is the following sentence true or false? The hardness of a mineral is the way in which its surface reflects light. _____

11. To determine the hardness of a mineral, geologists use _____ tests.

12. Is the following sentence true or false? The fracture of a mineral is how it breaks. _____

13. A type of fracture in which a mineral splits evenly is called _____.

14. Complete the table about the properties by which minerals can be identified.

Minerals and Properties	
Property	**Description**
Crystal Structure	
	The color of a mineral's powder
Luster	
	A mineral's mass divided by its volume
Hardness	
	How a mineral breaks
Cleavage	

Match each mineral to its property.

Mineral	Property
_____ **15.** calcite	a. Gives off visible light under an ultraviolet light
_____ **16.** Iceland spar	b. Becomes electrically charged when heated
_____ **17.** magnetite	c. Refracts light into two separate rays
_____ **18.** tourmaline	d. Is attracted by a magnet
_____ **19.** fluorite	e. Easily dissolved by acids

Section 22.3 Rocks and the Rock Cycle
(pages 670–675)

This section describes how rocks are classified. It also explains how rocks change form in the rock cycle.

Reading Strategy (page 670)

Comparing and Contrasting After you read, compare groups of rocks by completing the table. For more information on this Reading Strategy, see the **Reading and Study Skills** in the **Skills and Reference Handbook** at the end of your textbook.

Groups of Rocks		
Rock Group	**Formed by**	**Example**
Igneous		
		Sandstone
	Heat and pressure	

Classifying Rocks (page 670)

1. Circle the letters of the major groups into which rocks are classified.

    a. sedimentary   b. igneous

    c. calcite   d. metamorphic

2. Scientists divide rocks into groups based on _____.

Igneous Rock (page 671)

3. A rock that forms from magma is called a(n) _____.

4. A mixture of molten rock and gases that forms underground is called _____.

5. What is lava? _____

6. Is the following sentence true or false? Igneous rock is formed when molten material cools and solidifies either inside Earth or at the surface. _____

Match each type of igneous rock to its characteristics. Each type of rock will have more than one characteristic.

Igneous Rock	**Characteristic**
_____ 7. intrusive rock	a. Forms underground
_____ 8. extrusive rock	b. Forms at Earth's surface
	c. Has a fine-grained texture
	d. Has a coarse-grained texture
	e. Cools quickly
	f. Cools slowly

Chapter 22   Earth's Interior

Sedimentary Rock (pages 672–673)

9. The process of _____ breaks down rock at Earth's surface.

10. When sediment is squeezed and cemented together, _____ rocks are formed.

11. Circle the groups into which geologists classify sedimentary rocks.

    a. clastic rocks

    b. foliated rocks

    c. organic rocks

    d. chemical rocks

12. Sedimentary rocks formed from broken fragments of other rocks are called _____ rocks.

13. Is the following sentence true or false? Clastic rocks are classified mainly based on the number of fragments they have. _____

14. Minerals that precipitate out of solution form _____.

Metamorphic Rock (page 674)

15. Circle the ways a rock can be transformed into a metamorphic rock.

    a. by heat

    b. by precipitation

    c. by pressure

    d. by chemical reaction

16. Where do most metamorphic rocks form? _____

17. Is the following sentence true or false? Metamorphism can change the mineral content and texture of a rock. _____

18. Metamorphic rocks with crystals arranged in parallel bands or layers are called _____ rocks.

The Rock Cycle (pages 674-675)

19. Circle the letters of the sentences that are true about the rock cycle.

    a. A metamorphic rock that melts and cools to form a new rock becomes an igneous rock.

    b. Forces within Earth and at the surface cause rocks to change form in the rock cycle.

    c. In the rock cycle, rocks may wear away, undergo metamorphism, or melt and form new igneous rock.

    d. The rock cycle is a series of processes in which rocks change from one type to another continuously.

Chapter 22   Earth's Interior

Section 22.4 Plate Tectonics
(pages 676–683)

This section describes the theory of plate tectonics. It also examines sea-floor spreading, plate boundaries, and mountain building.

Reading Strategy (page 676)

Previewing Before you read this section, rewrite the headings as how, why, and what questions about plate tectonics. As you read, write answers to the questions. For more information on this Reading Strategy, see the **Reading and Study Skills** in the **Skills and Reference Handbook** at the end of your textbook.

Plate Tectonics
Questions on Plate Tectonics
What is the hypothesis of continental drift?

1. Is the following sentence true or false? According to the theory of plate tectonics, Earth's plates move about quickly on top of the crust. _____

2. What does the theory of plate tectonics explain about Earth's plates? _____

Continental Drift (page 677)

3. Explain Alfred Wegener's hypothesis about the continents. _____
_____

4. The process by which the continents move slowly across Earth's surface is called _____.

Sea-floor Spreading (pages 678–679)

5. The world's longest mountain chain is the underwater chain called the _____.

6. Is the following sentence true or false? The theory of sea-floor spreading explains why rocks of the ocean floor are youngest near the mid-ocean ridge. _____

7. Is the following sentence true or false? Old oceanic plates sink into the mantle at mid-ocean ridges in a process called subduction.
_____

8. A depression in the ocean floor where subduction takes place is called a(n) _____.

Chapter 22   Earth's Interior

9. Circle the letter that completes the sentence. Sea-floor spreading
   _____ new oceanic crust at mid-ocean ridges.

   a. creates   b. destroys

10. The process called _____ destroys old oceanic crust
    at subduction zones.

The Theory of Plate Tectonics (pages 679–680)

11. Is the following sentence true or false? The concept of sea-floor
    spreading supports the theory of plate tectonics by providing a
    way for the pieces of Earth's crust to move. _____

12. Heat from Earth's interior causes convection currents in Earth's

    _____.

13. Circle the sentences that are true about the theory of
    plate tectonics.

    a. The ocean floor sinks back into the mantle at subduction zones.

    b. The heat that drives convection currents comes from solar energy.

    c. Hot rock rises at mid-ocean ridges, cools and spreads out as
       ocean sea floor.

    d. Plate motions are the surface portion of mantle convection.

14. Describe the two sources of the heat in Earth's mantle.

    a. _____

    b. _____

Plate Boundaries (pages 681–682)

15. Identify each type of plate boundary.

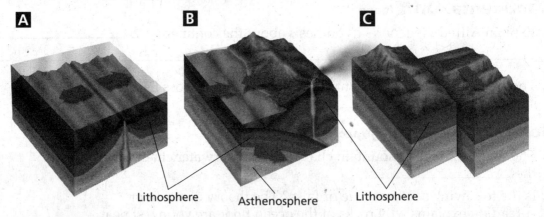

A   B   C

Lithosphere   Asthenosphere   Lithosphere

a. _____   b. _____   c. _____

Mountain Building (page 683)

16. Is the following sentence true or false? Most mountains form along
    plate boundaries. _____

17. Describe how the Himalayan Mountains were formed. _____
    _____

Chapter 22   Earth's Interior

Section 22.5 Earthquakes
(pages 684–689)

This section explains what earthquakes are, what causes them, and their effects.

Reading Strategy (page 684)

Building Vocabulary Copy the table on a separate sheet of paper and add more rows as needed. As you read, define each term for this section in your own words. For more information on this Reading Strategy, see the **Reading and Study Skills** in the **Skills and Reference Handbook** at the end of your textbook.

Earthquake Terms	
Vocabulary Terms	**Definitions**
Earthquake	
Seismic waves	
Stress	

1. An earthquake releases _____ energy that is carried by vibrations called _____.

Stress in Earth's Crust (page 685)

2. Name three ways that stress can affect rocks.

    a. _____

    b. _____

    c. _____

3. Is the following sentence true or false? Stress from moving tectonic plates produces faults and folds in Earth's crust. _____

Match each result of stress to its characteristics. Each result will have more than one characteristic.

Result of Stress	**Characteristic**
_____ 4. fault	a. A bend in layers of rock
_____ 5. fold	b. Many occur along plate boundaries
	c. A break in a mass of rock where movement happens
	d. Forms where rocks are squeezed but do not break

6. Is the following sentence true or false? Rocks tend to fold instead of break under low temperature or pressure. _____

Chapter 22   Earth's Interior

Earthquakes and Seismic Waves (pages 686–687)

7. Why do earthquakes occur? _____

_____

8. Is the following sentence true or false? The location underground where an earthquake begins is called the focus.

_____

9. The location on Earth's surface directly above the focus of an earthquake is called the _____.

10. Circle the sentences that are true about the physics of earthquakes.

   a. Stress builds in areas where rocks along fault lines snag and remain locked.

   b. In an earthquake, rocks break and grind past each other, releasing energy.

   c. Potential energy is transformed into kinetic energy in the form of seismic waves.

   d. Potential energy increases as rocks break and move.

Match each type of seismic wave to its characteristic.

Seismic Waves	Characteristic
_____ 11. P waves	a. Transverse waves that cannot travel through liquids
_____ 12. S waves	b. Slowest moving type of wave that develops when seismic waves reach Earth's surface
_____ 13. surface waves	c. Longitudinal waves similar to sound waves that cause particles in the material to vibrate in the direction of the waves' motion

14. Typically, the first seismic waves to be detected at a distance are _____ waves.

Measuring Earthquakes (page 687)

15. What devices do geologists use to record seismic waves? _____

_____

Seismographic Data (page 689)

16. Most earthquakes are concentrated along _____.

17. Is the following sentence true or false? Some earthquakes will occur in the interior of plates. _____

18. Is the following statement true or false? When seismic waves interact with boundaries between different kinds of rock within Earth, they can be reflected, refracted, or diffracted.

_____

Chapter 22   Earth's Interior

Section 22.6 Volcanoes
(pages 690–696)

This section describes volcanoes, how they form, and the different ways they erupt. It also describes the different types of volcanoes and other features created by magma.

Reading Strategy (page 690)

Sequencing As you read, complete the flowchart to show how a volcano forms. For more information on this Reading Strategy, see the **Reading and Study Skills** in the **Skills and Reference Handbook** at the end of your textbook.

Formation of a Volcano

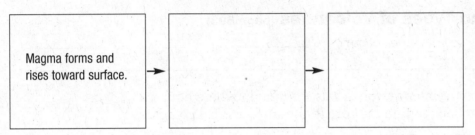

Magma forms and rises toward surface. →   →

1. A mountain that forms when magma reaches the surface is called a(n) _____.

Formation of a Volcano (page 691)

2. Is the following sentence true or false? Liquid magma is formed when small amounts of mantle rock melt. _____

3. Describe how a volcano forms. _____

_____

4. Describe how a volcano erupts. _____

_____

5. Magma collects in a pocket called the _____ before a volcanic eruption.

Match each feature of a volcano to its correct description.

Feature	Description
_____ **6.** pipe	a. A narrow, vertical channel where magma rises to the surface
_____ **7.** vent	b. An opening in the ground where magma escapes to the surface
_____ **8.** crater	
_____ **9.** magma chamber	c. A huge depression created if the shell of the magma chamber collapses
_____ **10.** caldera	d. A bowl-shaped pit at the top of a volcano
	e. A pocket where the magma collects

Chapter 22   Earth's Interior

Quiet and Explosive Eruptions (page 692)

11. Is the following sentence true or false? How easily magma flows depends on its viscosity. _____

12. List three factors that determine the viscosity of magma.

    a. _____

    b. _____

    c. _____

13. Is the following sentence true or false? Magma with higher temperatures has higher viscosity. _____

14. Hot, fast-moving lava is called _____ and cooler, slow-moving lava is called _____.

Location and Types of Volcanoes (page 693)

15. Where do most volcanoes occur? _____
    _____

16. Is the following sentence true or false? A region where hot rock extends from deep within the core to the surface is called a hot spot. _____

17. Is the following sentence true or false? A composite volcano is produced by a quiet eruption of low-viscosity lava. _____

18. An eruption of ash and cinders will produce a volcano called a(n) _____.

19. Is the following sentence true or false? A composite volcano is formed from an explosive eruption of lava and ash.
    _____

Other Igneous Features (page 696)

20. Circle the letters of the igneous features that are formed by magma.

    a. dikes

    b. sills

    c. volcanic necks

    d. batholiths

21. The largest type of intrusive igneous rock mass is called a(n) _____.

22. Is the following sentence true or false? A crack that has been filled in by magma and hardens parallel to existing rock layers is called a dike. _____

Chapter 22   Earth's Interior

WordWise

Use the clues below to identify vocabulary terms from Chapter 22. Write the terms below, putting one letter in each blank. When you finish, the term enclosed in the diagonal will reveal an important process on Earth.

Clues

1. A solid combination of minerals or mineral materials

2. The central layer of Earth

3. A type of fracture in which a mineral tends to split along regular, well-defined planes

4. A movement of Earth's lithosphere that occurs when rocks shift suddenly, releasing stored energy

5. A region where plates collide

6. The type of rock that forms when small pieces of sediment are squeezed together

7. A mountain that forms when magma reaches the surface

8. A bend in layers of rock

9. Wegener's hypothesis in which continents move slowly across Earth's surface

Vocabulary Terms

1. ◯ __ __ __

2. __ ◯ __ __

3. ◯ __ __ __ __ __ __ __

4. __ __ __ __ __ __ __ __ ◯ __ __

5. ◯ __ __ __ __ __ __ __ __ __   __ __ __ __ __ __ __ __ __

6. __ __ __ __ __ __ __ __ __ ◯ __   __ __ __ __

7. __ __ __ ◯ __ __ __

8. __ __ ◯ __

9. __ __ __ __ __ __ ◯ __ __ __ __   __ __ __ __ __ __

Hidden Word: __ __ __ __   __ __ __ __ __

Definition: _____

_____

Chapter 22   Earth's Interior

Calculating Wavelength and Frequency

An earthquake occurs 1000 km from seismograph station B. What is the difference in time between the arrivals of the first P wave and the first S wave at station B?

Math Skill:
Line Graphs

You may want to read more about this **Math Skill** in the **Skills and Reference Handbook** at the end of your textbook.

1. Read and Understand

What information are you given in the problem?
   Station B is 1000 km from where an earthquake occurred.

2. Plan and Solve

What does the question ask you to find?
   The difference in time between the arrivals of the first P wave and the first S wave at station B

Find the amount of time it took the first P wave to reach station B by following the 1000-km line up to where it meets the P wave curve.
   2 minutes

Find the amount of time it took the first S wave to reach station B by following the 1000-km line up to where it meets the S wave curve.
   4 minutes

Subtract the amount of time it took the P wave to travel to station B from the amount of time it took the S wave to travel to station B.
   4 minutes − 2 minutes = 2 minutes

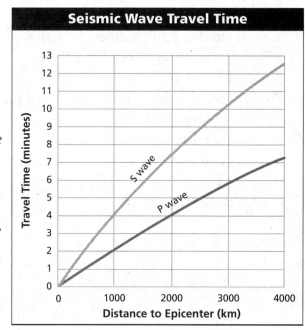

Seismic Wave Travel Time

3. Look Back and Check

Is your answer reasonable? Yes, because S waves move slower than P waves.

Math Practice

On a separate sheet of paper, solve the following problems. Use the graph.

1. An earthquake occurs 500 km from seismograph station B. What is the difference in time between the arrivals of the first P waves and the first S waves?

2. Station C is 2000 km from the epicenter of the earthquake. If P waves arrived there at 4:37 a.m., at approximately what time did the earthquake occur?

Chapter 23   Earth's Surface

Section 23.1 Fresh Water
(pages 704–708)

This section describes where water is found on Earth. It also explains the water cycle.

Reading Strategy (page 704)

Build Vocabulary Copy the table on a separate sheet of paper. As you read, add terms and definitions from this section to the table. For more information on this Reading Strategy, see the **Reading and Study Skills** in the **Skills and Reference Handbook** at the end of your textbook.

Earth's Fresh Water	
Vocabulary Term	**Definition**
Groundwater	
Water cycle	
Transpiration	

1. Water found underground in soil and within cracks in rocks is called _____.

The Water Cycle (pages 705–706)

2. Name five major processes of the water cycle.

    a. _____
    b. _____
    c. _____
    d. _____
    e. _____

Match each process with its correct description.

Description	Process
_____ **3.** When water droplets or ice crystals fall to the ground	a. evaporation
_____ **4.** The process through which a liquid changes into a gas	b. transpiration
_____ **5.** The process that forms clouds	c. condensation
_____ **6.** When water is released from a plant's leaves	d. precipitation

7. What is a glacier? _____
_____

Chapter 23   Earth's Surface

Fresh Water (pages 706–708)

8. Circle the letters of the places where portions of Earth's fresh water are located.

   a. in streams

   b. in the atmosphere

   c. in the oceans

   d. in lakes

9. Most of Earth's fresh water is located in _____ and

   _____.

10. What is runoff? _____

11. A smaller stream that flows into a river is called a(n)

    _____.

12. Circle the letters of the sentences that are true about watersheds.

    a. Watersheds are areas of land that contribute water to a river system.

    b. Watersheds can be large or small.

    c. The Mississippi River watershed drains most of the central United States.

    d. Watersheds are also called drainage basins.

13. Where do lakes and ponds form? _____

    _____

14. Is the following sentence true or false? Ponds usually form in large, deep depressions, but lakes form in smaller depressions.

    _____

15. An area underground where the pore spaces are entirely filled with water is called the _____.

16. Is the following sentence true or false? The water table is found at the bottom of the saturated zone. _____

17. Water cannot pass through _____ rocks.

18. Circle the letters of the sentences that are true about aquifers.

    a. They are permeable rock layers that are saturated with water.

    b. They are recharged or refilled as rainwater seeps into them.

    c. They are often made of shale and unbroken granite.

    d. Many people rely on aquifers for drinking water.

19. Where do glaciers form? _____

    _____

20. Circle the letter of each word that describes how ice is removed from a glacier.

    a. melting

    b. sublimation

    c. precipitation

    d. formation of icebergs

21. A large piece of ice that breaks off when a glacier reaches the ocean is called a(n) _____.

Chapter 23   Earth's Surface

Section 23.2 Weathering and Mass Movement
(pages 709–712)

This section describes how land is changed by weathering and erosion. It also discusses mass movement.

Reading Strategy (page 709)

Concept Map As you read, complete the concept map showing the key factors which affect the rate of weathering. For more information on this Reading Strategy, see the **Reading and Study Skills** in the **Skills and Reference Handbook** at the end of your textbook.

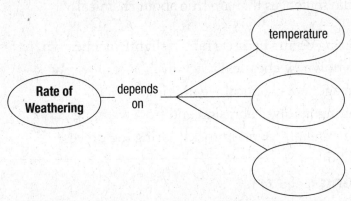

Erosion (page 709)

1. The process that wears down and carries away rock and soil is called _____.

2. Circle the letters of the sentences that are true about erosion.

   a. It acts through hoodoos.

   b. It acts through weathering.

   c. It acts through the force of gravity.

   d. It acts through the movement of glaciers, wind, or waves.

3. Is the following sentence true or false? The end product of erosion is sediment. _____

Weathering (pages 710–711)

4. The process by which rocks are chemically changed or physically broken into fragments is called _____.

5. Circle the letters of the sentences that are true about weathering.

   a. It can be mechanical.

   b. It can be chemical.

   c. It only breaks down soft rocks.

   d. It can break down rocks into fragments.

Chapter 23 Earth's Surface

6. Circle the letters of the sentences that are true about mechanical weathering.

   a. It occurs through frost wedging.

   b. It occurs from acidic rain.

   c. It occurs through rusting.

   d. It occurs through abrasion.

7. Is the following sentence true or false? Abrasion happens when rocks scrape against each other. _____

8. In the process of chemical weathering, rock is broken down by _____.

9. Circle the letters of the sentences that are true about chemical weathering.

   a. Chemical weathering occurs because rain is slightly acidic.

   b. Rocks are broken down by chemical reactions.

   c. Water is the main agent of chemical weathering.

   d. Chemical weathering involves abrasion and frost wedging.

10. What happens to the minerals found in rocks during the process of chemical weathering? _____

Rates of Weathering (page 711)

11. What factors determine the rate at which mechanical and chemical weathering take place?

   a. _____   b. _____

   c. _____

12. The kind of weathering that most likely occurs in places where temperature conditions alternate between freezing and thawing is _____ weathering.

Mass Movement (page 712)

13. In mass movement, rocks and soil move downhill because of _____.

Match each type of mass movement with its correct description.

Description	Mass Movement
_____ 14. Rapid mass movement of soil and other sediment mixed with water	a. creep
_____ 15. The rapid movement of large amounts of rock and soil	b. slumping
	c. mudflow
_____ 16. Weak layers of soil or rock suddenly moving down a slope as a single unit	d. landslide
_____ 17. Soil gradually moving down a slope	

Chapter 23   Earth's Surface

Section 23.3 Water Shapes the Land
(pages 713–717)

This section describes how water erodes the land. It also describes features created by water erosion and water deposition.

Reading Strategy (page 713)

Concept Map As you read, complete the concept map showing how moving water shapes the land. For more information on this Reading Strategy, see the **Reading and Study Skills** in the **Skills and Reference Handbook** at the end of your textbook.

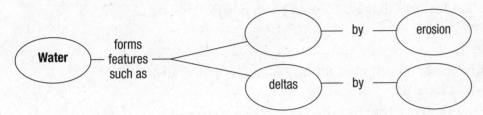

1. The process through which sediment is laid down in new locations is called _____.

Running Water Erodes the Land (pages 714–715)

Match each method that sediment is transported in streams with its correct description.

Description	Method of Transportation
_____ **2.** Dissolved sediment is carried this way	a. in suspension
_____ **3.** Large boulders can be moved this way during floods	b. in solution
_____ **4.** Tiny sediment grains move along with the water in a stream	c. by saltation
_____ **5.** Large particles bounce along the bottom of a stream	d. pushed or rolled

6. What does a stream's ability to erode mainly depend on? _____

_____

Features Formed by Water Erosion (pages 715–716)

7. A(n) _____ valley is formed by a fast-moving stream.

8. Is the following sentence true or false? A waterfall may develop where a stream crosses layers of rock that differ in hardness.

_____

Chapter 23   Earth's Surface

9. A flat area alongside a stream or river that is covered by water only during times of flood is called a(n) _____.

10. A loop-like bend in a river is called a(n) _____.

11. Is the following sentence true or false? Oxbow lakes form when an old meander is cut off from the rest of a river. _____

12. Circle the letters of features that are formed by water erosion.

   a. oxbow lakes   b. V-shaped valleys

   c. meanders   d. waterfalls

Features Formed by Water Deposition (page 716)

13. Name two main features that are formed by deposits made by flowing water.

   a. _____   b. _____

14. A fan-shaped deposit of sediment found on land is called a(n)

   _____.

15. Is the following sentence true or false? Deltas are masses of sediment that form where rivers enter large bodies of water.

   _____

Groundwater Erosion (page 717)

16. What type of weathering causes groundwater erosion?

   _____

17. Name two features that are formed by groundwater erosion.

   a. _____   b. _____

18. Identify the two types of cavern formations shown in the figure above.

   a. _____   b. _____

Chapter 23   Earth's Surface

Section 23.4 Glaciers and Wind
(pages 719–724)

This section describes how glaciers form and how landscape features are created. It also describes wind erosion and deposition.

Reading Strategy (page 719)

Sequencing As you read, complete the flowchart to show how a glacier forms and moves, and how it erodes and deposits sediment. For more information on this Reading Strategy, see the **Reading and Study Skills** in the **Skills and Reference Handbook** at the end of your textbook.

Snow is compacted to form glacial ice.

How Glaciers Form and Move (page 719)

1. Glaciers form in places where snow melts _____ than it falls.

Match the type of glacier to its description.

	Description	Glacier Type
_____	**2.** Found in high mountain valleys	a. valley glacier
_____	**3.** Covers a continent or large island	b. continental glacier

Glacial Erosion and Deposition (pages 720–722)

4. What are the two ways through which glaciers erode rock?

a. _____   b. _____

5. Circle the letters of the sentences that are true about glacial erosion.

a. Glacial ice widens cracks in bedrock beneath a glacier.

b. Pieces of loosened rock stick to the top of a glacier.

c. Rocks stuck to the bottoms and sides of a glacier act like sandpaper, scraping rock and soil.

d. As a glacier moves, it gently brushes the rocks and soil underneath it.

6. What are four distinctive features caused by glacial erosion?

a. _____

b. _____

c. _____

d. _____

Chapter 23   Earth's Surface

7. Large bowl-shaped valleys carved high on a mountainside are called _____.

8. How does a U-shaped valley form? _____
_____

9. Is the following sentence true or false? Continental glaciers fill depressions in the surface with water, where they create cirques.
_____

10. How does a glacier create landforms? _____
_____

11. Mounds of sediment at the downhill end of a glacier are called
_____.

Match each feature formed by glacial deposition to its correct description.

Description	Feature Formed
_____ 12. Long teardrop-shaped mounds of till	a. outwash plain
	b. erratics
_____ 13. A flat plain made of particles of rock that were deposited from glacial streams	c. eskers
	d. drumlins
_____ 14. A lake formed where large blocks of glacial ice become buried and melt	e. kettle lake
_____ 15. Ridges made from sand and gravel that were deposited in the bed of a glacial stream	
_____ 16. Boulders that a glacier has carried away from their place of origin	

Wind Erosion and Deposition (pages 723–724)

17. Name two ways that wind erodes the land.

a. _____   b. _____

18. Is the following sentence true or false? Deflation happens when the wind picks up and carries away loose surface material.
_____

19. Circle the letters of the features deposited by wind.

a. cirques   b. glacial lakes

c. sand dunes   d. loess deposits

20. Is the following sentence true or false? Deposits formed from windblown dust are called loess deposits. _____

Chapter 23   Earth's Surface

Section 23.5 The Restless Oceans
(pages 725–729)

This section describes the oceans and ocean currents. It also describes water erosion and deposition in the oceans.

Reading Strategy (page 725)

Relating Cause and Effect Copy the table on a separate sheet of paper. After you read, complete the table to compare ways that ocean water can move. For more information on this Reading Strategy, see the **Reading and Study Skills** in the **Skills and Reference Handbook** at the end of your textbook.

Ways Ocean Water Moves		
Movement Type	**Causes**	**Effects**
Surface current		
Density current		
Upwelling		
Longshore drift		

Exploring the Ocean (pages 725–726)

1. The proportion of dissolved salts in water is called _____.

2. Is the following sentence true or false? Salt is removed from the ocean by animals and plants and through deposition as sediment. _____

3. Circle the letters of the conditions that decrease with the ocean's depth.
   - a. pressure
   - b. light
   - c. temperature
   - d. salinity

4. What is the continental shelf? _____
   _____
   _____

Chapter 23   Earth's Surface

Ocean Currents (pages 726–728)

Match each type of ocean current with its correct description.

Description	Ocean Current
_____ **5.** A current responsible for a slow mixing of water between the surface and deeper ocean	a. surface current
_____ **6.** Movement of water from the deep ocean to the surface	b. density current
_____ **7.** A large stream of ocean water that moves continuously in about the same path near the surface	c. upwelling

8. What causes the continuous flow of surface currents? _____

_____

9. Winds blow warm surface water aside, allowing cold water to rise, in the process of _____.

10. What does each letter in the diagram below represent?

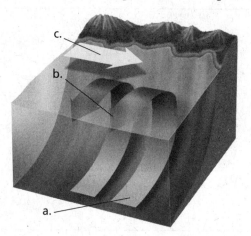

a. _____   b. _____   c. _____

Wave Erosion and Deposition (pages 728–729)

11. What are two hydraulic processes that can be responsible for wave erosion?

a. _____   b. _____

12. Circle the letters of the sentences that are true about hydraulic action.

a. A wave fills a crack with water.

b. Hydraulic action causes no changes to earth's coastlines.

c. Waves compress air as they slam into cracked rocks.

d. Pressure from waves causes cracks in rocks to get bigger.

13. Is the following sentence true or false? The process that moves sand along a shore is called hydraulic action. _____

Chapter 23   Earth's Surface

Section 23.6 Earth's History
(pages 732–738)

This section explains how scientists determine the age of rocks and how they use these methods to develop a time line for the history of Earth. It also describes the four major divisions of Earth history.

Reading Strategy (page 732)

Previewing Before you read, examine Figures 34 and 36 to help you understand geologic time. Write at least two questions about them in the table. As you read, write answers to your questions. For more information on this Reading Strategy, see the **Reading and Study Skills** in the **Skills and Reference Handbook** at the end of your textbook.

Questions on Geologic Time

1. What are fossils? _____
_____

Determining the Age of Rocks (pages 732–734)

2. Is the following sentence true or false? The relative age of a rock is its age compared to the ages of rocks above or below it. _____

3. Circle the letter that identifies the direction in which layers of sedimentary rocks form.

   a. vertically

   b. horizontally

   c. diagonally

   d. randomly

4. Circle the letter of the sentence that is true about the law of superposition.

   a. Younger rocks lie above older rocks if the layers are undisturbed.

   b. Older rocks lie above younger rocks if the layers are undisturbed.

   c. Rock layers are never disturbed.

   d. The youngest rock layers are typically at the bottom.

5. How do geologists use the law of superposition to determine the relative age of rocks?

   a. _____

   b. _____

Chapter 23 Earth's Surface

6. Organize and write the letters of the layers of rock in the diagram from oldest to youngest. If two rock layers are the same age, write them as a pair. _____

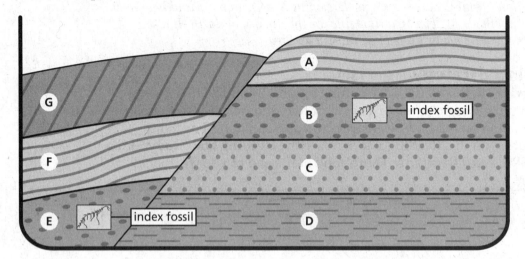

7. Circle the letters of the sentences that are true about index fossils.

a. They can be easily identified.

b. They help to determine the relative ages of rocks.

c. The organisms that formed them occurred over a large area.

d. The organisms that formed them lived during a well-defined time period.

8. Geologists use radioactive dating to determine the _____ of rocks.

A Brief History of Earth (pages 734–738)

9. What is the geologic time scale based on?

a. _____ b. _____

10. What is a mass extinction? _____
_____

Match each division of Earth's history to its correct description.

Description	Time
_____ **11.** Dinosaurs appeared.	a. Precambrian time
_____ **12.** Fishes and other animals first developed in the oceans.	b. Mesozoic Era
	c. Cenozoic Era
_____ **13.** Humans first appeared in Africa.	d. Paleozoic Era
_____ **14.** Earth was formed.	

Chapter 23   Earth's Surface

WordWise

Solve the clues to determine which vocabulary terms from Chapter 23 are hidden in the puzzle. Then find and circle the terms in the puzzle. The terms may occur vertically, horizontally, or diagonally.

```
t  a  v  f  n  o  l  k  w  e  f  r  z  h
g  b  i  m  e  t  l  o  e  s  s  k  d  r
s  i  y  b  r  r  w  f  a  d  u  o  l  u
b  a  x  a  s  a  d  q  t  w  i  d  m  j
p  r  l  l  c  n  p  t  h  r  p  e  p  d
s  j  e  i  n  s  g  i  e  a  q  p  y  e
u  a  k  p  n  p  j  p  r  u  n  o  f  f
p  x  l  v  c  i  b  x  i  a  b  s  c  l
w  g  i  t  q  r  t  c  n  s  f  i  p  a
e  z  e  f  a  a  z  y  g  q  a  t  j  t
l  n  b  o  r  t  x  f  o  s  s  i  l  i
l  f  p  j  g  i  i  o  p  d  f  o  g  o
i  d  a  n  b  o  l  o  e  m  k  n  c  n
n  z  g  d  e  n  r  q  n  i  g  f  s  d
g  l  j  q  c  i  s  o  n  a  z  l  x  j
m  a  s  s  m  o  v  e  m  e  n  t  n  a
```

Clues	Hidden Words
When water is released from the leaves of plants	_____
Water that flows over Earth's surface	_____
The process by which rocks are broken down into fragments	_____
The downward movement of rock and soil due to gravity	_____
The process through which sediment is laid down in new locations	_____
The process wherein pieces of sediment bounce and skip	_____
When wind picks up and carries away loose surface material	_____
Deposits formed from windblown dust	_____
The proportion of dissolved salts in water	_____
The movement of water from the deep ocean to the surface	_____
A preserved remain or trace of a once living thing	_____
A smaller unit of an era	_____

Chapter 23 Earth's Surface

Exploring Radioactive Dating

A fossil contains 100.0 milligrams of Thorium-232, which has a half-life of 14.0 billion years. How much Thorium-232 will remain after three half-lives?

Math Skill: Fractions
You may want to read more about this **Math Skill** in the **Skills and Reference Handbook** at the end of your textbook.

1. Read and Understand

How many milligrams of Thorium-232 does the fossil contain?
   100.0 milligrams

What is the half-life of Thorium-232?   14.0 billion years

What are you asked to find?   the amount of Thorium-232 that will remain in the fossil after three half-lives

2. Plan and Solve

During a half-life, one half of the original amount of a radioisotope decays. To find the amount of Thorium-232 left in the fossil after three half-lives, begin by multiplying $\frac{1}{2}$ by the number of half-lives.

$$\frac{1}{2} \times \frac{1}{2} \times \frac{1}{2} = \frac{1}{8}$$

This is the fraction of Thorium-232 that will be left in the fossil after three half-lives. Multiply this fraction by the original amount of Thorium-232 to find the amount of Thorium-232 that will remain.

$$100.0 \text{ milligrams} \times \frac{1}{8} = 12.5 \text{ milligrams}$$

3. Look Back and Check

Is your answer reasonable?

To check your answer, divide the number of milligrams in the fossil after three half-lives by the fraction of Thorium-232 left after three half-lives. Your answer should equal the original amount of Thorium-232 in the fossil.   100.0 milligrams

Math Practice

On a separate sheet of paper, solve the following problems.

1. A fossil contains 40.0 milligrams of Uranium-238, which has a half-life of 4.5 billion years. How much Uranium-238 will remain after two half-lives?

2. How long will it take for 50.0 milligrams of Thorium-232 in a rock to decay to 25.0 milligrams?

3. How long will it take for the amount of Rubidium-87 (which has a half-life of 48.8 billion years) in a rock to decay from 80.0 milligrams to 10.0 milligrams?

Section 24.1 The Atmosphere
(pages 746–751)

This section describes Earth's atmosphere, its composition, and its different layers. It also explains air pressure and the effects of altitude on air pressure.

Reading Strategy (page 746)

Relating Text and Diagrams As you read, refer to Figure 5 and the text to complete the table on the layers of the atmosphere. For more information on this Reading Strategy, see the **Reading and Study Skills** in the **Skills and Reference Handbook** at the end of your textbook.

Layers of the Atmosphere		
Layer	**Altitude Range**	**Temperature Change**
Troposphere		
	12–50 km	
		Temperature decreases as altitude increases.
Thermosphere		

Earth's Protective Layer (page 747)

1. Is the following sentence true or false? The layer of gases that surrounds Earth is called the atmosphere. _____

2. How does the atmosphere make Earth's temperatures suitable for life? _____

3. Name two gases in the atmosphere that are essential for life.

   a. _____   b. _____

Composition of the Atmosphere (page 747)

4. Is the following sentence true or false? The composition of the atmosphere changes every few kilometers as you move away from Earth. _____

5. Earth's atmosphere is a mixture of _____

   _____

6. What two gases together make up about 99% of Earth's atmosphere?   a. _____   b. _____

7. Is the following sentence true or false? Both water droplets and solid particles are suspended in the atmosphere. _____

Air Pressure (page 748)

8. What is air pressure? _____

   _____

9. As altitude increases, air pressure and density _____.

Chapter 24   Weather and Climate

10. Circle the letter of the instrument used to measure air pressure.

    a. a thermometer

    b. a barometer

    c. a psychrometer

    d. Doppler radar

Layers of the Atmosphere (pages 749–751)

11. Scientists divide the atmosphere into layers based on variations in _____.

12. List the four layers of the atmosphere.

    a. _____   b. _____

    c. _____   d. _____

13. Is the following sentence true or false? Weather is the average condition of the atmosphere in a particular place over a period of many years. _____

14. What is the ozone layer? _____

_____

15. How is ozone formed? _____

16. Is the following sentence true or false? Infrared radiation in sunlight is absorbed by ozone before it reaches Earth.

_____

17. The layer above the stratosphere is the _____.

18. Is the following sentence true or false? The temperature of the outer thermosphere is quite high. _____

Match the layer of the atmosphere with a characteristic that would best describe it.

Layer of the Atmosphere	Characteristic
_____ **19.** troposphere	a. Contains the ozone layer
_____ **20.** stratosphere	b. The outermost layer of the atmosphere
_____ **21.** mesosphere	c. The layer where most meteoroids burn up
_____ **22.** thermosphere	d. The layer where most weather occurs

23. What is the ionosphere? _____

_____

24. When charged particles from the sun are attracted to Earth's magnetic poles, a(n) _____ may appear.

Chapter 24   Weather and Climate

Section 24.2 The Sun and the Seasons
(pages 752–754)

This section describes the two major ways Earth moves. It also explains what causes the seasons.

Reading Strategy (page 752)

Building Vocabulary Copy the table on a separate sheet of paper. As you read, complete it by defining each vocabulary term from the section. For more information on this Reading Strategy, see the **Reading and Study Skills** in the **Skills and Reference Handbook** at the end of your textbook.

Vocabulary Term	Definition
Rotation	
Revolution	

1. What are the two major ways Earth moves?

   a. _____

   b. _____

2. The spinning of Earth on its axis, called _____, causes day and night.

3. Is the following sentence true or false? It takes Earth one year to complete one rotation. _____

4. The movement of one body in space around another is called _____.

5. Earth completes a full revolution around the sun in _____.

6. The path Earth takes around the sun is called its _____.

Earth's Latitude Zones (pages 752–753)

7. What is latitude? _____

8. Circle the letter that identifies the latitude of the North Pole.

   a. 70° north

   b. 80° south

   c. 90° north

   d. 100° south

Chapter 24   Weather and Climate

9. The part of Earth that receives the most direct sunlight is near the _____.

10. Is the following sentence true or false? Scientists use lines of latitude to mark out three different types of regions on Earth. _____

Match each type of region to its latitude.

Region	Latitude
_____ **11.** temperate zone	**a.** Falls between latitudes of 23.5° south and 23.5° north
_____ **12.** tropic zone	
_____ **13.** polar zone	**b.** From 66.5° north to the North Pole, and 66.5° south to the South Pole
	c. From 23.5° north to 66.5° north, and 23.5° south to 66.5° south

The Seasons (pages 753–754)

14. In which type of region is most of the United States located?

_____

15. Is the following sentence true or false? Earth's axis of rotation is tilted at an angle of about 25.3°. _____

16. The north end of Earth's axis points to _____.

17. The _____ are caused by the tilt of Earth's axis as it moves around the sun.

18. Circle the letter of each sentence that is true about a solstice.

   a. A solstice occurs when the sun is directly above the North Pole.

   b. A solstice occurs when the sun is directly above the South Pole.

   c. A solstice occurs when the sun is directly above the latitude 23.5° north or 23.5° south.

   d. A solstice occurs when the sun is directly above the latitude 66.5° north or 66.5° south.

19. Is the following sentence true or false? When the winter solstice begins in the Northern Hemisphere, the Southern Hemisphere is tilted toward the sun. _____

20. Is the following sentence true or false? Earth is closer to the sun when it is summer than when it is winter in the Northern Hemisphere. _____

21. Circle the letter that identifies the season that begins with the vernal equinox.

   a. summer   b. spring

   c. autumn   d. winter

Chapter 24   Weather and Climate

Section 24.3 Solar Energy and Winds
(pages 755–759)

This section explains what happens to solar energy that reaches Earth's atmosphere and how it is transferred within the troposphere. It also describes the different winds on Earth and what causes them.

Reading Strategy (page 755)

Comparing and Contrasting After you read, complete the table to compare and contrast sea and land breezes. For more information on this Reading Strategy, see the **Reading and Study Skills** in the **Skills and Reference Handbook** at the end of your textbook.

Sea and Land Breezes		
	Day or Night?	**Direction of Air Movement**
Sea breeze		
Land breeze		

Energy in the Atmosphere (page 755)

1. What happens to the solar energy that reaches Earth's atmosphere?

   a. _____   b. _____

   c. _____

2. Is the following sentence true or false? The atmosphere is heated mainly by energy that is reradiated by Earth's surface. _____

3. The process where certain gases in the atmosphere radiate absorbed energy back to Earth's surface, warming the lower atmosphere, is called the _____.

4. Circle the letter of each way energy can be transferred within the troposphere.

   a. convection   b. radiation

   c. precipitation   d. conduction

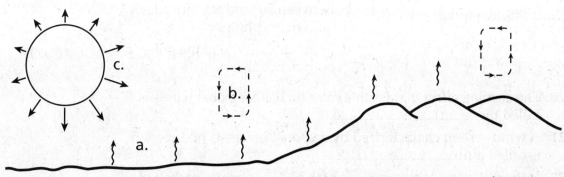

5. Name the type of energy transfer in the troposphere that each type of arrow on the diagram represents.

   a. _____   b. _____   c. _____

Chapter 24   Weather and Climate

6. Is the following sentence true or false? The air that directly contacts Earth's surface is heated by conduction. _____

7. Heat is circulated through the troposphere by _____.

Wind (page 757)

8. Is the following sentence true or false? Air flows from areas of high pressure to areas of low pressure. _____

9. What causes winds? _____

10. Is the following sentence true or false? The equal heating of Earth's surface causes differences in air pressure. _____

11. What happens to air as it warms, expands, and becomes less dense? _____

Local Winds (page 757)

12. Is the following sentence true or false? A local wind blows over a long distance. _____

13. Circle the letter of each example of a local wind.

   a. a sea breeze   b. a trade wind

   c. a jet stream   d. a land breeze

14. Would you expect to find a land breeze on the beach during the day or during the night? _____

Global Winds (pages 758–759)

15. Is the following sentence true or false? Winds that blow over short distances from a specific direction are global winds. _____

16. Global winds move in a series of circulating air patterns called _____.

Match the global winds to their locations.

Global Winds	Location
_____ **17.** polar easterlies	a. Just north and south of the equator
_____ **18.** tradewinds	b. Between 30° and 60° latitude in both hemispheres
_____ **19.** westerlies	c. From 60° latitude to the poles in both hemispheres

20. The curving effect that Earth's rotation has on global winds is called the _____.

21. A wind system characterized by seasonal reversals of direction is called a(n) _____.

22. Is the following sentence true or false? A jet-stream is a belt of high-speed wind in the upper troposphere. _____

Chapter 24   Weather and Climate

Section 24.4 Water in the Atmosphere
(pages 760–764)

This section discusses the water in the atmosphere. It explains the effect water has on processes in the atmosphere such as cloud formation and precipitation.

Reading Strategy (page 760)

Sequencing As you read, complete the flowchart to show how a cloud forms. For more information on this Reading Strategy, see the **Reading and Study Skills** in the **Skills and Reference Handbook** at the end of your textbook.

Cloud Formation

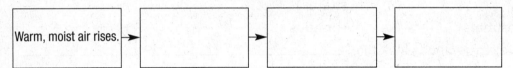

Warm, moist air rises.

Humidity (pages 760–761)

1. The amount of _____ in the air is called humidity.

2. Is the following sentence true or false? The ratio of the amount of water vapor in the air to the amount of water vapor the air can hold at that temperature is relative humidity. _____

3. What is the dew point? _____

4. Name what water vapor may condense into.

   a. _____   b. _____

   c. _____   d. _____

5. When water vapor in air changes directly from a gas to a solid, _____ forms.

Cloud Formation (page 761)

6. What is a cloud? _____

   _____

7. Is the following sentence true or false? Clouds are formed when cool, dry air rises and water vapor condenses. _____

8. Clouds may form when moist air rises and the temperature cools below the _____.

9. Besides water vapor, what must be present for a cloud to form?

   _____

Classifying Clouds (pages 762–763)

10. Scientists classify clouds based on their form and

    _____.

Chapter 24   Weather and Climate

11. What are the three basic cloud forms?

a. _____ b. _____ c. _____

12. A cloud that is near or touching the ground is called _____.

13. Is the following sentence true or false? Flat layers of clouds that cover much of the sky are stratus clouds. _____

14. The letters _____ are added to a cloud's name to mean that the cloud produces precipitation.

15. Is the following sentence true or false? Altostratus clouds are low-level clouds similar to fog. _____

16. Circle the letter of the cloud form that looks like puffy, white clouds with flat bottoms.

a. fog   b. stratus

c. altostratus   d. cumulus

17. What do cirrus clouds look like? _____

_____

18. Circle the letter of each type of cloud you often see on sunny days.

a. cumulonimbus   b. cumulus

c. altostratus   d. cirrus

Match each cloud to its description.

Cloud	Description
_____ **19.** cumulus	a. Thin, high-altitude clouds that generally produce no rain
_____ **20.** cirrus	b. "Fair-weather clouds" that look like piles of cotton balls
_____ **21.** altostratus	
_____ **22.** cumulonimbus	c. Clouds that produce heavy precipitation and are sometimes called thunderheads
	d. Middle-level clouds that can produce light rain

Forms of Precipitation (page 764)

23. What are the five most common types of precipitation?

a. _____ b. _____

c. _____ d. _____

e. _____

24. Is the following sentence true or false? Snow is precipitation in the form of ice crystals. _____

25. How does hail form? _____

_____

26. Rain that freezes as it falls is called _____.

Chapter 24   Weather and Climate

Section 24.5 Weather Patterns
(pages 765–771)

This section describes the weather patterns on Earth. It explains how air masses form and create fronts, low and high-pressure systems, and storms.

Reading Strategy (page 765)

Outlining Complete the outline with information from the section. Use the green headings as the main topics and the blue headings as subtopics. As you read, add supporting details to the subheadings. For more information on this Reading Strategy, see the **Reading and Study Skills** in the **Skills and Reference Handbook** at the end of your textbook.

Weather Patterns
I. Air Masses
II. Fronts
A. Cold fronts
B.
C.
D.

Air Masses (pages 765–766)

1. A large body of air that has fairly uniform physical properties such as temperature and moisture content at any given altitude is a(n) _____.

2. When do air masses form? _____
_____

Match the classifications of air masses to where they form.

	Classification of Air Mass	**Where They Form**
_____	**3.** maritime	a. Originates where it is very warm
_____	**4.** tropical	b. Forms over water transpiration
_____	**5.** polar	c. Forms over land
_____	**6.** continental	d. Originates where it is very cold

Fronts (pages 767–768)

7. When a continental polar air mass collides with a maritime tropical air mass, a(n) _____ forms.

8. Circle the letters of the weather conditions often associated with cold fronts.

   a. large amounts of precipitation   b. clear skies

   c. severe thunderstorms   d. strong winds

Chapter 24   Weather and Climate

Match each front to the way it forms.

Front	How It Forms

_____ **9.** cold front

_____ **10.** warm front

_____ **11.** stationary front

_____ **12.** occluded front

a. Occurs when a warm air mass is caught between two cooler air masses

b. Occurs when a warm air mass overtakes a cold air mass

c. Occurs when a cold air mass overtakes a warm air mass

d. Occurs when two unlike air masses have formed a boundary and neither is moving

Low- and High-Pressure Systems (page 769)

13. A weather system around a center of low pressure is called a(n) _____.

14. Circle the letter of each weather condition associated with cyclones.

   a. precipitation   b. clouds

   c. stormy weather   d. clear skies

15. Is the following sentence true or false? An anticyclone is a weather system with a swirling center of low pressure. _____

16. What kind of weather conditions are associated with an anticyclone?

_____

_____

Storms (pages 770–771)

17. Is the following sentence true or false? A thunderstorm is a small weather system with thunder and lightning. _____

18. Circle the letter of each characteristic of a thunderstorm.

   a. strong winds and heavy rain or hail

   b. only occurs on cool days

   c. forms when columns of air rise within a cumulonimbus cloud

   d. thunder and lightning

19. Is the following sentence true or false? A tornado is a small, intense windstorm in the shape of a rotating column that touches the ground. _____

20. How does a tornado form? _____

_____

21. A hurricane is a large tropical _____ with winds of at least 119 kilometers per hour.

Chapter 24   Weather and Climate

Section 24.6 Predicting the Weather
(pages 774–777)

This section explains some of the technology meteorologists use to predict the weather. It also explains some of the symbols found on weather maps.

Reading Strategy (page 774)

Identifying the Main Idea As you read the text, write the main idea for each heading of this section in the table. For more information on this Reading Strategy, see the **Reading and Study Skills** in the **Skills and Reference Handbook** at the end of your textbook.

Heading	Main Idea
Weather forecasting	
Weather maps	

Weather Forecasting (pages 774–776)

1. What is meteorology? _____

2. Is the following sentence true or false? Scientists who study weather are called weatherologists. _____

3. What are four technologies that help meteorologists predict the weather?

   a. _____   b. _____

   c. _____   d. _____

4. With Doppler radar, _____ waves are bounced off particles of precipitation in moving storms.

5. Scientists can calculate a storm's _____ by calculating how much the frequency of Doppler radar waves changes.

6. The types of weather data that can be collected by a typical weather station include _____.

7. Meteorologists use high-speed computers to analyze data and create short- and long-term _____.

8. Meteorologists can accurately forecast the movement of large weather systems for a period of _____ days.

9. Why is it difficult for meteorologists to predict the weather beyond a week? _____
_____

Weather Maps (pages 776–777)

10. What does a weather map show? _____
_____

Chapter 24   Weather and Climate

11. Circle the letter of each type of information that a typical weather map shows.

   a. temperatures

   b. mountain altitudes

   c. symbols for cloud cover

   d. areas of precipitation

12. Is the following sentence true or false? Weather maps often include symbols for fronts and areas of high and low pressure.
_____

Look at the weather map and the key to answer questions 13–15.

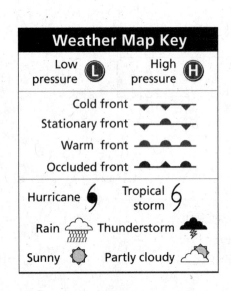

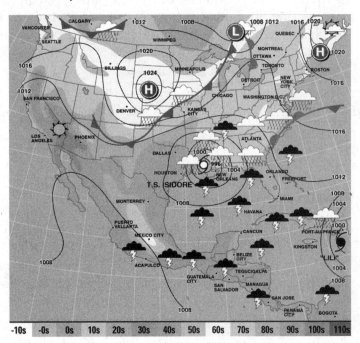

13. What type of front is shown near Calgary, Canada?
_____

14. What are the weather conditions in Los Angeles?
_____

15. What is the highest air pressure shown on the map?
_____

16. A line on a map that connects points of equal air temperatures is called a(n) _____.

17. How is a map with isotherms helpful to meteorologists? _____
_____

18. Is the following sentence true or false? An isobar is a line that connects points of unequal air pressure. _____

19. Circle the letter of each type of weather information that isobars help meteorologists to identify.

   a. areas of cloud cover

   b. centers of low-pressure systems

   c. locations of fronts

   d. centers of high-pressure systems

Chapter 24   Weather and Climate

Section 24.7 Climate
(pages 778–782)

This section describes climate and climate changes. It also describes factors
that affect the patterns of temperature and precipitation of a region.

Reading Strategy (page 778)

Building Vocabulary As you read, complete the concept map with
terms from this section. For more information on this Reading
Strategy, see the **Reading and Study Skills** in the **Skills and
Reference Handbook** at the end of your textbook.

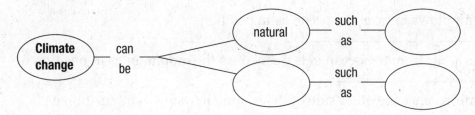

1. What is climate? _____

Classifying Climates (pages 778–779)

2. What are the six major climate groups?

   a. _____   b. _____

   c. _____   d. _____

   e. _____   f. _____

3. Circle the letters of the two main factors that determine a
   region's climate.

   a. elevation   b. temperature

   c. precipitation   d. winds

Factors Affecting Temperature (pages 779–780)

4. What are four factors that affect a region's temperature?

   a. _____   b. _____

   c. _____   d. _____

5. What factors influence the temperature of coastal regions? _____

   _____

6. Is the following sentence true or false? As altitude increases,
   temperature generally increases. _____

Factors Affecting Precipitation (page 780)

7. Circle the letter of each factor that can affect a region's precipitation.

   a. the existence of a mountain barrier   b. distribution of air pressure systems

   c. distribution of global winds   d. latitude

8. Precipitation is generally higher near the _____ than the poles.

Chapter 24   Weather and Climate

Use the diagram below to answer the questions that follow.

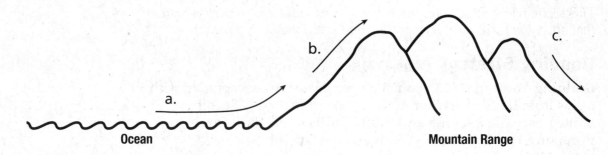

Ocean   Mountain Range

9. What type of air blows in from the ocean as in position a?
   _____

10. What happens as air from the ocean gets pushed up the mountain as in position b?
   _____

11. What type of air reaches the other side of the mountain range as in position c?
   _____

Natural Climate Change (page 781)

12. Is the following sentence true or false? The climate of a region never changes. _____

13. Circle the letters of two factors that may contribute to changes in climate.

   a. human activities   b. animal activities

   c. meteorologists   d. natural forces

14. Glaciers covered a portion of Earth's surface and temperatures were colder than usual during _____.

15. Is the following sentence true or false? El Niño is the periodic cooling of water in the central and eastern Atlantic Ocean.
   _____

Global Warming (page 782)

16. The addition of _____ and certain other gases to the atmosphere may cause global warming.

17. The _____ effect occurs when certain gases absorb radiation from Earth's surface and then radiate energy back toward the surface.

18. The process called _____ refers to an increase in the worldwide temperature of the lower atmosphere.

19. Circle the letters that identify some possible strategies to limit the effects of global warming.

   a. increasing use of fossil fuels

   b. increasing use of solar and geothermal energy

   c. increasing use of nuclear energy

   d. increasing energy conservation efforts

Chapter 24   Weather and Climate

WordWise

Complete the sentences by using one of the scrambled vocabulary terms from Chapter 24.

mertpoheas   ria superers   prehopotres
trainoot   quieoxn   hoeusegren tefefc
ase zebere   rilocosi ceteff   wed tinpo
rai sams   dunterh   mosthrei
emailtc

The lower-most layer of the atmosphere is called the

_____.

A description of the pattern of weather over many years in a place
or region is its _____.

A time when neither hemisphere is tilted toward the sun and lengths
of daylight and sunlight are approximately equal is called a(n)

_____.

A large body of air that has fairly uniform physical properties such
as temperature and moisture content at any given altitude is a(n)

_____.

The process by which gases in the atmosphere radiate absorbed
energy back to Earth's surface, warming the atmosphere is known
as the _____.

The layer of gases that surrounds Earth is called the _____.

The spinning of Earth on its axis is called its _____.

A local wind that blows from sea to land is a(n) _____.

The curving effect that Earth's rotation has on all free-moving objects
is the _____.

A line on a map that connects points of equal air temperature is called
a(n) _____ .

The force exerted by the weight of a column of air on a surface
is called _____.

The temperature at which air becomes saturated is its _____.

The sound produced by rapidly expanding air along the path of a
lightning discharge is called _____.

Calculating Volume of Gases

About 78% of the volume of dry air is composed of nitrogen. About how much nitrogen would there be in a 500 m³ volume of dry air?

Math Skill: Percents and Decimals

You may want to read more about this **Math Skill** in the **Skills and Reference Handbook** at the end of your textbook.

1. Read and Understand

What information are you given in the problem?
  Dry air = 78% nitrogen

2. Plan and Solve

What unknown are you trying to calculate?
  500 m³ volume of dry air contains __?__ m³ of nitrogen

Convert the percent of nitrogen in dry air (78%) to a decimal.
  Move the decimal point in 78% two places to the left and drop the percent sign.   = 0.78

To find the amount of nitrogen in a 500 m³ volume of dry air, multiply 500 by the decimal conversion of 78%.   0.78 × 500 m³ = 390 m³

About how much nitrogen will a 500 m³ volume of dry air have?
  500 m³ volume of dry air contains about 390 m³ nitrogen

3. Look Back and Check

To check your answer, find what percent of 500 m³ your answer is. To do this, first divide your answer by 500.

$$\frac{390 \text{ m}^3}{500 \text{ m}^3} = 0.78$$

Then, convert the decimal to a percent by moving the decimal point two places to the right and placing a percent symbol after the number. If the percent is the same as the percentage of nitrogen found in dry air, your answer is correct.   0.78 becomes 78%

Math Practice

On a separate sheet of paper, solve the following problems.

1. Helium makes up 0.00052% of dry air. About how much helium would there be in a 10,000 m³ volume of dry air?

2. A 500 m³ volume of dry air contains 0.185 m³ of carbon dioxide. What percent of this sample of air is made up of carbon dioxide?

3. Oxygen makes up 20.946% of dry air. Argon makes up 0.934% of dry air. About much more oxygen than argon would you find in a 1000-m³ volume of dry air?

Chapter 25   The Solar System

Section 25.1 Exploring the Solar System
(pages 790–794)

This section explores early models of our solar system. It describes the components of the solar system and scientific exploration of the solar system.

Reading Strategy (page 790)

Comparing and Contrasting After you read, compare the geocentric and heliocentric systems by completing the table below. For more information on this Reading Strategy, see the **Reading and Study Skills** in the **Skills and Reference Handbook** at the end of your textbook.

Solar System Models		
	Location of Earth	Location of Sun	Developer(s) of Theory
Geocentric System	Center of universe		
Heliocentric System			Aristarchus, Copernicus

Models of the Solar System (pages 790–791)

1. Is the following sentence true or false? In the Northern Hemisphere, the stars appear to circle around the North Star. _____

2. Name the five planets besides Earth that ancient observers could see with the unaided eye.

    a. _____   b. _____

    c. _____   d. _____

    e. _____

3. Many ancient Greeks thought _____ was the center of the universe.

4. Circle the letter of each sentence that is true about a geocentric model.

    a. Earth is stationary at the center.

    b. Objects in the sky move around Earth.

    c. The sun is the center of the solar system.

    d. The planets revolve around the sun.

5. Name the center of the solar system in a heliocentric model.

    _____

6. Is the following sentence true or false? The first heliocentric model was widely accepted by most ancient Greeks. _____

Chapter 25   The Solar System

7. Is the following sentence true or false? The sun, moon, and stars appear to move because the Earth is rotating on its axis. _____

Planetary Orbits (page 792)

8. Planets move around the sun in orbits that are in the shape of a(n) _____.

9. The plane containing Earth's orbit is called the _____.

10. Name the two factors that combine to keep the planets in orbit around the sun. _____

_____

Components of the Solar System (pages 792–793)

11. Circle the letters that identify objects in our solar system.

   a. moons of the planets   b. nine planets

   c. the sun   d. the stars other than the sun

12. Name three planets that were identified after the invention of the telescope in the early 1600s.

   a. _____   b. _____   c. _____

13. Is the following sentence true or false? All of the planets have moons. _____

14. Unlike the sun, planets and moons do not produce their own _____.

15. Is the following sentence true or false? The sun's mass is smaller than the combined mass of the rest of the solar system. _____

Exploring the Solar System (pages 793–794)

16. Name three examples of types of modern technology that scientists use to explore the solar system.

   a. _____   b. _____   c. _____

17. Circle the letter that identifies the first person to walk on the moon.

   a. Alan Shepard   b. Yuri Gagarin

   c. Chuck Yeager   d. Neil Armstrong

18. An unpiloted vehicle that sends data back to Earth is called a(n) _____.

19. Describe the space shuttle. _____

_____

20. Is the following sentence true or false? The International Space Station is a permanent laboratory designed for research in space. _____

Chapter 25   The Solar System

Section 25.2 The Earth-Moon System
(pages 796–801)

This section describes Earth's moon, how it was formed, and its phases. It also explains solar and lunar eclipses and tides on Earth.

Reading Strategy (page 796)

Building Vocabulary As you read, complete the concept map with terms from this section. Make similar concept maps for eclipses and tides. For more information on this Reading Strategy, see the **Reading and Study Skills** in the **Skills and Reference Handbook** at the end of your textbook.

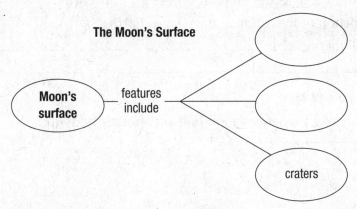

1. What is the force of gravity on the moon's surface compared to the force of gravity on Earth's surface? _____

   _____

Earth's Moon (pages 796–797)

2. How does the moon's lack of an atmosphere affect its temperatures? _____

   _____

3. Evidence of ice on the moon has been found near the moon's _____.

Surface Features (page 797)

4. Circle the letter of each major surface feature of the moon.

   a. highlands   b. maria

   c. seas   d. craters

Match each lunar surface feature with its correct description.

Description	Surface Feature
_____ 5. A round depression caused by a meteoroid	a. maria
_____ 6. Low, flat plains formed by ancient lava flows	b. crater
_____ 7. A rough, mountainous region	c. highland

Chapter 25   The Solar System

Formation of the Moon (page 798)

8. Explain the leading hypothesis of how the moon formed. _____

_____

Phases of the Moon (pages 798–799)

9. Circle the letter of each sentence that is true about phases of
   the moon.

   a. The moon's phases change according to an irregular cycle.

   b. Phases are the different shapes of the moon visible from Earth.

   c. Phases are caused by changes in the relative positions of the
      moon, sun, and Earth as the moon revolves around Earth.

   d. The sunlit portion of the moon always faces Earth.

10. When does a full moon occur? _____

_____

Eclipses (pages 799–800)

11. When the shadow of a planet or moon falls on another body in
    space, a(n) _____ occurs.

Solar Eclipse

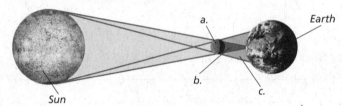

12. Look at the diagram showing a solar eclipse and label the parts.

   a. _____   b. _____   c. _____

13. Circle the letter of each sentence that is true about a lunar eclipse.

   a. A lunar eclipse occurs when Earth casts a shadow on the moon.

   b. A lunar eclipse occurs when the moon casts a shadow on a
      portion of Earth's surface.

   c. A lunar eclipse occurs during a full moon, when Earth is
      between the sun and moon.

   d. A lunar eclipse occurs during a new moon, when the moon is
      between the sun and Earth.

Tides on Earth (page 801)

14. Describe the cause of tides. _____

_____

15. Is the following sentence true or false? A spring tide is produced
    when the change between daily high and low tides is the greatest.

_____

Section 25.3 The Inner Solar System
(pages 803–809)

This section describes the terrestrial planets found in the inner solar system.

Reading Strategy (page 803)

Summarizing Copy the table on a separate sheet of paper. Write all the headings for the section in the table. Write a brief summary of the text for each heading. For more information on this Reading Strategy, see the **Reading and Study Skills** in the **Skills and Reference Handbook** at the end of your textbook.

The Terrestrial Planets

I. The Terrestrial Planets

  • Four planets closest to the sun

  • Small, dense, with rocky surfaces

II.

  a.

III. Venus

  b. Thick atmosphere, very hot surface, many volcanoes

The Terrestrial Planets (pages 803–804)

1. Identify the four terrestrial planets.

  a. _____   b. _____

  c. _____   d. _____

2. Circle the letter of each sentence that is true about the terrestrial planets.

  a. They all are relatively small and dense.

  b. They all have rocky surfaces.

  c. They all have thick atmospheres.

  d. They all have a crust, mantle, and iron core.

Mercury (pages 804–805)

3. Circle the letter of each sentence that is true about Mercury.

  a. It is the closest planet to the sun.

  b. It is the smallest of the terrestrial planets.

  c. It is geologically dead.

  d. It is the slowest-moving planet.

4. Is the following sentence true or false? Mercury has a large number of craters, suggesting that the surface has been largely unchanged for billions of years. _____

Chapter 25   The Solar System

Venus (page 805)

5. Circle the letter of each sentence that is true about Venus.

   a. It rotates in the direction opposite to which it revolves.

   b. It is the brightest object in Earth's night sky besides the moon.

   c. It rotates once every 24 hours.

   d. Its rotation rate is very fast.

6. Describe the effect that carbon dioxide in Venus's atmosphere has on its temperature. _____

_____

Earth (pages 805–806)

7. Circle the letter of each sentence that is true about Earth.

   a. Its atmosphere is very thin and composed mostly of carbon dioxide.

   b. It supports millions of different species of living things.

   c. It has a suitable atmosphere and temperature for liquid water to exist.

   d. Its core has cooled down to the point where it is geologically dead.

8. Why does Earth's surface continue to change? _____

_____

Mars (pages 807–808)

9. Circle the letter of each sentence that is true about Mars.

   a. The largest volcano in the solar system is on Mars.

   b. Iron-rich rocks on Mars's surface give it a reddish color.

   c. It has a thick atmosphere that keeps the planet warm.

   d. The surface of Mars is colder than Earth's surface.

10. Is the following sentence true or false? Mars shows evidence of once having liquid surface water. _____

Asteroids (page 809)

11. Small, rocky bodies in space are called _____.

12. Circle the letter of each sentence that is true about asteroids.

    a. Most small asteroids have irregular forms.

    b. The asteroid belt formed when a giant planet was shattered by a collision with a meteoroid.

    c. Most asteroids are found in the asteroid belt between Earth and Mars.

    d. Most asteroids are less than 1 kilometer in diameter.

13. What do scientists hypothesize about how the asteroids formed? _____

_____

Chapter 25   The Solar System

Section 25.4 The Outer Solar System
(pages 810–815)

This section describes the planets in the outer solar system. It also describes comets and meteoroids and the edge of the solar system.

Reading Strategy (page 810)

Summarizing Copy the table on a separate sheet of paper. Fill in the table as you read to summarize the characteristics of the outer planets. For more information on this Reading Strategy, see the **Reading and Study Skills** in the **Skills and Reference Handbook** at the end of your textbook.

The Outer Planets	
Outer Planets	**Characteristics**
Jupiter	Largest; most mass; most moons; Great Red Spot

Gas Giants (page 811)

1. Circle the letter of each sentence that is true about Jupiter, Saturn, Uranus, and Neptune compared to the terrestrial planets.

   a. Their years are shorter than the terrestrial planets.

   b. They are colder than the terrestrial planets.

   c. They are further from the sun than the terrestrial planets.

   d. They are much larger than the terrestrial planets.

2. Why are the outer planets called the gas giants? _____

   _____

3. Describe the cores of the gas giants. _____

   _____

Jupiter (pages 811–812)

4. The _____ is a huge storm on Jupiter.

5. Circle the letter of each sentence that is true about Jupiter's moons.

   a. Callisto and Ganymede are Jupiter's largest moons.

   b. Scientists hypothesize that Europa could support life.

   c. Ganymede has a metal core and rocky mantle.

   d. Io is covered with ice.

Chapter 25   The Solar System

Saturn (pages 812–813)

6. Saturn has the largest and most visible _____ in the solar system.

7. Is the following sentence true or false? Saturn has the largest atmosphere and the lowest average density of all the planets in the solar system. _____

Uranus (page 813)

8. Is the following sentence true or false? Uranus gets its distinctive blue-green appearance from large amounts of methane in its atmosphere. _____

9. Uranus's _____ is tilted more than 90°.

Neptune (page 814)

10. Circle the letter of each sentence that is true about Neptune.

    a. It has visible cloud patterns in its atmosphere.

    b. It has only five known moons.

    c. It has large storms in its atmosphere.

    d. It has no rings.

11. The _____ in Neptune's atmosphere causes its bluish color.

Pluto (page 814)

12. Is the following sentence true or false? Pluto is both larger and denser than the other outer planets. _____

13. Describe Pluto's probable composition. _____

_____

Comets and Meteoroids (page 815)

14. A(n) _____ is made of ice and rock that partially vaporizes when it passes near the sun.

15. Chunks of rock, usually less than a few hundred meters in size, that travel through the solar system are called _____.

16. The radioactive dating of ancient meteoroids has allowed scientists to establish that the age of the solar system is

_____.

The Edge of the Solar System (page 815)

17. The _____ contains tens of thousands of objects made of ice, dust, and rock that orbit the sun beyond Pluto.

18. The thick sphere of comets encircling the solar system out to a distance of about 50,000 AU is called the _____.

Chapter 25   The Solar System

Section 25.5 The Origin of the Solar System
(pages 818–820)

This section explains a theory of how the solar system originated. It also describes how this theory explains the composition and size of the planets.

Reading Strategy (page 818)

Identifying Main Ideas As you read, write the main idea for each topic. For more information on this Reading Strategy, see the **Reading and Study Skills** in the **Skills and Reference Handbook** at the end of your textbook.

Theories on the Origin of the Solar System	
Topic	**Main Idea**
The Nebular Theory	
Formation of the protoplanetary disk	
Planetesimals and protoplanets	
Composition and size of the planets	

The Nebular Theory (pages 818–819)

1. The generally accepted explanation for the formation of the solar system is called the _____.

2. Circle the letter of each sentence that is true about the nebular theory.

   a. The solar nebula formed from the remnants of previous stars.

   b. The explosion of a nearby star likely caused the solar nebula to start to contract.

   c. As the solar nebula contracted, it began to spin more slowly.

   d. The solar system formed from a rotating cloud of dust and gas.

3. Describe a solar nebula. _____

   _____

4. A large, spherical cloud of dust and gas in space is called a(n)

   _____.

5. Is the following sentence true or false? Most planets and moons are revolving now in the direction that the protoplanetary disk was spinning. _____

Chapter 25   The Solar System

6. Circle the letter of each sentence that is true about the formation of the protoplanetary disk.

   a. The disk was densest in the center and thinner toward the edges.

   b. At the center of the disk, nuclear reactions fused hydrogen and helium and the sun was formed.

   c. The temperature at the center of the disk was extremely low.

   d. Nearly all of the mass of the solar nebula became concentrated near the outer edge of the disk.

7. Asteroid-like bodies that combined to form planets were called _____.

8. The process by which planetesimals grew is called _____.

9. Put the following events about the formation of planetesimals and protoplanets in correct order. Number the events 1–5 in the order that they occurred.

   _____ Balls of gas and dust collided and grew larger.

   _____ Planetesimals became large enough to exert gravity on nearby objects.

   _____ Planetesimals grew by accretion.

   _____ Protoplanets joined to form the current planets in a series of collisions.

   _____ Planetesimals grew into protoplanets.

Composition and Size of the Planets (page 820)

10. At _____ pressures, such as those found in space, cooling materials can change from a gas directly into a solid.

11. Ice-forming materials _____ at temperatures between 500 K and 1200 K.

12. Why are the terrestrial planets relatively small and rocky? _____
    _____
    _____

13. Circle the letter of each sentence that is true about the formation of the gas giants.

   a. The gravity of the gas giants decreased as they grew larger.

   b. Ice-forming material could condense in the outer solar system.

   c. The planets grew large and were able to capture hydrogen and helium from nearby space.

   d. Less material was available for the gas giants to form than was available for the terrestrial planets.

14. Is the following sentence true or false? Scientists have found planets in orbit around distant stars that provide support for the nebular theory.
    _____.

Chapter 25   The Solar System

WordWise

Test your knowledge of vocabulary words from Chapter 25 by completing this crossword puzzle.

Clues across:

3. A model where Earth is stationary while objects in the sky move around it

4. A small natural body in space that revolves around a planet

6. Asteroid-like bodies that eventually combined to form planets

9. The regular rise and fall of ocean waters

10. A chunk of rock that moves through the solar system

Clues down:

1. The event that occurs when the shadow of one body in space falls on another

2. Dusty pieces of ice and rock that partially vaporize when they pass near the sun

5. Small, rocky bodies that travel through the solar system

7. Low, flat plains on the moon

8. A disk made of many small particles of rock and ice in orbit around a planet

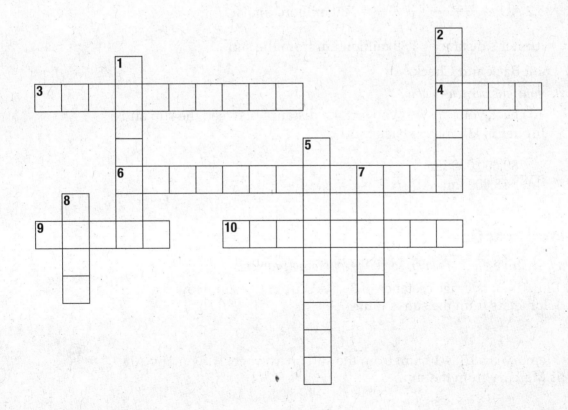

Chapter 25   The Solar System

Calculating Distances Between Objects in Space

Jupiter is, on average, 5.2 astronomical units (AU) from the sun. About how many kilometers is Jupiter from the sun?

1. Read and Understand

What information are you given?

   Jupiter's distance = 5.2 AU from the sun

2. Plan and Solve

What are you asked to find?

   Jupiter's distance = ? kilometers from the sun

How many kilometers are in one AU?

   149,598,000 kilometers

Write a conversion factor that can be used to change AU to kilometers.

$$\frac{149{,}598{,}000 \text{ km}}{1 \text{ AU}}$$

Multiply the distance from the sun to Jupiter in AU by the conversion factor.

$$5.2 \text{ AU} \times \frac{149{,}598{,}000 \text{ km}}{1 \text{ AU}} = 780 \text{ million km}$$

   Jupiter's distance = 780 million km from the sun

3. Look Back and Check

Is your answer reasonable?

   To check your answer, convert the distance between the sun and Jupiter in kilometers back to AU.

$$\frac{780{,}000{,}000 \text{ km}}{149{,}598{,}000 \text{ km/AU}} = 5.2 \text{ AU}$$

© Pearson Education, Inc., publishing as Pearson Prentice Hall. All rights reserved.

Math Practice

On a separate sheet of paper, solve the following problems.

1. Pluto is an average distance of 39.5 AU from the sun. How many kilometers from the sun is Pluto?

2. Mercury is 58.3×10^6 km from the sun on average. How many AU is Mercury from the sun?

3. Mars is 1.52 AU from the sun on average. Saturn is 9.54 AU. About how far apart, in kilometers, are Mars and Saturn when they are closest to each other?

Chapter 26 Exploring the Universe

Section 26.1 The Sun
(pages 828–833)

This section describes how the sun produces energy. It also describes the sun's interior and atmosphere.

Reading Strategy (page 828)

Build Vocabulary Copy the table on a separate sheet of paper and add more lines as needed. As you read, write a definition of each vocabulary term in your own words. For more information on this Reading Strategy, see the **Reading and Study Skills** in the **Skills and Reference Handbook** at the end of your textbook.

The Sun	
Vocabulary Term	**Definition**
Core	
Radiation zone	
Convection zone	

Energy from the Sun (pages 828–829)

1. The sun gives off a large amount of energy in the form of _____ radiation.

2. Circle the letter of each sentence that is true about nuclear fusion in the sun.

    a. Less massive nuclei combine into more massive nuclei.

    b. The end product of fusion is hydrogen.

    c. Fusion is a type of chemical reaction.

    d. Hydrogen nuclei fuse into helium nuclei.

Forces in Balance (page 829)

3. For the sun to be stable, inward and outward forces within it must be in _____.

4. Is the following sentence true or false? The sun remains stable because the inward pull of gravity balances the outward push of thermal pressure from nuclear fission. _____

The Sun's Interior (pages 830–831)

5. Circle the letter of each layer of the sun's interior.

    a. the radiation zone   c. the convection zone

    b. the photosphere   d. the core

Chapter 26   Exploring the Universe

6. Circle the letter of each way that energy moves through the sun.

a. gravity   b. convection

c. radiation   d. nuclear fusion

7. List the layers of the sun's interior shown on the diagram.

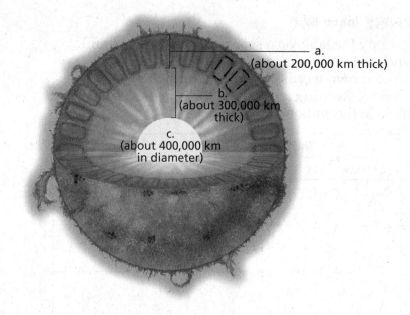

a. _____

b. _____

c. _____

The Sun's Atmosphere (page 831)

8. Circle the letter of each layer of the sun's atmosphere.

a. photosphere   b. chromosphere

c. corona   d. core

9. When can the corona be seen? _____

_____

Features of the Sun's Atmosphere (pages 832–833)

Match each description to a feature of the sun's atmosphere.

Description	Feature of Sun's Atmosphere
_____ **10.** Spectacular features of the sun's atmosphere that occur near sunspots	a. solar flares
_____ **11.** Areas of gas in the atmosphere that are cooler than surrounding areas	b. prominences
_____ **12.** Sudden releases of energy that produce X-rays and hurl charged particles into space	c. sunspots

Chapter 26   Exploring the Universe

Section 26.2 Stars
(pages 834–839)

This section discusses how scientists classify stars. It also describes other important properties of stars.

Reading Strategy (page 834)

Using Prior Knowledge Add what you already know about stars to the concept map. After you read, complete your concept map, adding more ovals as needed. For more information on this Reading Strategy, see the **Reading and Study Skills** in the **Skills and Reference Handbook** at the end of your textbook.

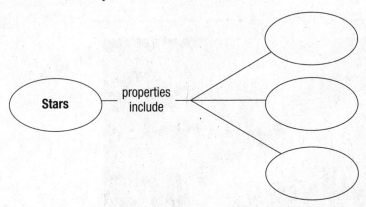

Distances to the Stars (pages 834–836)

1. Circle the letter of each sentence that is true about a light-year.

   a. It is a typical unit of measure for distances on Earth.

   b. It is a distance of about 9.5 trillion kilometers.

   c. It is the distance that light travels in a vacuum in a year.

   d. It is a unit of time.

2. Is the following sentence true or false? Parallax is the apparent change in position of an object with respect to a distant background. _____

3. Astronomers measure the parallax of a nearby star to determine its _____.

Properties of Stars (pages 836–837)

4. Circle the letter of each property that astronomers use to classify stars.

   a. brightness   b. distance

   c. color   d. size

5. Is the following sentence true or false? The brightness of a star as it appears from Earth is called its absolute brightness. _____

6. A star's _____ can be used to identify different elements in the star.

7. Describe the chemical makeup of most stars. _____

_____

The Hertzsprung-Russell Diagram (pages 838–839)

8. Circle the letter of each way that Hertzsprung-Russell (H-R) diagrams might be used.

   a. to study sizes of stars

   b. to study distant planets

   c. to determine a star's absolute brightness

   d. to determine a star's surface temperature or color

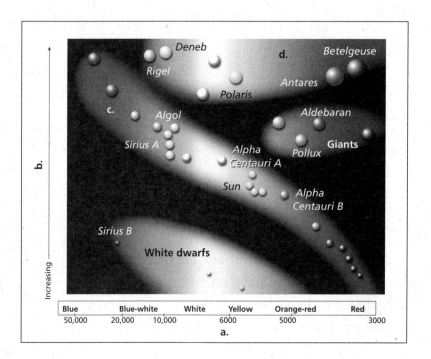

9. Provide labels for each of the letters shown on the H-R diagram above.

   a. _____   b. _____

   c. _____   d. _____

10. Circle the letter of each sentence that is true about supergiants.

    a. They are found at the upper right of the H-R diagram.

    b. They are much brighter than main sequence stars of the same temperature.

    c. They are 100 to 1000 times the diameter of the sun.

    d. They are smaller and fainter than giants.

11. How does the brightness of white dwarfs compare to the brightness of main sequence stars? _____

_____

Chapter 26   Exploring the Universe

Section 26.3 Life Cycles of Stars
(pages 840–844)

This section explains how stars form, their adult stages, and how they die.

Reading Strategy (page 840)

Sequencing Copy the flowchart on a separate sheet of paper. As you read, extend and complete it to show how a low-mass star evolves. For more information on this Reading Strategy, see the **Reading and Study Skills** in the **Skills and Reference Handbook** at the end of your textbook.

Evolution of a Low-Mass Star

How Stars Form (pages 840–841)

1. A large cloud of dust and gas spread out over a large volume of space is called a(n) _____ .

2. Circle the letter of each sentence that is true about a protostar.

    a. Nuclear fusion is taking place within it.

    b. It has enough mass to form a star.

    c. Its internal pressure and temperature continue to rise as it contracts.

    d. It is a contracting cloud of dust and gas.

3. Describe how a star is formed. _____
   _____

Adult Stars (page 841)

4. A star's _____ determines the star's place on the main sequence and how long it will stay there.

5. Circle the letter of each true sentence about adult main-sequence stars.

    a. High-mass stars become the bluest and brightest main-sequence stars.

    b. Low-mass stars are usually short-lived.

    c. Yellow stars like the sun are in the middle of the main sequence.

    d. Red stars are the hottest and brightest of all visible stars.

The Death of a Star (pages 842–844)

6. The core of a star starts to shrink when the core begins to run out of

   _____ .

Chapter 26   Exploring the Universe

7. Name three possible end stages of a star.

a. _____ b. _____ c. _____

8. Is the following sentence true or false? The final stages of a star's life depend on its mass. _____

9. Circle the letter of each sentence that is true about the death of low-mass and medium-mass stars.

a. The dying stars are called planetary nebulas.

b. They remain in the giant stage until their supplies of helium and hydrogen are gone and there are no other elements to fuse.

c. The energy coming from the stars' interiors decreases and the stars eventually collapse.

d. The cores of the stars shrink and only their atmospheres remain.

10. The glowing cloud of gas that surrounds a dying low- or medium-mass star is called a(n) _____.

11. List the stages in the evolution of a low-mass star shown in the diagram below.

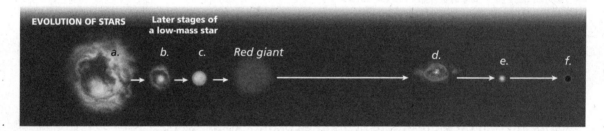

a. _____   b. _____

c. _____   d. _____

e. _____   f. _____

12. Is the following sentence true or false? A high-mass star dies quickly because it consumes fuel rapidly. _____

13. An explosion so brilliant that a dying high-mass star becomes more brilliant than an entire galaxy is called a(n) _____.

Match each final stage of a high-mass star to its correct description.

Description	Final Stage of a High-Mass Star
_____ 14. Surface gravity is so great that nothing can escape from it	a. pulsar
	b. black hole
_____ 15. A spinning neutron star that gives off strong pulses of radio waves	c. neutron star
_____ 16. The remnant of a high-mass star that has exploded as a supernova, which begins to spin more and more rapidly as it contracts	

Chapter 26   Exploring the Universe

Section 26.4 Groups of Stars
(pages 846–849)

This section describes star systems, star clusters, and galaxies.

Reading Strategy (page 846)

Comparing and Contrasting After you read, compare types of star clusters by completing the table. For more information on this Reading Strategy, see the **Reading and Study Skills** in the **Skills and Reference Handbook** at the end of your textbook.

Types of Star Clusters		
Cluster Type	Appearance	Age and Type of Stars
Open cluster		
		Bright, young stars
	Spherical, densely packed	

1. A group of stars that seems to form a pattern as seen from Earth is called a(n) _____.

2. Is the following sentence true or false? Constellations are important to astronomy because they help to form a map of the sky. _____

Star Systems (pages 846–847)

3. A group of two or more stars that are held together by gravity is called a(n) _____.

4. Is the following sentence true or false? Astronomers have concluded that more than half of all stars are members of groups of two or more stars. _____

5. A star system with two stars is called a(n) _____.

Star Clusters (page 847)

Match each basic kind of star cluster to its description.

Description	Star Cluster
_____ **6.** A loose grouping of no more than a few thousand stars that are well spread out	a. globular cluster
	b. open cluster
_____ **7.** Loose groupings of bright, young stars	c. associations
_____ **8.** A large group of older stars	

Chapter 26   Exploring the Universe

9. Is the following sentence true or false? Astronomers estimate that the oldest globular clusters are at least 20 billion years old.

_____

Galaxies (pages 848–849)

10. A huge group of individual stars, star systems, star clusters, dust, and gas bound together by gravity is called a(n) _____.

11. Our galaxy is called the _____.

12. Galaxies that have a bulge of stars at the center with arms extending outward like a pinwheel are called

_____.

13. Is the following sentence true or false? The arms of spiral galaxies contain very little gas and dust. _____

14. A spiral galaxy that has a bar through the center with the arms extending outward from the bar on either side is called a(n)

_____.

15. Circle the letter of each sentence that is true about elliptical galaxies.

   a. They are spherical or oval shaped.

   b. They typically have lots of dust and gas.

   c. They come in a wide range of sizes.

   d. They usually contain only old stars.

16. A(n) _____ galaxy has a disorganized appearance and is typically smaller than other types of galaxies.

Match each type of galaxy to its description.

Description	Galaxy
_____ **17.** Spherical or oval, no spiral arms, and usually contains only old stars	a. barred-spiral galaxy
_____ **18.** Bulge of stars at the center with arms extending outward like a pinwheel	b. elliptical galaxy
_____ **19.** Composed of many young stars, comes in many shapes, and has a disorganized appearance	c. spiral galaxy
_____ **20.** Has a bar through the center with arms extending outward from the bar on either side	d. irregular galaxy

21. Is the following sentence true or false? The Milky Way appears as a band from Earth because we are looking at it edgewise.

_____

22. The enormously bright centers of distant galaxies are called

_____.

Section 26.5 The Expanding Universe
(pages 852–855)

This section describes Hubble's Law. It also explains the big bang theory.

Reading Strategy (page 852)

Previewing Before reading, examine Figure 26 and write at least two questions to help you understand the information in it. As you read, write answers to your questions. For more information on this Reading Strategy, see the **Reading and Study Skills** in the **Skills and Reference Handbook** at the end of your textbook.

The Evolution of the Universe
Questions on the Evolution of the Universe

Hubble's Law (pages 852–853)

1. Is the following sentence true or false? The apparent change in frequency and wavelength of a wave as it moves towards or away from an observer is known as the Doppler effect. _____

2. How can astronomers use the Doppler effect? _____ _____

3. Circle the letter of each sentence that is true about spectrums of stars or galaxies.

   a. As a star or galaxy circles the Earth, the lines in its spectrum shift toward the middle of the spectrum.

   b. As a star moves toward Earth, the lines in its spectrum are shifted toward shorter wavelengths.

   c. As a star or galaxy moves away from Earth, the lines in its spectrum are shifted toward longer wavelengths.

   d. The greater the observed shift in spectrum, the greater the speed the star or galaxy is moving.

4. The shift in the light of a galaxy toward the red wavelengths is called a(n) _____.

5. Describe Hubble's Law. _____ _____

6. Is the following sentence true or false? The most distant galaxies that can be seen from Earth are moving away at more than 90% of the speed of light. _____

Chapter 26   Exploring the Universe

7. Describe what the observed red shift in the spectra of galaxies shows.

_____

_____

The Big Bang Theory (page 854)

8. Astronomers theorize that the universe came into being in an event called the _____.

9. Circle the letter of each sentence that is true according to the big bang theory.

   a. The matter and energy in the universe was once concentrated in a very hot region smaller than a sentence period.

   b. The universe began billions of years ago with an enormous explosion.

   c. The universe came into existence in an instant.

   d. The matter and energy in the universe has taken billions of years to form.

10. After the big bang, it is theorized that the universe

_____.

11. How large was the universe when the sun and solar system formed?

_____

12. Circle the letter of each sentence that gives evidence that supports the big bang theory.

   a. The existence of cosmic microwave background radiation.

   b. The red shift in the spectra of distant galaxies.

   c. The fact that the sun is about 20 billion years old.

   d. The pulling of atoms together into gas clouds by gravity.

13. Recent measurements of the microwave background radiation have led astronomers to estimate that the universe is

_____.

Continued Expansion (page 855)

14. Matter that does not give off radiation is known as

_____.

15. Circle the letter of each sentence that is true about dark matter.

   a. Astronomers currently don't know what it is or how it is distributed.

   b. It cannot be seen directly.

   c. It can be measured using the Doppler effect.

   d. It can be detected by observing how its gravity affects visible matter.

16. Why is it significant that the galaxies contain as much as ten times more dark matter than visible matter? _____

_____

Chapter 26   Exploring the Universe

WordWise

Answer the questions by writing the correct vocabulary terms from the chapter in the blanks. Use the circled letter in each word to find the hidden word.

Clues	Vocabulary Terms
What is the central region of the sun?	Ⓞ _ _ _
What is the surface layer of the sun?	_ Ⓞ _ _ _ _ _ _ _ _
What is a dramatic eruption on the sun that produces X-rays and hurls charged particles into space at nearly the speed of light?	_ _ _ Ⓞ _ _ _ _
What is a contracting cloud of gas and dust with enough mass to form a star?	_ _ Ⓞ _ _ _ _ _ _
What is the diagonal band of stars on the H-R diagram?	Ⓞ _ _ _ _ _ _ _ _ _ _
What is the dense remnant of a high-mass star that has exploded as a supernova?	_ _ _ _ _ Ⓞ _ _ _ _ _
What are the very bright stars at the upper right of the H-R diagram?	Ⓞ _ _ _ _ _ _ _ _ _
What is the apparent change in position of an object with respect to a distant background?	Ⓞ _ _ _ _ _ _ _
What is an object whose surface gravity is so great that nothing, not even light, can escape from it?	_ _ _ _ _ Ⓞ _ _ _
What is the distance that light travels in a vacuum in a year?	_ _ _ _ _ - _ Ⓞ _ _
What is a large glowing ball of gas in space?	_ _ _ Ⓞ
What is a large cloud of gas and dust spread out over a large volume of space?	_ Ⓞ _ _ _ _

Hidden Word: _ _ _ _ _ _ _ _ _ _ _ _

Definition: _____

_____

Calculating Distances to Stars

A star is 3.6×10^{19} kilometers from Earth. How many light-years is this?

Math Skill: Exponents

You may want to read more about this **Math Skill** in the **Skills and Reference Handbook** at the end of your textbook.

1. Read and Understand

How many kilometers from Earth is the star?

Star = 3.6×10^{19} kilometers from Earth

What are you asked to find?

Star = ? light-years from Earth

2. Plan and Solve

Write the number of kilometers in a light-year using scientific notation.

9.5×10^{12} kilometers

To find the number of light-years the star is from Earth, divide its distance by the number of kilometers in a light-year. Begin by dividing 3.6 by 9.5. Round your answer to the nearest hundredth.

0.38

To divide numbers with exponents, subtract the exponents. What will the exponent of the answer be?

7

To write your answer in scientific notation, a number other than zero must be in the ones place. Move the decimal one place to the right and subtract one from the exponent. How many light-years is the star from Earth?

3.8×10^{6} light-years

3. Look Back and Check

Is your answer reasonable?

To check your answer, multiply the number of light-years away the star is by the number of kilometers in a light-year. Remember to add the exponents when you multiply. Your answer should be the distance from Earth to the star in kilometers.

3.6×10^{19} kilometers

Math Practice

On a separate sheet of paper, solve the following problems.

1. A star is 8.6×10^{14} kilometers from Earth. How many light-years away is the star? Round your answer to the nearest tenth.

2. The star Proximi Centauri is about 4.3 light-years from Earth. How many kilometers from Earth is it?

3. A star is 6.8×10^{8} light-years from Earth. How many kilometers from Earth is the star?